Israel C. Russell

Rivers of North America

A Reading lesson for students of geography and geology

Israel C. Russell

Rivers of North America
A Reading lesson for students of geography and geology

ISBN/EAN: 9783337239558

Printed in Europe, USA, Canada, Australia, Japan

Cover: Foto ©Andreas Hilbeck / pixelio.de

More available books at **www.hansebooks.com**

RIVERS OF NORTH AMERICA

A READING LESSON FOR STUDENTS
OF GEOGRAPHY AND GEOLOGY

BY

ISRAEL C. RUSSELL

PROFESSOR OF GEOLOGY IN THE UNIVERSITY OF MICHIGAN
AUTHOR OF "LAKES OF NORTH AMERICA," "GLACIERS OF NORTH AMERICA,"
"VOLCANOES OF NORTH AMERICA," ETC.

———

NEW YORK
G. P. PUTNAM'S SONS
LONDON
JOHN MURRAY

" Every river appears to consist of a main trunk, fed from a variety of branches, each running in a valley proportioned to its size, and all of them together forming a system of valleys, communicating with one another, and having such a nice adjustment of their declivities, that none of them join the principal valley either on too high or too low a level ; a circumstance which would be infinitely improbable if each of these valleys were not the work of the streams that flow through them."—*Illustrations of the Huttonian Theory of the Earth : by John Playfair. Edinburgh, 1802. p. 102.*

TO THE READER

EVERY person is familiar with the beating of the rain upon the surface of the land, and the gathering of the waters that fall into rills, rivulets, and brooks which frequently unite to form larger rivers. Everyone is aware, also, that streams are turbid after heavy rains. But, although these facts have been known to us from childhood, yet comparatively few people have thought out the chain of events of which they form a part, or recognised the results toward which they lead.

Standing by the side of a river, we see its waters flowing continually in one direction and in many instances bearing along a load of sediment. We know that the mud which discolours the waters was derived from the lands bordering the stream and is journeying to the sea. So far as we can ordinarily discern, there is no compensation for this removal. Evidently, if the process goes on without being counteracted by other agencies, all of the material forming land areas will in time be removed, and the hills and even the grandest mountains will be degraded to the level of the sea. We know of no reason why this process of soil removal may not have been in operation since rain first fell on land, or why it may not continue so long as continents and islands exist. As the land has not been reduced to sea-level, one of two conclusions seems evident: either the time that has elapsed since the process began has not been sufficiently long to bring about the final result, or else there is some compensating process by which land areas are renewed.

A person who wanders along a river bank with these and kindred thoughts in mind naturally seeks for evidences of the work the rivers have accomplished and endeavours to learn how it has been carried on. One observes the river flowing through a narrow, steep-sided trench, or perhaps meandering in broad, graceful curves over the bottom of a wide, fruitful valley. In all directions the view is limited by hills or steeply ascending slopes. On gaining a commanding station on a hilltop, the broader prospect, including both hills and valleys, very likely will reveal the fact that the hills, ridges, and more or less isolated peaks rise to the same general height, and appear as a level plain when the eye, nearly on a level with their summit, ranges over them; and sunken in this plain is the river valley. If the river has been engaged for ages in carrying away the material of the land in the way it is now doing, the valley must represent a part or the whole of the work done. The thought that the river is older than the valley, and that the valley has been excavated by the river, comes to one like a revelation. In fancy we see the valley filled with rocks like those in the bordering hills and the plain restored. Evidently the surface of the region, less diversified than now, must have been a plain or plateau before the stream excavated its valley. When this idea has taken root in the mind, our powers of observation are stimulated and our faith strengthened in what has been termed the scientific use of the imagination.

As our vision ranges over valleys and hills, the fact is recognised that the neighbouring mountains are but uplands of larger size, separated one from another by gorges and valleys, in each of which a stream is flowing, and we are startled by the vividness of the pictures that crowd themselves on our fancy, each portraying a different stage in the development of a landscape which had previously charmed us simply by its assemblage of attractive forms and its harmonious blendings of colour.

The mental pictures of the loiterer by a stream-side or the dreamer on a hilltop are not confined to the region immediately before him. What is true of the stream at his feet must also pertain in general to other streams in whatever clime. Again, a curtain is lifted and he sees that every stream on the earth's surface is engaged in changing the aspect of the land. Valleys have been excavated on every continent and island. Every mountain has been sculptured. Changes due to running water are everywhere in progress. If these conclusions are well founded, it is evident that valleys and mountains are but transient forms in a long process of topographical development, and the history of past changes should find expression in the relief of the land.

The leading idea which absorbs the attention when a living interest is once awakened in the meaning of the many and diversified features of the earth's surface, is that they are not fixed and changeless forms, but have undergone many orderly modifications in the past and will continue to change under the action of definite laws in the future. It is not the shape of the earth as it exists to-day, the present distribution of land and water on its surface, or the relief of the land, or of the floor of the sea, but the changes that each of these conditions has passed through in order to reach its present state, and the modifications still in progress, which claim the greatest share of the geographer's attention. Evolution is the leading theme of the inanimate as well as of the animate world. The features of the earth's surface, from the continents and oceans to the smallest islands and tiniest rills, all have what may be termed their life histories. It is the recognition of this fact that has given new interest and imparted a fresh impetus to geographical study.

When once the idea is grasped that each and every one of the elements in a landscape has a history which can be read, and that the end is not yet, but still other transformations are to come, an insatiable desire is awakened for more knowledge concerning especially the work of the streams to which so many of the changes that have been made on the earth's surface are due. What laws do the streams obey ? What conditions modify their normal behaviour ? What are the various stages in the transformations they are making everywhere about us ? Are there other forces in action, tending to counteract their destructive work ? Are the conditions to which man has become adjusted to pass away ? What changes are to come ? Is the re-modelling of the land to be continued for ever, or will there be a final condition beyond which the expression of the face of Nature will become sphinx-like and unchanging ? These and many more queries crowd themselves on the mind when once an interest in the daily scenes about us is awakened. Many, but by no means all, of the questions which we wish to ask of the mountains and streams can be satisfactorily answered at the present day.

It is with the hope of assisting the reader both in questioning the streams and in understanding their answers, and at the same time creating a desire for more light on other and related chapters of the earth's history, that the book before you was written.

The study of the earth's surface should be of especial interest to American students not only because of the magnificent and varied scenery of our native land, but for the reason that new life and vividness have been given the subject by the labours of men who are still among us.

The marked advances made during the present century both in the study of the ancient life on the earth and of the surface changes still in progress, show the influence of environment. The Geological Survey of the State of New York gave a marked impetus to the study of the invertebrate life of distant ages, largely for the reason that the rocks of the New York series are rich in such relics. When geologists visited the central and western portions of the United States, the sediments of ancient lakes, rich in vertebrate fossils, were discovered. The veritable menagerie of marvellous birds, reptiles, and mammals that has been made to appear from these cemeteries is more varied than the most fantastic dreams of fable. We feel that the uncouth procession has only begun to pass in review, but are at a loss to imagine what as yet unknown commingling of fish, reptile, bird, and mammal in one and the same individual can possibly be found. When investigators of surface geology and geography made their bold explorations into the vast

arid region of the south-west, they discovered a land of
wonders, where the mask of vegetation which conceals so
many countries is absent, and the features of the naked land
are fully revealed beneath a cloudless sky. The facts in
the earth's history which there impress themselves most
forcibly on the beholder are such as have resulted from the
action of streams and of atmospheric agencies. It was in
this arid region of strong relief that a revival of interest in
the surface forms of the earth was engendered. The seeds
of what is practically a new science,—physiography,—
gathered in this desert land by J. S. Newberry, J. W.
Powell, G. K. Gilbert, C. E. Dutton, and others, when
carried to other regions bore abundant fruit. It was found
that the surface of the land, when once suggestion had enabled men to see topographic forms and interpret their
meaning, is a manuscript on which wonderful events are
recorded.

A younger generation of active workers has extended the
study of the earth's surface, so greatly stimulated by the
pioneer explorers just named, and has read for us the histories of valleys, plains, hills, and mountains throughout the
length and breadth of the land. Of these younger investigators we are indebted to none so much as to W. M. Davis,
Professor of Physical Geography at Harvard, who has made
New England, New Jersey, and Pennsylvania classic ground
to all future students of physiography. Gilbert has extended his studies to the basins of the Laurentian lakes and
other regions. The writings of J. C. Branner, M. R. Campbell, T. C. Chamberlin, N. H. Darton, J. S. Diller, C. W.
Hayes, Arthur Keith, W J McGee, R. D. Salisbury, R.

S. Tarr, Bailey Willis, and others, have greatly enlarged our knowledge of the laws governing streams, and of the origin of topographic forms.

The publications of the United States Geological Survey and of the earlier national surveys of which it is a continuation, the Geological and Natural History Survey of Canada, various State surveys, the Geological Society of America, and the National Geographic Society, together with the *Journal of Geology*, the *American Journal of Science*, etc., are the sources of published information drawn on most largely in the preparation of this book.

In the following chapters many references are given to the writings of the distinguished investigators named above, but all of the help derived from them while writing this book can scarcely be acknowledged. Much assistance has also been derived from conversation and correspondence with my colleagues, and, although fully appreciated, the portion derived from each one is scarcely known even to myself. My part in presenting this book is largely that of a guide who points out the routes others have traversed. My reward will be ample if even a few students follow the paths indicated and are led to explore their many as yet unknown branches.

ISRAEL C. RUSSELL.

UNIVERSITY OF MICHIGAN,
December 10, 1897.

CONTENTS

PAGE

TO THE READER v

CHAPTER I

THE DISINTEGRATION AND DECAY OF ROCKS 1
Mechanical Disintegration—Chemical Disintegration or Rock Decay
—Removal and Renewal of Surface Debris.

CHAPTER II

LAWS GOVERNING THE STREAMS 13
How Streams Obtain their Loads—Transportation—Debris Carried
by Ice — Corrasion — Pot-Holes — Lateral Corrasion — Meandering
Streams—Other Curves—Deflection of Streams Owing to the Earth's
Rotation—Questioning the Rivers—Erosion—Baselevel of Erosion—
Peneplains—Influence of Vegetation on Erosion.

CHAPTER III

INFLUENCE OF INEQUALITIES IN THE HARDNESS OF ROCKS ON RIVER-
SIDE SCENERY 52
Waterfalls—The Migration of Waterfalls—Bluffs Bordering Aged
Streams.

CHAPTER IV

MATERIAL CARRIED BY STREAMS IN SUSPENSION AND IN SOLUTION . 67
The Visible Loads of Streams—Bottom Load—Measures of Material
in Suspension—The Invisible Loads of Streams—Rate of Land
Degradation—Mechanical Degradation—Chemical Degradation—
Rate of Both Mechanical and Chemical Degradation—Underground
Streams.

xiii

CHAPTER V

STREAM DEPOSITS 97

Alluvial Cones—Talus Slopes—Flood-Plains—Natural Levees—Deltas: Deltas of High-Grade Streams—Deltas of Low-Grade Streams—Effects of Changes in the Elevation of the Land on the Growth of Deltas—Variations in Normal Stream Deposition—Influence of Elevation and Depression of the Land on Stream Deposition—Influence of Variations in Load on Stream Deposition—Influence of Changes of Climate on Stream Deposition—The General Process of Stream Corrasion and Deposition—Profiles of Streams—The Longitudinal Profile—Cross-Profiles.

CHAPTER VI

STREAM TERRACES 152

Origin of Terraces during the Process of Normal Stream Development—Terraces Due to Climatic Changes—Terraces Due to Elevation of the Land—Bottom Terraces—Delta Terraces and Current Terraces—Glacial Terraces—Relative Age of Terraces—Other Terraces—General Distribution of Stream Terraces.

CHAPTER VII

STREAM DEVELOPMENT 184

Consequent Streams—Subsequent Streams—Ideal Illustration of Stream Adjustment and Development—Examples of Stream Development and Adjustment in the Appalachian Mountains—Influence of Folds in the Rocks on Stream Adjustment—Water-Gaps and Wind-Gaps—Stream Conquest—Ancient Peneplains—Synclinal Mountains and Anticlinal Valleys—Effects of Elevation and Subsidence on Stream Development—Some of the Effects of Elevation—Some of the Effects of Subsidence—Some of the Influences of Volcanic Agencies on Stream Development—Some of the Modifications in Stream Development Due to Climatic Changes—Variations in Precipitation—Variations in Temperature—Fluctuations of Streams—Some of the Influences of Glaciers on Stream Development—Some of the Influences of Vegetation on Stream Development—Driftwood—Superimposed Streams—Migration of Divides.

CHAPTER VIII

PAGE

SOME OF THE CHARACTERISTICS OF AMERICAN RIVERS   254

Drainage Slopes : Atlantic, St. Lawrence, Hudson Bay, Arctic, Bering, Pacific, Great Basin, Gulf, and Caribbean—Leading Features of the Several Drainage Slopes—New England Rivers—A Drowned River—Appalachian Rivers—Rivers of Glaciated Lands—Southern Rivers—Alluvial Rivers—The Mississippi—Canyon Rivers—Sierra Nevada Rivers—" Where Rolls the Oregon "—Rivers of the Far North-West—Glacier-Born Rivers—Arctic Rivers—Rivers of the " Great Lone Land "—Rivers Flowing to Fresh-Water Seas—Niagara—Retrospect.

CHAPTER IX

THE LIFE HISTORY OF A RIVER 301

INDEX   321

ILLUSTRATIONS IN THE TEXT

FIGURE   PAGE

1. A POT-HOLE BEING SCOURED OUT BY A STREAM 33

2. A YOUNG STREAM NEAR ITHACA, NEW YORK 55

3. PROFILE OF NIAGARA FALLS 60

4. CROSS-PROFILE OF A FLOODPLAIN 118

5. MAP OF THE LOWER MISSISSIPPI SHOWING CREVASSES . . . 119

6. RADIAL SECTION OF A DELTA 126

7. LONGITUDINAL PROFILE OF A YOUNG STREAM 147

8. SUCCESSIVE CHANGES IN THE PROFILE OF A DIVIDE . . . 148

9. IDEAL PROFILE OF A DIVIDE 149

10. CROSS-PROFILE OF A TERRACED VALLEY 152

11. ALLUVIAL TERRACES 156

12. ALLUVIAL TERRACES 157

13. CROSS-SECTION OF A VALLEY WITH TERRACES IN SOLID ROCK . 165

14. CROSS-SECTION OF A CURRENT-BUILT TERRACE 168

15. SECTION OF TILTED PENEPLAIN 186

16. SKETCH-MAP, SHOWING YOUNG STREAMS 187

17. SKETCH-MAP, ILLUSTRATING STREAM DEVELOPMENT . . . 189

18. SKETCH-MAP, SHOWING MATURE STREAMS 190

19. ANTICLINAL AND SYNCLINAL 198

20. MAP ILLUSTRATING RIVER PIRACY 200

21. SECTION THROUGH LOOKOUT MOUNTAIN, ETC., ALABAMA . . 212

22. MAP OF CHESAPEAKE BAY 219

23. CROSS-PROFILE OF COLORADO CANYON 272

TABLE A. ANALYSIS OF AMERICAN RIVER-WATERS . . *facing* 78

FULL-PAGE ILLUSTRATIONS

PLATE   FACING PAGE

I. *a.* Marion River, New York. *b.* Ingall's Ceeek, Washington 12

II. Views on the Yukon, Alaska 24

III. *a.* Ray Brook, Adirondacks, New York. *b.* Moccasin Bend, Tennessee River 38

IV. *a.* Fall on Black Creek, near Gadsden, Alabama. *b.* Echo River, Mammoth Cave, Kentucky . . . 60

V. Map of the Delta of the Mississippi 98

VI. *a.* Sketch of Alluvial Cones. *b.* Indian Creek, California 102

VII. *a.* Big Goose River, Wyoming. *b.* New River, Tennessee, 108

VIII. *a.* Terraces on Fraser River, British Columbia. *b.* Terraces in Connecticut Valley 154

IX. Map of the Northern Appalachians 196

X. Map of Western Portion of the Anthracite Basin, Pennsylvania 204

XI. Map illustrating Stream Adjustment 210

XII. *a.* Beaver Dam, Wyoming. *b.* Dam of Drift-wood, West Fork of Teanaway River, Washington . . . 238

XIII. Map of a Portion of the Catskill Mountains, New York, 250

XIV. Map of North America showing Drainage Slopes . . 256

XV. *a.* Columbia River. *b.* Hudson River 262

XVI. *a.* An aggraded Valley near Fort Wingate, New Mexico. *b.* Shenandoah Peneplain, near Harper's Ferry, West Virginia 268

XVII. Canyon of the Colorado 274

RIVERS OF NORTH AMERICA

CHAPTER I

THE DISINTEGRATION AND DECAY OF ROCKS

THE study of rivers, from the point of view of the geographer, necessitates the consideration of the nature and origin of many topographic forms; the reason being that streams are among the most important agencies which give form and expression to the surface of the land. The study of streams, therefore, involves, to a great extent, the consideration of the origin of hills and mountains, plains and valleys, and the changes they pass through.

One of the principal tasks performed by streams is the moving of rock fragments and their transportation to the sea. Another function of streams is the deepening and widening of their channels and valleys. These propositions will be demonstrated later. It will be shown, also, that clear water has but little power to wear away the rocks over which it flows. In order to do this, the flowing water must be charged with hard particles or rock fragments of greater or less size. That is, the streams must be supplied with tools with which to excavate. It is now well under-

1

stood that the tools used by streams in abrading the rocks are mainly silt, sand, gravel, and stones, which are carried in suspension or rolled and pushed along the bottom. One of the primary questions, therefore, in order to understand how streams are enabled to remove material from the land, and, in so doing, to deepen and broaden their valleys, is: How are the rocks broken or otherwise prepared for stream transportation ?

The soil which nearly everywhere forms the surface of the land is composed mainly of disintegrated rock. This loose surface layer of more or less comminuted and decayed material, much of it, however, far too coarse to be termed soil, is the storehouse from which the streams derive the principal part of their loads.

The study of the agencies at work in breaking and otherwise disintegrating the earth's crust has shown that they may be classified in two groups: 1st, those acting mechanically; and 2d, those whose influence is principally chemical. Although the various agencies in these two groups co-operate and are frequently in action at the same time, it is convenient to consider them separately.

Mechanical Disintegration.—Changes of temperature, as between day and night, or from season to season, cause unequal expansion and contraction of the minerals and grains of which rocks are composed. Various and complex stresses are thus produced which cause even the most compact granite to crumble. The freezing of water contained in crevasses in rocks or in the interspaces between grains or crystals, is accompanied by expansion, which exerts a powerful force tending to fracture and disintegrate them.

The roots of trees enter crevices in the rocks, and as they enlarge, force off fragments frequently of large size. The undercutting of cliffs and banks by streams and by the waves and currents of lakes and of the ocean, causes the dislodgment of vast quantities of earth and stone. The fall of rocky material produced by these and still other causes, leads to still further breakage. Rock masses are also loosened or caused to fall by earthquake shocks. Volcanoes discharge a great volume of fragmental material into the air, and the cooling of lavas causes them to become fractured and jointed. When molten lava enters surface-water bodies, steam and gas explosions occur, and the rock is perhaps blown to dust. Rain-drops, snow crystals, and hail by beating on the rocks exert a force tending to break off fragments loosened by other and principally chemical agencies, and to wear, and frequently to polish, exposed surfaces. Sand and dust, blown by the wind, on coming in contact with rock exposures, wear away the softer parts and loosen the harder grains and crystals. Glaciers as they flow down mountain valleys or move over the surface of more level land, tear away projecting ledges, and when charged with sand and stones abrade and grind away the rock over which they move. Avalanches and landslides rush down declivities, carrying destruction in their paths, and sweep along loosened rock fragments which are broken still finer and in part ground to powder. The streams themselves, under certain conditions, roll along stones and even large boulders, which become rounded and broken, at the same time abrading the rocks over which they are carried, and thus aid in the general process of rock disintegration which

prepares the material composing the land for stream transportation.

All of the agencies just enumerated are mechanical in
their action, although accompanied by chemical changes,
and are confined to the surface, or, at most, to an extremely
superficial portion, of the earth's crust. There are also important mechanical agencies which act deep below the surface and lead to the fracturing of the rocks in such manner
as greatly to facilitate the agencies producing disintegration
in operation at the surface. And, besides, on account of
the continual lowering of the surface in many regions owing
to the removal of material, rock fragments originating at a
greater or less depth become mingled with those produced
at the surface in the several ways just enumerated, and thus
become of interest in the study of the manner in which
rocks are reduced to fragments of such size that they can
be moved by streams.

Of the mechanical agencies leading to the fracturing of
rocks below the reach of frost and of normal changes in
temperature, the most important are movements in the
earth's crust, the nature of which it is impracticable to discuss at this time, which cause even the most massive layers
to become folded and broken. These movements are frequently accompanied by the crushing of the rocks in zones
of various widths, as when a fracture is formed and its walls
ground against each other. Such breaks, accompanied or
followed by differential movements of their walls, are
termed faults, and the rock fragments produced are designated *fault breccias*.

The world over and to a great but indefinite depth, the

rocks are divided by what are known as joints, the origin of which is obscure. These dividing planes are similar, we may fancy, to gashes made by a sharp blade without appreciable thickness, drawn through the rocks. There are frequently two series of joints nearly at right angles to each other, and more or less nearly vertical; these are intersected many times by approximately horizontal cuts of the same character, and frequently also by planes of bedding. The rocks are divided in this manner into masses that are sometimes nearly true cubes. In many instances the joints cross each other irregularly and divide the rocks into blocks of many shapes. Joint blocks of whatever form vary in size, from a small fraction of a cubic inch to many cubic feet. In some instances these are contributed directly to streams, as when they fall from the face of a precipice, but more commonly they are broken and variously modified by atmospheric agencies before being fed to the flowing waters. The joints in rocks, although of inappreciable width deep below the surface, are planes of weakness along which chemical and mechanical agencies find favourable lines of attack. They open when the rocks are exposed to the weather, and greatly favour the further disintegration resulting from changes of temperature, the freezing of water, etc. The jointing of rocks is one of the primary and most important methods by which they become divided into blocks, thus exposing greater surfaces to the attack of chemical agencies, and in many regions, particularly in rugged mountains and in canyon walls, exerts a direct and pronounced influence on topographic forms.

Among the agencies that lead to the fracturing and mechanical disintegration of rocks deep below the surface, should be noted, also, injections of molten rocks forced upward into the earth's crust, earthquake shocks, the friction of debris carried by subterranean streams, and the falling of cavern roofs.   Still another agency, as has been pointed out by G. P. Merrill, in part chemical and in part mechanical in its action, results from the combination of water with certain mineral substances, producing what is termed hydration. This is accompanied by an increase in the bulk of the minerals affected, and the consequent production of stresses in the rocks containing them.   In some instances, apparently unaltered rock, when removed from mines and tunnels, rapidly crumbles from this cause when exposed to the air. In nature, the lowering of the surface by erosion and the exposure of previously deeply buried rocks would bring about similar changes.   There are yet other alterations in progress in the rocks due to chemical action, that promote mechanical disintegration, which cannot be noted at this time.

By the several processes just enumerated, the rocks are broken into blocks of all shapes and dimensions, some of which are of the size of gravel, sand, and dust grains, and are thus rendered suitable for stream transportation, and to act as tools by means of which flowing water promotes the process of rock breakage.

Chemical Disintegration or Rock-Decay.—Water is a solvent for probably all substances that occur in the earth's crust, although in many instances acting with extreme slowness.   The readiness with which most substances are taken into solution by water is enhanced by an increase of temperature, and in nature is also greatly assisted by various substances, especially organic acids, with which it becomes charged.

Even rain-water is never pure, but contains various salts and gases derived from the air. Principal among these is carbon dioxide, or carbonic acid. Rain-water on reaching the earth flows over the surface, or percolates for a time through the soil and rocks, and thus comes into intimate relations with the great store of organic acids supplied by the waste and decay of animal and vegetable life. The chemical energy of the water is thus greatly enhanced, and it becomes an active solvent for most mineral substances. Some of the minerals composing rocks are more soluble than others, and, being removed, allow those that remain to crumble and fall apart. The mineral substances taken in solution are, for the most part, contributed to streams and by them carried to the sea as an invisible load; but a portion is taken below the surface by downward-percolating waters and undergoes many changes in composition and at the same time produces various alterations in the rocks through which it passes.

The chemical changes produced in the rocks by percolating waters, while most active near the surface, occur also at considerable depths, and are there augmented by the internal heat of the earth. There is a lower limit to this process, however, due to the increasing density of the rocks with pressure and to the rise of temperature with increase in depth. There are good reasons for concluding that surface waters cannot descend more than twenty thousand or thirty thousand feet below the surface.

The chemical changes due to percolating water are influ-

enced in a variety of ways by temperature. The rocks are
dissolved most readily in warm, moist regions. It is in such
regions also that vegetation is most luxuriant and animal
life most abundant, and hence the waters are most highly
charged with organic acids. Chemical action, in most instances, is retarded by cold; vegetation is less abundant
and decay less rapid in cold than in warm climates; it is,
therefore, in cold regions that the decay of the rocks is at
a minimum.

In warm, humid countries, deep rock-decay has usually
taken place, but a thick surface sheet of decomposed material is not necessarily found, as the loosened debris may
be carried away as fast as it is produced. In the southern
Appalachians, and in many other warm temperate or equatorial regions, the rocks are so broken and decayed, even at
a depth of one hundred and fifty or two hundred feet from
the surface, that they may be crumbled between the fingers
or moulded like clay. In such instances the soil usually
shows various tints of red and yellow, the colours being due
to the oxidation and hydration of iron present in them.

In warm, dry countries chemical changes in the surface
material are retarded, although the rocks may be greatly
shattered by changes of temperature. In such regions the
soils are seldom red.

Chemical changes produced by percolating water below
the superficial portion of the earth—that is, below, perhaps, one hundred feet—increase with depth, on account of
progressively increasing temperature, but these changes
are beyond the immediate subject under discussion. An
important agency in rock disintegration and decay having

its source deep within the earth, however, is manifest especially in volcanic regions where steam charged with various acids rises through fissures and other openings. During volcanic eruptions, but more particularly after a volcano has passed to the condition of a fumarole or a solfatara, heated vapour and gases charged with sulphuric, hydrochloric, carbonic, and other acids escape in large volumes, sometimes continuously for centuries, and produce conspicuous changes in the rocks through which they rise. Similar but usually less copious exhalations occur from lava streams, and produce alterations in the lava which influence the character of the soil resulting from them.

The chemical alterations produced by percolating water, and less commonly by volcanic gases, in rocks near the surface, are in part by solution, and in part oxidation, hydration, precipitation, etc. These changes, except the last mentioned, may be grouped, at least in a general way, under the term *rock-decay*. In decaying, the rocks are more or less disintegrated, however, since the more soluble minerals are removed, thus allowing the less soluble rock constituents to crumble and fall apart. The processes of rock-disintegration and rock-decay mutually assist each other, and progress at the same time. The result is that the surface layer of the earth's crust is profoundly altered, and a sheet of modified material is produced, which is designated in part as soil and in part as rock detritus.[1]

The Removal and Renewal of Surface Debris.—The sur-

---

[1] The name *Regolith*, meaning blanket-stone, has recently been proposed for the superficial material covering the earth, by G. P. Merrill, *A Treatise on Rocks, Rock-Weathering and Soils*, 1897, p. 299.

face changes just considered have been in progress since the first appearance of land, and will continue as long as continents and islands exist.   In former geological periods the agencies enumerated, particularly those of a chemical nature, were more active than now, and have varied from time to time, in probably all portions of the earth's surface, with climatic and other changes.   Throughout all geological ages, the streams have been actively engaged in removing the disintegrated and more or less chemically altered surface portions of the earth's crust.   In places and at certain times, the debris has been removed as fast as formed, and bare, hard rock surfaces have been exposed; at other times, the supply has been in excess of the demand, and deep accumulations have resulted.   The surface sheet of debris has been continually wasting and continually renewed.   Throughout the history of the earth, topographic changes have been in progress.   Mountain ranges and systems have been upraised, the rocks composing them fractured and chemically altered, and borne away by streams.   Where once a magnificent mountain range reared its battlements among the clouds, there is now a plain but little elevated above the sea.   Not only one, but several such *geographical cycles* have run their courses in many lands.

During the cycles still in progress human agencies have been added to those previously in action.   This new element in the earth's history has become more and more important as man has advanced in civilisation.   In part, human industries have retarded the work of physical and chemical agencies, but in the main man has been a destroyer.

The removal of the portion of the earth's crust rising

above the sea, during each cycle, has been done almost wholly by streams. The manner in which the rocks are prepared for transportation, however, is quite as important to the geographer as the methods employed for their removal, but the brief review given above of this division of the general process must suffice for the present.

The student who may wish to continue the studies outlined in this chapter will find assistance in the books mentioned below.[1]

[1] GEORGE P. MERRILL. *A Treatise on Rocks, Rock-Weathering and Soils*, pp. 172–398. The Macmillan Co., 1897.

ISRAEL C. RUSSELL. *The Decay of Rocks and the Origin of the Red Colour of Certain Formations.* U. S. Geological Survey, Bulletin No. 52, 1889.

ISRAEL C. RUSSELL. "A Reconnoissance in South-Eastern Washington." U. S. Geological Survey, *Water-Supply and Irrigation Papers*, No. 4, pp. 57–69, 1897.

GEORGE P. MARSH. *The Earth as Modified by Human Action.* Charles Scribner's Sons, 1885.

JOHN C. BRANNER. "Decomposition of Rocks in Brazil." *Bulletin of the Geological Society of America*, vol. vii., pp. 255–314, 1896.

ALEXIS A. JULIEN. "On the Geological Action of the Humus Acids," in *American Association for the Advancement of Science, Proceedings*, vol. xxviii., pp. 311–410, 1879.

WALTER MAXWELL. *Lavas and Soils of the Hawaiian Islands.* Honolulu, 1898.

CHAPTER II

LAWS GOVERNING THE STREAMS

THE water which flows off from the land, as is well known, is supplied by the condensation of vapour in the air. A part of the water reaching the earth flows over the surface and gathers into rills which unite to form larger streams, and a part sinks below the surface and, after following an underground course, usually by percolation through porous soil or rocks, emerges in springs, many of which join the surface flow.

It is also well known that streams ranging in size from the smallest rills to the mightiest rivers are engaged either occasionally, as during floods, or continually, in carrying away material that was previously a portion of the land. The manner in which this material is acquired by the streams, the way it is transported, the effects it has on the flow of the streams, and on their bottoms and sides, the modifications in the configuration of the surface of the land due to the removal and re-deposition of debris, etc., are all phenomena that obey definite laws and are variously modified by conditions. If one can ascertain the laws governing the behaviour of a single stream, they should also apply not only to the streams of North America, but to those of all land areas.

PLATE I.

FIG. A.   Marion River, Adirondacks, New York.

Summer stage, showing stones which are moved during high-water.   (Photograph by S. R. Stoddard.)

FIG. B.   Ingall's Creek, Washington.

Showing boulders too large for the stream to move even during high-water stages.

No one stream, perhaps, in the limited time that an individual student is enabled to examine it, will furnish illustrations of all of the modifying conditions influencing the life of a great river. By selecting typical examples, however, affected by different modifying conditions, we may sketch a composite picture which will represent the various phases in the life history of a single river that has carried on its work for tens of thousands of years.

How Streams Obtain their Loads.—Rain-drops strike the earth with a certain force, dependent on their size, the distance they descend, the direction and force of the wind, etc. If rain-drops fall on the surface of a still pool we may see them rebound. If we face a rain-storm, the sting of the beating drops again assures us that they exert a considerable force on the objects against which they strike. When the drops fall on a solid rock surface, they gather in rills of clear water, but if they fall on loose soil, as a newly ploughed field, for example, the finer particles of earth are disturbed, and as the waters gather into rills and flow away in obedience to gravity, they are turbid with earth particles held in suspension. The turbid rills unite in brooks, and these again combine to form larger streams. The fine silt disturbed by the impact of the rain-drops is carried by the rills to the brooks and thence onward, perhaps with many halts, to the sea. After heavy rains even large rivers become muddy. The lakes and large areas in the sea near the mouths of rivers are then discoloured. This happens during every storm the world over, and evidently, if sufficient time be allowed, must lead to changes of great magnitude both in the topography of the land from which material is removed and in the shape of the basins where it is deposited.

When the surface of the land is dry, and especially when bare of vegetation, earth particles are moved by the wind in much the same manner that streams take up and transport the flakes and grains of rock which they are competent to transport. The dust and sand carried by the wind and falling in streams is another source from which they obtain material suitable for removal.

The fine rock powder, or glacial meal as it is termed, produced by the grinding of stones held in the ice against each other and on the rocks over which the glaciers flow, is contributed directly to the waters formed by the melting of the ice. For this reason nearly every glacier-born stream is turbid and heavy with silt.

Volcanoes during times of violent eruption discharge vast quantities of fine dust, and in many instances equally abundant rock fragments of the size of sand and gravel. When material extruded in these forms falls in streams, or is carried in by tributary rills and by the wind, another source is furnished from which streams receive their initial loads. There are yet other methods by which streams are supplied with material in a suitable condition to be transported. Among these may be noted the fall of cosmic dust, disturbances produced by avalanches and landslides, the uprooting of trees, the impact of driftwood and floating ice on the bottoms and sides of stream channels, the movement of roots and overhanging branches by the wind and by the currents of the streams themselves, disturbances of the material forming the bottoms and sides of stream channels by animals,—as by beavers, for example,—contributions of shells and siliceous cases from organisms like mollusks and diatoms living in the waters, etc. Man promotes the transfer of solid matter to the streams in various ways, more especially by ploughing and otherwise disturbing the soil, and by the removal of forests. All of the methods mentioned in this paragraph, however, are of secondary importance in comparison with the influence of rain, wind, and glaciers.

The particles carried in suspension by streams tend to fall to the bottom, being continually pulled down by gravity, but in flowing water there are various currents, some of which tend upward and exert an influence on the falling particles in opposition to gravity. The currents in the water move the suspended particles in various directions and retard their fall to the bottom, but the resultant movement is in the direction of the flow of the stream.

The particles carried by streams fall to the bottom many times during their journeys, and rest there for a period perhaps brief but possibly long, and are again lifted by upward currents and brought within the influence of the onward flow. Material thus transported by a stream may for convenience be termed its *load*. Streams not only receive their initial loads in the various ways just stated, but there are other methods by which the same result is reached. As will be considered later, flowing water exerts a pressure on objects against which it strikes. If this force be great enough to move the objects in the path of a stream, they will be pushed along, rolled over, or, with the assistance of upward currents, taken in suspension. The strength of the water current determines the size of the particles it can carry, so that a stream of a given velocity, but without an initial load, would be able to remove from its channel all of the loose particles it is competent to carry and thereafter would run clear unless its velocity were increased.

The principal methods by which streams receive their initial loads insure a waste of the land between the drainage lines, and consequently this land changes in topographic form. The deepening and broadening of the stream channels is accomplished principally by the friction of the debris carried through them, aided also by solution. The laws governing this complex process will be considered later.

Transportation.—The debris acquired by streams in the several ways considered above is carried along by them. A convenient term for this process is *transportation*. Light objects like leaves, wood, pumice, etc., are floated on the surface, but meet with various delays, and undergo more or less chemical and mechanical changes during their journeys, and sooner or later sink to the bottom. Material like fine sand and silt remains in suspension to a great extent and is carried bodily onward. Heavier objects, like pebbles and boulders, are either rolled or pushed along the bottom, or remain at rest until they are reduced in size by the friction and solution, or shattered by the impact, of material swept against them. The size, weight (specific gravity), and form of the loose material within the influence of a stream determine whether or not it will be moved by a current of a given velocity. The smaller the divisions into which a mass of rock is broken, the larger the ratio of surface to weight. The force which a current of a given velocity exerts against objects in its path varies as the area of the opposing sur-

face. The smaller the parts into which a rock mass becomes divided, therefore, the greater the tendency of the
current to move them.

The ability of the stream to carry debris in suspension,
however, depends not only on its velocity and the degree of
comminution of the material within its influence, but also,
as previously stated, on the presence of secondary and especially of upward currents which tend to lift the particles
brought within their influence. While a particle is in suspension the onward currents bear it along, but gravity is all
the while acting, and, unless counteracted, finally pulls it
to the bottom. The journey of a rock fragment from the
mountains to the sea consists of a great number of upward
and onward excursions, with rests of greater or less length
between. More definitely, the ability of a stream to hold
debris in suspension is due to the fact that different layers
of water are actuated by different velocities, and these exert
different pressures upon the different sides of the suspended
particles. Hence, the greater the differences in the velocities of consecutive layers, the greater will be the tendency
to hold material in suspension. It is stated by Humphreys
and Abbot, from whose report on the Mississippi much of
this discussion of the mechanics of stream flow is taken,
that the change in the velocity of the waters of streams in
horizontal planes is greatest near the shore and least near
the thread of maximum current; and in vertical planes, is
greatest near the bottom and surface and least at about one-
third of the depth of the stream—that is, where the abso-
lute velocity is greatest. If, then, the water be either
charged to its maximum capacity or overcharged with sedi-

ment, the highest percentage of material in suspension will be found near the banks and near the surface and bottom, and the least amount near the thread of the maximum current and at a depth of about one-third of that of the stream. If, however, the water is undercharged with material in suspension, the distribution will not follow any law, the amount at any locality being determined by what may be considered as accidental swirls, boils, etc. As most streams are undercharged, it follows that samples of water from several points in a cross-section should be examined in order to ascertain approximately the amount of material that is being carried. Rock fragments too heavy to be lifted may be rolled or pushed along the bottom, or perhaps turned over from time to time by the resultant onward current. There is thus an adjustment between the strength of the current and the specific gravity of the material transported.

It is well known that the power flowing water has to transport rock debris increases with increase of velocity. Experiments have shown that if water is made to flow through an even channel and the rate of flow is gradually increased by increasing the inclination of the channel, it will move material added to it approximately as follows [1]:

VELOCITY OF CURRENT.	SIZE OF MATERIAL MOVED.
3 inches per second.	Fine clay and silt.
6 " " "	Fine sand.
12 " " "	Pebbles ½ inch in diameter.
2 feet " "	" 1 " " "

[1] David Stevenson, *Canal and River Engineering*, p. 315; A. J. Jukes-Browne, *Physical Geology*, 1892, p. 130; Archibald Geikie, *Text-Book of Geology*, 2d edition, 1885, p. 354; Joseph Le Conte, *Elements of Geology* 4th edition, 1896, pp. 18–20. See also other elementary works on geology.

VELOCITY OF CURRENT.	SIZE OF MATERIAL MOVED.
2.82 feet per second.	Pebbles 2 inches in diameter.
3.46 " " "	" 3 " " "
4 " " "	" 4 " " "
4.47 " " "	" 5 " " "
4.90 " " "	" 6 " " "
5.29 " " "	" 7 " " "
5.65 " " "	" 8 " " "
6 " " "	" 9 " " "

It must be understood that the currents referred to in this table are bottom currents, and in general may be taken at about one-half the central surface current.

An important fact shown by these and other similar experiments is that the transporting power of running water increases in a greater ratio than the increase in velocity.

It has been demonstrated that if the surface of an object opposed to a current of water, as the pier of a bridge, for example, remains constant, the force of current striking it varies as the square of its velocity. Also, that the *transporting* power of a current, or the weight of the largest fragment it can carry, *varies as the sixth power of the velocity.*[1] Under this law it will be seen that doubling the velocity of a current increases its transporting power sixty-four times. If a stream flowing with a given velocity is able to move stones weighing one pound, by doubling the velocity boulders weighing sixty-four pounds can be carried; and if the velocity were increased ten times, rocks weighing one million pounds could be moved. This enables us to see how streams are capable of producing such striking results during floods, when their velocities are increased on account of an increase in volume. The gradient of a river, or its average

[1] A demonstration of this proposition may be found in Joseph Le Conte's *Elements of Geology*, 4th edition, pp. 19, 20. Appleton & Co., 1896.

fall in a given distance, as a rule, progressively decreases from near its source to its mouth. With this general decrease in gradient there is a decrease in velocity, and consequently a loss in transporting power and a diminution or total check of friction on the stream's bottom. As a result of these conditions, we usually find that the streams are actively engaged in deepening their channels in their upper courses, and are consequently able to extend their branches farther and farther, thus acquiring new territory, and at the same time to deposit material in their lower and less steep courses nearer their mouths. Variations in this process occur not only from season to season but from day to day, on account principally of variation in velocity due to changes in volume.

The carrying of debris consumes some of the energy of flowing water. As an extreme example, it is readily seen that an excessive quantity of fine mud contributed to a stream will entirely check its flow. If but little mud is added, however, it is carried forward without sensibly diminishing the strength of the current. Without attempting to present a complete analysis of the laws governing stream transportation, it will be sufficient at this time to note that streams exert a selective power, taking up and carrying forward the finer and lighter material within their reach, and, if this be sufficient to consume their available energy, leaving the larger and heavier masses, although they may not be too heavy to be removed if the energy of the stream is not otherwise taxed.

The principal laws governing stream transportation may be briefly formulated as follows:

1. The greater the slope of a stream channel, the greater the amount of material in suspension the stream can carry; the reason being that the greater the slope the swifter is the flow of the water descending it, other conditions remaining unchanged. The increase in transporting power with increase of slope is greater than a single ratio. That is, if the declivity of a stream is double, its transporting power is more than double.

2. An increase in the volume of a stream increases its ability to transport. The greater the volume of a stream, the greater will be its velocity, and the less its loss of power due to friction in proportion to its energy. Here, again, the increase in transporting power is greater than a simple ratio.

3. The capacity of a stream to transport is greater for fine debris than for coarse; for the reason that to move fine material requires less power for the same weight than for coarser material, and, also, when the material is fine a greater portion of the stream's energy can be utilised than when the load is coarse.

One of the most important principles connected with stream transportation is that flowing water assorts the debris delivered to it. Fine particles are more easily carried than coarser ones of the same specific gravity, and are first removed. This is true both of particles in suspension and of material rolled along the bottom. If the fine material is sufficient to consume the available energy of a stream, all coarser debris is left until its energy is increased, as during storms, or until the fragments too large to be removed are reduced in size. There is a delicate adjustment between the velocity of a stream and the size of the debris it can carry, which may be termed the selective power of currents. The influence of this selective power is seen not only in the character of the material moved by streams, and in the debris left on their bottoms, but in the deposits which they make, whether on their border, or in the lakes and sea to which they contribute their loads. As most sedimentary rocks are formed of stream-born debris, this assorting process must evidently be of vast geological importance.

Debris Carried by Ice.—An interesting and at times an important factor in stream transportation is the assistance furnished by ice, which frequently enables streams to move objects that would otherwise exceed their power.

During winter the water of streams frequently freezes to the bottom, more especially along their margins, and stones, gravel, sand, etc., forming the beds of their channels, become firmly attached to the ice. In spring, when the streams are swollen, the ice, on account of its buoyancy, breaks away from the bottom, but frequently retains large quantities of debris, which is carried with it down-stream, and may make a long journey before being dropped or deposited by the stranding of the ice.[1] Stones carried in this manner are frequently of large size. A rudely spherical boulder measured by me on the bank of the Yukon, which had certainly travelled scores of miles from its parent ledge, was a little over six feet in diameter. Many others very nearly as large were seen which had recently been forced several yards up the banks of the river. All of these were

---

[1] An account of the method of transportation here discussed may be found in Lyell's *Principles of Geology* (11th edition, vol. i., pp. 359–363, Appleton & Co., 1873), accompanied by an illustration of large boulders along the shores of the St. Lawrence, which had been moved through the agency of ice..

far beyond the reach of former glaciers, and, without question, had been deposited in their present positions at a very recent date; some of them, in fact, during the floods of the preceding spring.

Another method by which the ice of a large river sometimes becomes freighted with debris may be observed where high-grade tributaries occur. In such an instance, when spring approaches, the small streams may first become freed of ice and be able to sweep down debris upon the still frozen surface of the river. Again, when a river is bordered by steep bluffs, material loosened from the faces of the cliffs falls upon the ice and is ready for removal when freshets occur. Avalanches may also bring debris to a frozen river in the same way that they do to glaciers.

The assistance in transportation rendered to streams by ice is, of course, greatest in high latitudes, but is not inconsiderable as far south as Virginia. Along the Potomac there are frequently boulders much too large for the unaided waters to move, and which it is presumed have been buoyed up by ice during a part at least of their journeys, since they are well beyond where the river loses velocity on passing from its high-grade upper course to the plain near the sea. In the method of transportation here considered it is not necessary that a river should freeze from side to side. The ice that forms about a partially submerged boulder near the shore of a stream tends to buoy it up. When the water surface is raised, if sufficient ice has formed about the stone, it will be floated away.[1] In the terraces of the Potomac

---

[1] The weight of a cubic foot of water at 32° F. is 62.417 pounds; a cubic foot of ice weighs 57.2 pounds.

about Washington, there are boulders two to three feet or
more in diameter, resting on fine sand and clay, which it is
thought were attached to ice-cakes at the time of their removal to their present sites.   The locality referred to, it
will be remembered, is south of the southern limit of former
glaciers.

The stone-charged ice carried each spring by the rivers in
high latitudes acts much like a glacier in grinding the bottom and sides of the channel down which it moves.   In the
case of a large river this action is most pronounced near its
borders, where the water is shallow, and probably does not
occur at all in the deeper portions.   On the border of Porcupine River, Alaska, I have seen large areas exposed
during low water where the bottom consisted of stones embedded in tenacious clay so as to form a veritable pavement.
The ice charged with debris had previously moved over this
pavement, and not only pressed down the stones so as to
produce a generally even surface, but ground their exposed
portions so as to make facets which were polished and
striated.   The pebbles and in some cases flat stones a foot
or more in diameter, bearing these markings, have a remarkable resemblance to glaciated boulders.

In other instances along the Yukon I found the solid
rock, on prominent points, to a height of twenty feet or
more above the summer level of the river, smoothed and
striated by the action of river ice in much the same manner
that is familiar in formerly glaciated valleys.[1]

During spring floods in northern rivers, ice-blocks are fre-

[1] I. C. Russell, " Notes on the Surface Geology of Alaska," in *Bulletin of
the Geological Society of America*, vol. i., pp. 116–122, 1890.

PLATE II.

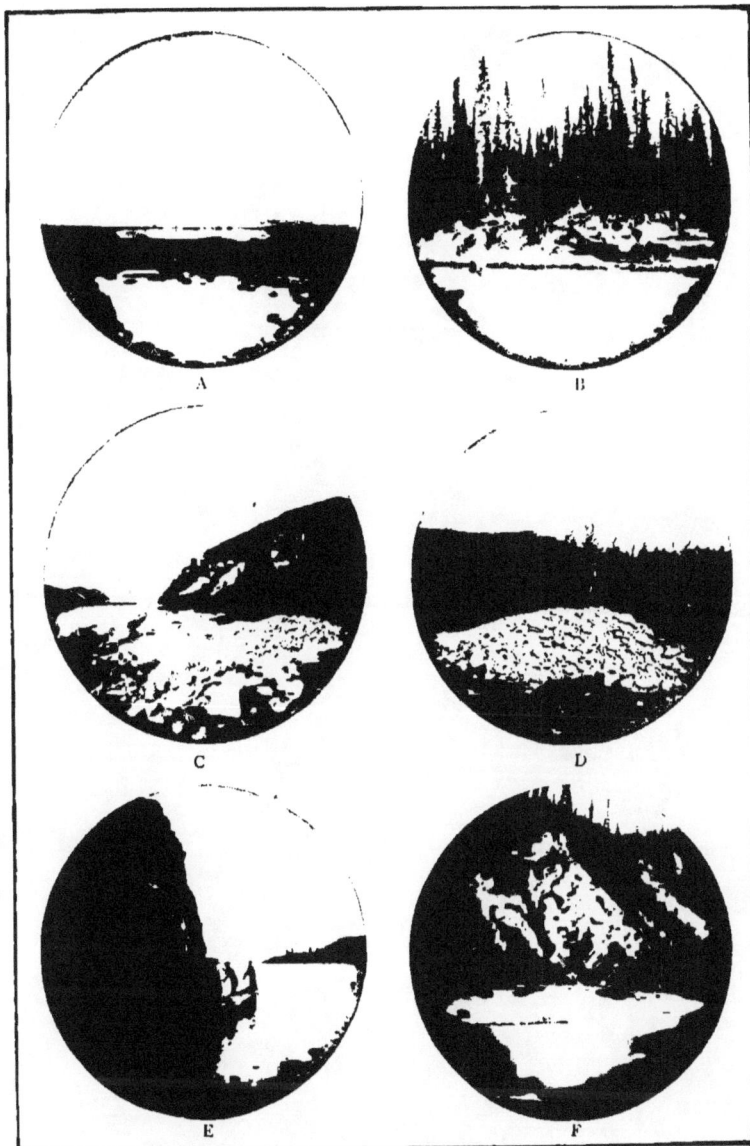

Views on the Yukon, Alaska.

A.—Looking from the river across a portion of its delta.
B.—River-bank of perennially frozen gravel.
C. and D.—Stones left by floating ice during spring floods.
E.—Bluff of hard rock on the border of a deeply cut valley.
F.—Small cut-terraces in sand deposited during high-water.

quently stranded and even forced far up the banks. Where flat cakes of ice accumulate in this manner, they sometimes have gravel and sand washed over them; this material lodges in the cracks and openings between the cakes, and is left in curious heaps and ridges when the ice is melted. Sometimes these deposits surround small areas so as to make shallow basins.

There is yet another method by which ice assists streams in moving debris down their channels, and one which operates in midstream, where the current is swift. I refer to the formation, during excessively cold weather, of what is termed *anchor ice*, or *ground ice*, at the bottom of streams, especially where the waters plunge over small obstructions and comparatively quiet bottom-eddies are produced. This bottom ice forms about stones, and by its buoyancy tends to lift them from the bottom, and thus to assist the currents in carrying them away.

An instructive account of the formation of anchor ice in one of the rivers of New Brunswick, during the winter of 1869–70, has been recorded by W. G. Thompson,[1] one of the engineers of the Intercolonial Railway. In this account, quoted below, it is stated that not only were small stones lifted from the bottom and floated down-stream, but, what is of still greater interest, the ice increased in thickness in some instances until it formed dams, and the stream was turned from its course. Mr. Thompson's account is as follows:

" The Matapediac, which is fed by large fresh-water springs, runs over a rocky bottom covered with loose stones, ranging in

[1] *Nature*, vol. i., p. 555, 1870.

size from coarse gravel to boulders as large as a hogshead, and the average current is about four miles an hour.

" Early in November last the temperature went down in one night to 12° F., and on going out of camp the following morning I noticed large quantities of what appeared to be snow saturated with water floating down the stream, but not a particle of snow had fallen near us for many miles round, as far as I could see by the mountain-tops, nor had any ice formed on the surface of the river.

" The water opposite where I stood was about six feet deep, and perfectly clear, so that I could see every stone on the bottom, and, with the exception of the floating slush, the river was as it had been the previous day when the temperature was about 50° F. I got into a canoe and paddled with the current for half a mile or so, and in shooting some small rapids, where the water in places was not more than two or three feet deep, I noticed on the bottom masses of the slush clustered round and between the boulders, and a slight touch with the paddle was sufficient to free these clusters, when they rose to the surface, and were carried away by the current. I continued down the stream for three or four miles, and noticed the same thing in every rapid, where the water was shallow and ruffled by stones at the bottom.

" The buoyancy of this slush was such that when detached from the bottom it rose so rapidly as to force itself well out of the water, and then floated off about half submerged.

" I watched this forming of slush for many days, and in several cases found small stones embedded in the floating slush, having been torn from the bottom when the buoyancy of the slush, aided by the running water, caused it to rise.

" The temperature continued getting lower daily, and the slush in the rapids formed more rapidly than it was carried away, so much so that a bar or dam was formed across the river at each rapid, backing up the water in some cases five or six feet, when it generally found an outlet over the adjoining land, and into its natural bed again, or the head of water became sufficient to tear away the obstruction, which by this time had become a solid frozen mass.

" All this time, no properly crystallised ice had formed on the surface of the river, the current being too rapid, but the slush of 'anchor ice,' as the trappers call it, was forming in deeper water than it had formed in before, indeed all over the river bottom, and was rising and floating away as I have already described. Eventually the temperature got down to two and three degrees below zero, when the river *surface* began to freeze in the eddies and along the edges, and the open-water space became narrower every day, and was filled with floating 'anchor ice' and detached masses of solid ice, which here and there became jammed and frozen together, so as to form ice-bridges on which we could cross.

" These ice-bridges served as booms to stop much of the floating ice, which froze solid the moment it came to rest; and in this manner the river at last became completely frozen over for about forty miles of its length, but not until after we had experienced five weeks of steady cold, with the thermometer never above 12° F., and frequently down to − 16° F."

When we recall the fact that the conditions of temperature described above recur every winter throughout nearly one-half of North America, it becomes evident that anchor ice must play an important part in stream transportation. But little attention has been directed to this matter, however, and it is highly desirable that someone favourably located for such studies should make a careful record, especially as to the number and size of the stones picked up from the bottom of stream channels, owing to the buoyancy of the ice formed about them. It will be noted that this process of transportation is brought into operation simply by a lowering of temperature, and does not require a rise of the water in order to float the debris attached to the ice, as is the case when surface ice becomes fastened to the bottom. Anchor ice operates in the way

described in midstream, where the water is not only swift
but may be comparatively deep; while the similar work of
surface ice is practically confined to the shallow water on
the margins of streams.

Corrasion.—Clear streams, as we ordinarily see them, are
such as have removed from their channels all of the particles
within their reach which they are competent to transport,
although they may still roll and push coarse fragments along
their bottoms. It is to be noted, however, that clear
streams, when of a given velocity, may become muddy if the·
velocity is increased. The friction of clear running water
is but slight, hence streams not charged with material in
suspension wear their channels very slowly. In such instances chemical solution of the rocks over which the waters
flow may be in excess of mechanical abrasion.

When a stream receives an initial load of silt and sand
from rain-wash, the action of the wind, glacial abrasion,
etc., an important change in its behaviour occurs. The
transported fragments on being brought in contact with the
bottom and sides of the channel of the stream produce
abrasion. The flowing waters charged with silt and sand
act not unlike a strip of sandpaper that is drawn over an
object continually in one direction. The transported fragments abrade the rocks with which they are brought in
contact, and are themselves worn and broken. Gravel and
larger rock fragments too heavy to be carried in suspension,
except during floods, are worn and broken by smaller frag·
ments coming in contact with them, and when moved during
high-water stages, assist in a marked way in promoting the
process of channel enlargement. The friction and impact

of the particles that are carried forward tend to loosen and dislodge other fragments, and thus increase the amount of material available for transportation.

It is convenient to consider the process of stream abrasion due to the friction of transported material and to chemical solution, as a part of the general process of land degradation, and to give it a separate name. To meet this want, the term *corrasion* has been proposed.[1]

The deepening and widening of a stream channel—that is, corrasion—is carried on mainly by mechanical wear due to the friction of silt, sand, gravel, boulders, etc., carried through it by the flowing waters, but is assisted, many times in an important manner, by solution.

There are conditions that limit or modify the competency of a stream to transport debris, as has already been briefly considered. In a similar way there are conditions which modify and limit the rate of stream corrasion. Streams, as is well known, vary in rate of flow, in volume, in declivity, in the degree to which they are loaded, in chemical composition, etc. Changes in any one of these conditions will manifestly exert an influence on the rate at which a stream is enabled to deepen and widen its channel.

The nature of the load carried by a stream also varies in different instances, and even from month to month and

---

[1] As the nomenclature of dynamical geology and physical geography is not yet definitely fixed, it may be suggested that *corrasion* furnishes a convenient generic term, and may be made to include the processes of abrasion by stream-like movements of other substances than water, when charged with rock fragments. The grinding of rocks by glaciers may be designated as *glacial corrasion ;* the process of wearing of rocks by dust and sand transported by air-currents becomes *æolian corrasion ;* and lake and ocean shores furnish examples of wave and current corrasion.

from day to day in the same stream. The particles or fragments carried are fine or coarse, hard or soft, rounded or
angular; all of these conditions have an influence on the
amount of friction exerted on the stream bed, and hence
modify the rate of corrasion. Again, the rate at which a
stream channel is enlarged under the supposition that the
velocity of the stream, the character of its load, etc., remain
constant, will vary with the nature of the rocks over which
it flows. Hard rocks are worn more slowly than soft rocks,
easily soluble rocks are more rapidly removed than those of
difficult solubility. There are still other conditions pertaining to the beds of streams which influence corrasion. Massive rocks yield less readily than those perhaps of equal
hardness and equally soluble, but which are much jointed, or
occur in thin layers. Rock texture thus exerts an important influence on corrasion, as does also the inclination of
the rocks or their dip. When hard and soft beds alternate,
other conditions being the same, corrasion is more rapid
when they are inclined than when they are horizontal.

It is unnecessary to trace the effects of variations in these
several conditions, as the student may do this for himself,
and thus have the pleasure of making independent dis-
coveries. In the case of a stream flowing under stated conditions, let the student postulate an increase in volume, in
declivity, in character of load, in hardness of the rocks
forming its channel, etc., other conditions remaining the
same in each case, except so far as the reaction on them of
the postulated change is concerned, and trace the effects on
the rate of corrasion.

The principal laws governing corrasion are, briefly:

1. The rate at which a stream corrades its channel, other conditions remaining the same, increases with increase in load to a certain point which varies with the character of the load. If the load continues to increase, friction on the bottom decreases, and ceases when the entire energy of the stream is consumed in transportation.

2. Other conditions remaining the same, corrasion increases with declivity and with volume of water, since each of the changes increases velocity.

For a more detailed discussion of the laws governing stream transportation and corrasion than it is practicable to present at this time, the reader is referred to Gilbert's[1] admirable analysis of land sculpture, already cited many times in the present treatise.

The conditions controlling the amount of detritus a stream can transport are mainly velocity and volume. Velocity is increased by an increase in volume and also by increased declivity. In nature we find that streams ordinarily vary in volume with seasonal changes and also from day to day, and hence their ability to transport, and consequently to corrade, undergoes many fluctuations. The gradients of stream channels vary from place to place along their courses, and hence their ability to deepen their channels is not the same in all parts. The load that a stream carries in one portion of its course may be too great a burden in another portion, and some of it, always the coarser portion, will be dropped. The journeys of stream-borne debris are thus far from being continuous. The transported material

---

[1] G. K. Gilbert, *Report on the Geology of the Henry Mountains*, 4to, pp. 99–150. Department of the Interior, U. S. Geographical and Geological Survey of the Rocky Mountain Region, J. W. Powell in charge. Washington, 1877.

is laid aside from time to time in bars and flood-plains. It may require tens of thousands of years for a given rock fragment loosened on a mountain-side to reach its final resting-place in the sea.

In nature we find, as a rule, that the gradients of streams decrease from their sources to their mouths, but it must be remembered that this is the result of the action of the streams themselves and follows a long period of development and adjustment. As increased declivity favours corrasion, it is to be expected that the mountain tracts of streams will be deepened at a greater rate than their valley tracts, and that they will be enabled to extend their branches farther and farther, and thus acquire new territory. This, in fact, is the case, as we know, for the great majority of rivers are corrading their channels in the highlands and depositing in the lowlands. Rivers are ordinarily supplied by many branches, however, which means that the volume of water in the branches is less than in the trunk stream, and accompanying decreased volume, other conditions remaining the same, is a decreased corrasion. The behaviour of a stream in reference to corrasion and deposition is thus a resultant of many and frequently opposing conditions. As will be shown later, the ability of a stream to corrade or deposit in a given portion of its course varies ordinarily with its age, or, more accurately, with its stage of development. The portion of a stream channel where corrasion is in active progress during its youth, may become a region of deposition at a more advanced stage in its history under the process of normal development which streams experience even if no changes occur in land elevation.

Pot-Holes.—One of the minor phases of stream corrasion is illustrated by the cylindrical holes frequently worn in the beds of streams by stones swept about by strong currents. These holes are sometimes saucer-shaped, but more frequently have steep sides and rounded bottoms, and resemble the insides of the familiar cast-iron kettles used for culinary purposes; this similarity has suggested the name *pot-hole*, by which they are commonly designated. Their walls are usually smooth, and sometimes exhibit grooves and ridges

FIG. 1.   A Pot-Hole being Scoured out by Stream Action.
(After R. S. Tarr.)

in horizontal planes or arranged more or less spirally. In these grooved holes one sometimes finds well-worn pebbles, or even large boulders, and discovers a relation between the size of the grooves and of the stones that made them. In many instances, also, these mills are still in working order, and a stream of water is plunging into them, as is shown in the accompanying photograph.

Pot-holes are of all sizes, from shallow depressions a few inches in depth to vertical borings five or six feet across and fifteen or twenty feet or more deep. From these well defined examples there is a gradation up to the basins produced by the stones swirled about at the bases of waterfalls, as the pool into which Niagara plunges, for example, which might perhaps be termed compound pot-holes.

In the making of these characteristic depressions the millstones may be worn out, but new ones are supplied from time to time, and the process goes on. Similar excavations are made also beneath glaciers, where streams flowing on the surface of the ice plunge into crevasses, or deep well-like openings termed *moulins*, and reach the rocks below. In fact, any strong current by being deflected may cause loose stones to be whirled about so as to grind the rocks on which they rest, and produce depressions of the nature here considered. Favourable conditions result when pebbles and boulders of hard material occur in a stream where the bottom is of soft rock, and where also the current is swift, and eddies, swirls, whirlpools, etc., are produced.

Lateral Corrasion.—Streams in moving material along their channels not only wear away the rocks over which they flow, but abrade the sides of their channels as well.

It is difficult to formulate the laws governing lateral corrasion, but the general manner in which it is accomplished may be readily understood.

In considering the process of vertical corrasion the influence of upward currents in flowing water was recognised. But besides the upward currents there are also lateral currents. In fact, the flow of water, even through smooth, straight troughs, is complex, and many secondary currents are generated. This complexity is vastly increased when the channel is rough and irregular. If we watch a swift-flowing stream, we shall be enabled to see that there are many swirls and eddies due to, or accompanied by, currents moving in all directions. Along the sides of a stream channel the secondary currents strike the rocks and dash against them whatever material the waters may hold in suspension. Friction results from the impact of the floating particles, and tends to wear away the sides of the channel. The larger fragments rolled along the bottom of the stream can take but little part, directly, in this process of channel-widening. It is the finer material—the silt and sand held in suspension—which does most of the work. Moreover, the courses of stream channels are seldom, if ever, straight for any considerable distance, but are a succession of concave and convex curves. The water is alternately thrown against one bank, and the direction of the current being deflected, impinges on the opposite bank lower down-stream. At the locality where the thread of swiftest flow nears the bank, the rocks are worn away, and the irregularity of the stream's course increased. The material removed is carried down-stream, and in part deposited in the slack water on the concave side of the next bend. Swift streams are not so easily turned aside as those which flow less impetuously. Hence the former maintain straighter courses than the latter.

Lateral corrasion may go on when vertical corrasion is checked by decrease in declivity, deposition, or for other reasons. After a stream has cut down its channel at its mouth to the level of the still water into which it discharges and established a low gradient, lateral corrasion may continue. It is under these conditions that the widening of river valleys is mainly accomplished. In general, vertical is so far in excess of lateral corrasion in the case of high-grade streams, that the valleys produced are narrow, and V-shaped in cross-section, while under similar conditions in respect to climate, rock texture, etc., in a low-grade stream, although its actual rate of lateral corrasion may be less than in the first instance cited, the ratio of lateral to vertical corrasion is greater, and a flat-bottomed valley results. The cross-profile of a valley widened by lateral corrasion is U-shaped, and if the process is long continued becomes broad-bottomed. The statement frequently made that a stream-cut valley is V-shaped in cross-profile, in distinction from the U-shape of valleys formerly occupied by glaciers, is not strictly true, as it considers only young stream-valleys.

Meandering Streams.—The serpentine courses followed especially by sluggish streams, just referred to, is a matter of more than passing interest to the student of geography. Much of the charmingly picturesque which enters into and many times forms the leading feature of stream-side scenery, as well as the secret of the process by which valleys are broadened, and the adjacent uplands removed, results from the meandering and lateral migration of streams. By this same general process, too, as will be considered later, the flood-plains of rivers are spread out. Illustrations of the curves characteristic of many streams, are given on Plate 3.

The causes leading to the meandering of streams have been studied by various observers. As stated by Fergus-

PLATE III.

FIG. A.   Ray Brook, Adirondacks, New York.
(Photograph by S. R. Stoddard.)

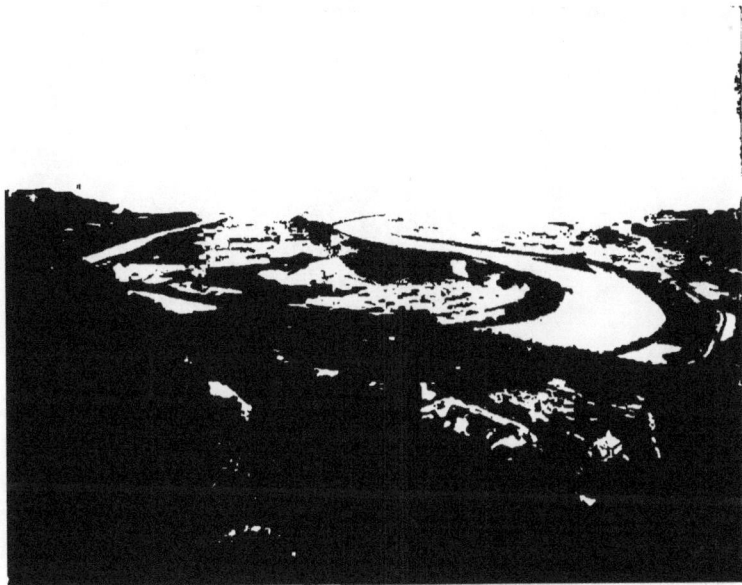

FIG. B.   Moccasin Bend, Tennessee River, from Lookout Mountain ;
Chattanooga at the Right.

son,[1] a river is a body of water in unstable equilibrium, whose normal condition is that of motion down an inclined plane, and if all inequalities in the material forming the bottom and sides of its channel could be removed, it would flow continuously in a straight line. (It is to be noted, however, that the influences of the earth's rotation is not considered in this discussion.) Any obstruction or inequality, however, necessarily induces an oscillation, and, the action being continuous, the effects are cumulative, and the oscillation goes on increasing till it reaches a mean between the force of gravity tending to direct the current in a straight line, and the force due to the obstruction tending to give a direction more or less at right angles to the former. In nature not one but many disturbing conditions occur, and the streams flow in a series of curves, each of which bears a definite relation to their volumes and the gradients of their channels.

The stage in the lives of rivers when they meander in broad curves through rich bottom-lands, is usually, or most commonly, reached late in their lives, when the task of reducing their channels to the level of the still water into which they discharge has been nearly completed. They then flow sluggishly, and may be said to be enjoying the rest to which a long life of activity entitles them. A slack current and a tortuous course are not infallible indications of old age, however. Young streams flowing across an abandoned lake bed, for example, or over lands recently raised from the sea, may have these characteristics. A

[1] James Fergusson, "On Recent Changes in the Delta of the Ganges," in *The Quarterly Journal of the Geological Society of London*, vol. xix., p. 323, 1863.

winding course may be retained by a river which has been
given renewed energy by a re-elevation of the land, even
after it has cut a deep trench and is a hurrying torrent.
The tendency to meander is strongest in streams that are
heavily loaded and are depositing a portion of their burdens
in flood-plains.   •

Although the tendency to meander characterises all
streams, for the reason that their channels are never
straight or composed of homogeneous material for any considerable distance, yet the process carries with it certain
limitations, as will be shown in discussing the origin and
nature of flood-plains and terraces in a subsequent chapter.

Other Curves.—Not only do streams bend to the right
and left of their general courses, as where a river meanders
through a broad, partially alluvial-filled valley, but, as will
be described later, form curves in a vertical plane as well.
Where corrasion is in progress, the longitudinal profile of
the channel produced is concave to the sky, and where deposition occurs, curves convex upward result.   More or less
complete spiral curves about vertical or inclined axes, like
the twists of a corkscrew, may be seen when a high-grade
stream is excavating soft clays, and where a brook on the
surface of a glacier plunges into a well-like opening in the
ice.   The influence of the graceful sweep of stream-curves,
on the beauty of many landscapes, is due to their infinite
variety; no two in the course of even a great river being
identical.   This marvellous diversity, produced by simple
means, becomes still more impressive when it is remembered
that no one of these many curves remains the same for any
considerable period of time.

The several classes of curves in the channels of streams are supplemented in an interesting manner by other curves in the surfaces of the streams themselves. Not only are graceful curves produced by the flow of water in eddies and swirls, or when they arch over or circle about obstacles, and are thrown into waves by the wind and other causes, but the surface of a stream in cross-section is not a straight line, although this condition is very nearly reached when the current is gentle, and the waters deep. If there is a strong central current, however, the surface there forms a convex curve, which rises well above the more gently flowing waters on either side. In swift rivers this difference in level frequently amounts to five or six feet, and in certain instances, as at the whirlpool below Niagara, is reported to be two or three times these measures. In such examples the surface line of a cross-profile would show a pronounced upward curve in the central part, bordered on each side by a downward curve. The bordering downward curves are gentle, but may be recognised, although they probably depart but little from a straight line.

Driftwood carried by a stream with a swift central current, as will be described more fully in advance, tends to leave the elevated central part and collect along the banks. This tendency may be seen especially when swift streams are rising; when the waters fall, however, driftwood leaves the slack water adjacent to the shore, and tends to concentrate in mid-stream. At such times the stream in cross-profile probably presents a concave surface-line.

Deflection of Streams Owing to the Rotation of the Earth.— The earth, as is well known, makes one rotation from west to east about an axis passing through the poles, in 23 hours 56 minutes and 4 seconds. The circumference of the earth being about 24,000 miles, any point on the equator must, therefore, travel over 1000 miles an hour. North and south of the equator this motion gradually decreases, and becomes zero at the poles. This motion has an influence on the flow of streams, and tends to cause them to follow curved instead of straight courses. This may be most readily understood in the case of streams having either north or south directions, but affects all streams on the earth's surface, unless they follow strictly the path marked out by the equator.

Water flowing northward from the equator would start with the motion from west to east, which pertains to that location, but as it advanced would cross regions which have progressively less and less motion from west to east. The current due to gravity, we will assume, tends due north, but the waters have also a motion from west to east, due to the earth's rotation, which is in excess of the similar motion of the region necessarily invaded. The resultant of these two forces will carry the stream to the east of the meridian on which it started, and the stream will curve to the right of its initial course. In a similar way, a stream in the northern hemisphere, flowing toward the equator, would be continually invading territory having greater and greater motion from west to east and would curve to the west of the path it would follow if influenced only by gravity. Thus, in the northern hemisphere, the tendency of the earth's rotation is to cause the streams, no matter what their direction of flow, to corrade their right more than their left banks. In the southern hemisphere the direction of curvature due to the earth's rotation is reversed, and the streams, no matter what their direction, tend to corrade their left more than their right banks. This is an application to streams of Ferrel's law, namely: " *If a body moves in any direction on the earth's surface, there is a deflecting force arising from the earth's rotation which deflects it to the right in the northern hemisphere, but to the left in the southern hemisphere.*" [1]

The tendency of a stream to maintain a straight course as it invades territory having a progressively changing rate of motion is greater the greater the velocity of the stream; the same is true of the parts of a stream. The thread of maximum current in a stream following an approximately straight course, is in the centre near the surface. The change in direction owing to rotation is, therefore, less quickly manifest in the thread of maximum current than in the more sluggish waters on either side, and the current undergoes greater deflection. Where streams follow winding courses this tendency leads to an increase in their meanderings to the right, in the northern hemisphere, more than to the left of their general direction. There is thus a tendency, due to the earth's rotation, for them to excavate their right more than their left banks, and to migrate to the right of their initial courses. This tendency is slight, but all the time operative. Owing, however, to inequalities in hardness of the banks of streams, and other disturbing conditions, it is difficult to discover examples where the earth's rotation has

---

[1] William Ferrel, " The Motions of Fluids and Solids Relative to the Earth's Surface," in *The Mathematical Monthly*, vol. i., p. 307, 1859. The influence of the earth's rotation on air-currents is clearly explained in W. M. Davis's *Elementary Meteorology*, pp. 101–111. Ginn & Co., Boston, 1894.

plainly controlled their migrations.   An illustration of such
a result is thought to be furnished, however, by the streams
on the south side of Long Island, where there is a plain
with a remarkably even descent and gentle slope.   This
plain is crossed by a number of small streams which have
excavated shallow valleys in essentially homogeneous
gravel.   Each of these little valleys is bordered on the
west, or right side, by a bluff from ten to twenty feet high,
while its gentle slope on the left side merges imperceptibly
with the general plain.   The stream in each case follows
closely the bluff at the right.   As stated by Elias Lewis,
and affirmed by Gilbert,[1] there seems to be no room for
reasonable doubt that these peculiar features result from
the influence of terrestrial rotation.

It is to be remembered that the force of rotation, like
gravity, is all the time operative, but its influence is greatest
on streams flowing north or south, is greater in high than
in low latitudes, and increases with the rapidity with which
the waters are transferred from an area having a certain
motion to another area having a different motion.   The
results of this influence, although not conspicuous, are nev-
ertheless important.   There is a slight tendency throughout the length of every stream in America and at all times,
to erode its right more rapidly than its left bank.   In the
case of the Mississippi, shown by Gilbert in the article

---

[1] G. K. Gilbert, " The Sufficiency of Terrestrial Rotation for the Deflection
of Streams," in *American Journal of Science*, vol. xxvii., pp. 427–432, 3d
series, 1884.   An abstract of this paper, accompanied by an extension of the
discussion, may be found in *Science*, vol. iv., pp. 28, 29, 1884.   See, also, W.
M. Davis, " An Early Statement of the Deflective Effect of the Earth's Rotation," in *Science*, vol. i., p. 98, 1883.

cited above, the selective tendency thus determined toward the right bank is nearly nine per cent. greater than toward the left bank.

Questioning the Rivers.—To illustrate the laws governing the behaviour of streams, let us see how some of the leading features of the rivers of North America can be accounted for.

Why, for example, are the waters of the St. Lawrence clear and those of the Missouri usually muddy ? The former is obviously a clear stream for the reason that the Great Lakes it drains act as settling basins and retain the sediment brought down by countless tributaries. Many small streams join the St. Lawrence below Lake Ontario, but most of these also have lakes in their courses, and the amount of the sediment reaching the main river from rills and brooks is not sufficient to materially change its character. The clear waters of the St. Lawrence have but little power to corrade. The current is swift in places, but all of the fragments in its bed which the current is competent to move have long since been carried away. Corrasion has gone on with extreme slowness throughout the present geographical cycle, and the river has not yet entrenched itself, but is practically a surface stream.

The reader will, no doubt, at once remark that the Missouri and the Platte are also surface streams, although heavily loaded with silt and sand. These rivers, however, rise in high mountains and flow across a broad plateau. Their many branches in the mountains are swift and bear along heavy loads of detritus. On leaving the mountains and entering their plain tracts, velocity is checked, and the less swift waters are no longer able to carry the loads they pre-viously transported with ease, and deposition occurs. Then, too, the surfaces of the Great Plateaus are composed of easily eroded rocks. During every rain quantities of soil, etc., are washed into the rivers, and during the long, dry summers, the winds are busy in performing a similar task. At present not only is corrasion *nil* throughout the plain tracts of the Missouri and the Platte, but sedimentation is in progress. These rivers are aggrading previously eroded valleys.

The question of how deep and how wide a river valley shall be, depends not alone on the elevation of the land above sea-level, but also on the ratio of stream corrasion to the general waste or erosion of the bordering lands. When the rate of stream corrasion is in marked excess of the rate at which the general surface of the land is being eroded, deep, narrow stream channels result. But if the erosion progresses at nearly the same rate as corrasion, the relief of the region will be mild. Between these two ex-tremes there are many intermediate stages. Overloaded streams, by dropping a portion of their burdens, may not only spread out broad flood-plains, but also elevate their channels so as to flow at a higher level than the sur-rounding land. The Platte and the Missouri are now de-positing material throughout their courses across the Great Plateaus, and, as just stated, are aggrading previously formed broad-bottomed valleys.

Many conditions besides those just noticed exert an influ-ence on the character and expression of stream-cut valleys. When the rocks are hard, they tend to form precipitous bluffs; when soft, they crumble, and the valleys have flaring sides. When the climate is arid, the wasting away of cliffs is long delayed, and if corrasion is actively progressing, steep-sided gorges, or canyons, result. Vegetation retards surface erosion, although favouring rock decay, and has a varied influence on the lives and character of the streams. These and still other influences modify the results of stream corrasion, which find expression in the scenery of the land.

It may be asked, why is it that the Colorado has carved the most magnificent canyon in North America, while the Platte, rising in the same mountains, is bordered throughout much of its course by perhaps the least picturesque scenery of any large river on the continent ? Much of the answer has already been given. The Platte, as we have seen, is aggrading its channel to the east of the Rocky Mountains. The Colorado is still corrading from its source, with the exception of certain slack-water reaches in soft rocks, all the way to its place of discharge. The rocks through which the Platte flows are soft; while those cut by the Colorado are hard. The region of the High Plateaus crossed by the Colorado has experienced a somewhat recent uplift of several thousand feet; while the country traversed by the Platte to the east of the Rocky Mountains has, so far as is known, undergone but slight changes in elevation during the same period. The climate of the Colorado region is arid, and surface waste from rains and the action of the wind probably less than in the region of the Platte. It is in these and perhaps still other contrasts of conditions that the striking differences in the scenery along the border of these two rivers may be accounted for.

By comparing the scenery of various other regions and seeking for the underlying causes to which their differences are due, the student may arrive at a juster appreciation of the characteristics of river work than a formal statement of the subject will furnish.

Erosion.—Weathering, transportation, and corrasion are three agencies which by their combined action lead to the removal of land upraised above the sea, and the production of a vast array of ever-changing topographic forms. To this far-reaching and highly complex process, the name *erosion* has been given.

Briefly stated, the removal of material from land areas is accomplished by: 1st. The disintegration of the rocks by both mechanical and chemical means, through the action of the varied and complex process termed *weathering*. 2d. The removal especially of the finer products produced by weathering, by the wind, general rain-wash, and rills, and of both fine and coarse debris by brooks and rivers, by a process termed *transportation*. 3d. The friction and impact of the material transported, accompanied by solution, lead to the deepening and broadening of stream channels, or *corrasion*.

A necessary accompaniment of erosion is the deposition of the material removed, or *sedimentation*. A temporary phase of sedimentation is the laying aside of stream-carried detritus in flood-plains and stream channels, but its final resting-place, so far as a single geographical cycle is involved, is on the floor of the sea.

Baselevel of Erosion.—The depth to which a stream, flowing into a lake or the sea, can lower its channel by mechanical corrasion is limited by the surface level of the receiving water-body. As mechanical corrasion decreases in more than a simple ratio with decrease in declivity, the final stages in the lowering of a stream channel to the level of the still water into which it flows must be extremely slow. Corrasion is not limited to mechanical processes, however, but includes solution as well. The final reduction of a stream channel to sea-level must, therefore, be by solution. Every stream, when its entire history is reviewed, will be found to be engaged in deepening its channel to the horizon referred to, or else has accomplished a part or the whole of the task. The datum-plane limiting downward corrasion is reached first at the mouth of a stream and is then continued progressively towards its source. When many streams are considered, various stages in this process may be recognised. The depths to which streams may excavate their channels is evidently a matter of great importance in their development and in the history of the topographic changes of the land. This fundamental principle was first clearly defined by Powell,[1] who employed the term *baselevel* to designate the lower limit of stream action. It is the baselevel of corrasion. A lake determines the baselevel for the streams flowing into it, but as lakes are short-lived, the real baselevel toward which all streams are working is the surface level of the sea.

To use Powell's own words in this connection:

"We may consider the level of the sea to be a grand baselevel, below which the dry land cannot be eroded; but we may

[1] J. W. Powell, *Exploration of the Colorado River of the West and its Tributaries*, p. 203, 4to. Washington, D. C., 1875.

also have, for local and temporary purposes, other baselevels of erosion, which are the levels of the beds of the principal streams which carry away the products of erosion.   I take some liberty in using the term level in this connection, as the action of a running stream in wearing its channel ceases, for all practical purposes, before its bed has quite reached the level of the lower end of the stream.   What I have called the baselevel would, in fact, be an imaginary surface, inclining slightly in all its parts toward the lower end of the principal stream draining the area through which the level is supposed to extend, or having the inclination of its path raised in direction as determined by tributary streams.''

When a stream has lowered its channel nearly to baselevel, downward corrasion is retarded, but lateral corrasion continues.   Low-grade streams, as we have seen, are the ones most inclined to meander, and to broaden their valleys. If this process is continued for a sufficient time in any region, it will lead to the removal of all land within reach of the streams, down to their own level.   Baselevel of corrasion thus becomes practically the baselevel of erosion.   The ultimate result of erosion is to reduce a land area to a plain at sea-level.   Such perfect plains, however, are exceedingly rare, but approximations to the ultimate result are common, and plains in this penultimate stage have been named *peneplains* by Davis.

A peneplain is the normal result of the erosion of the land, provided elevation or depression do not occur to check the process.   If a portion of the earth crust remains essentially stable for a sufficient length of time to allow the streams flowing from it to broaden their channels, a more or less extensive peneplain is produced.   Such periods of

stability, when movements in the earth's crust are not sufficient to check the normal process of baselevelling, are termed
geographical cycles. A peneplain may be defined as an approximately perfect plain produced by erosion during a
geographical cycle. If, after a portion of a land area has
been reduced to a peneplain, elevation occurs, a new geographical cycle will be initiated, and the process of baselevelling again begun.

During one geographical cycle all of the land may not be
reduced to a plain, but isolated uplands between broad
valleys remain. These remnants are left as an inheritance
to the next succeeding geographical cycle. Mount Monadnock, in southern New Hampshire, is an example of such a
remnant, and forms a prominent feature on the surface of
an elevated peneplain. The study of the relief of the land
in various regions has shown that there are many such remnants, left by incomplete planation. A name is needed
for such topographic features, and to meet this want Davis
has proposed that they be termed *monadnocks*, after the
typical example just referred to. A monadnock, then, is a
hill or mountain left standing on a peneplain, owing to
incomplete planation.

The laws, just stated, governing the reduction of land
areas to baselevel, although wide-reaching and fundamental
to the student of geography, are not strictly true, or, rather,
exceptions to them may be found. The downward limit of
mechanical corrasion is not in all cases the sea-level. Glaciers may enter the sea and continue their destructive work
at a depth of a few hundred feet below its surface. Ice-
bergs may also disturb the bottom of the sea at considerable

4

depths.   Currents in the sea sometimes corrade the bottom ; the downward limit to which this process may be
carried is unknown, but may be hundreds of fathoms.   The
removal of rocks in solution may be carried on deep below
sea-level ; the lower limit has not been determined, but is
certainly many thousands of feet.   Change in the position
of rock material through the agency of plants and animals
is not limited downward, by the surface level of the sea, but
goes on below that horizon.   All of these processes, however, are of minor importance, and need not be considered
as sensibly modifying the conclusion that the downward
limit to which land areas may be reduced is the horizon of
the surface of the sea.   Strictly speaking, baselevel is the
lower limit of the mechanical corrasion of streams, but practically, as we say, it is also the downward limit of erosion.

Influence of Vegetation on Erosion.—The influence of
vegetation on the general process of denudation is varied,
and both retards and accelerates the process.   Vegetation
breaks the force with which rain-drops strike the earth, and
besides, when the ground is covered with leaves, or with
grasses, moss, or other plants of low growth, the surface
waters are filtered of such debris as they may have taken
in suspension.   Vegetation thus retards transportation and
decreases mechanical corrasion.   On the other hand, vegetation furnishes the percolating water with organic acids,
principally humus acids, which greatly enhance their solvent
power.   Hence vegetation favours chemical corrasion in a
high degree.

The roots of plants bind the soil together, and thus assist
it in resisting mechanical agencies tending to remove it.

But roots furnish organic acids as they decay, and besides open passageways for descending water, thus facilitating chemical changes. The student may readily observe other modifications in the lives of streams due to vegetation and to climate. Interesting results would no doubt be obtained from the study of the vegetation which grows in the streams themselves, such as the algæ and certain higher forms of plant life. The direct influence of driftwood and of fallen timber is considered in a subsequent chapter.

Although the summary of the laws governing the behaviour and work of streams just presented is confessedly incomplete, yet it is the writer's hope that it will serve to interest the reader in the processes of land sculpture nearly everywhere in progress where the earth's surface rises above the sea, and suggest questions to which more technical treatises, or, better still, the rills and rivers themselves will furnish answers.

NOTE.—Since this chapter was written, a highly instructive paper by Huntington Hooker has appeared, on " The Suspension of Solids in Flowing Water," *Transactions of the American Society of Civil Engineers*, vol. xxxvi., 1897, pp. 239-340, which the reader is recommended to study.

CHAPTER III

INFLUENCE OF INEQUALITIES IN THE HARD-NESS OF ROCKS ON RIVER-SIDE SCENERY

IF we watch a hillside rill which is born during a heavy shower and runs dry when the sun again shines, it will be noted that in the steeper portion of its descent it cuts a narrow trench and deposits much of the material removed farther down its course. It soon becomes apparent that the little stream is corrading where its descent is steep, and raising its bed by depositing the material brought from above where the grade becomes gentle. The processes of corrasion, transportation, and deposition may all be seen in operation in a stream only a few rods in length. The topographic forms resulting are, on a minute scale, the same as those which give grandeur to many far-reaching views of river-side scenery.

The process of excavation and deposition carried on by a rill leads to the making of a uniform grade down which the waters continue to carry debris. This gradient, as will be shown later in discussing the profiles of streams, is not an inclined plane, but in longitudinal profile is a curve, steepest near the source of the stream, and flattening out and approaching nearer and nearer a straight line the nearer the mouth of the rill is approached. The immediate task of the rill may be said to be the making of a certain gradient, which is best suited to its volume and other conditions.

In the portion of the rill channel where corrasion is in progress, the waters are broken by little cascades and miniature rapids, and it is evident that a uniform gradient in that portion of its bed is far from perfect. The reason is that the clay, earth, or other material in which the rill is working is of varying degrees of hardness. When a boulder is crossed, a cascade results. When the material is soft the channel is quickly deepened. Each passage from a hard to a soft layer is marked by a cascade. Evidently the character of the material which the rill is removing exerts a controlling influence on the miniature scenery along all of its upper course.

If we enlarge our field of observation, similar characteristics will be found in many brooks, creeks, and rivers. The study of many streams will soon show, however, that some of them are broken by cascades and rapids, while others, except on their extreme headwaters, have even descents and flow with a generally uniform current. Those which are broken by cascades, we soon learn, for the most part occupy narrow, steep-sided trenches, and are apt to have lakes along their courses; while those with a uniform descent from near their sources to their mouths, are not associated with lakes, except perhaps such as are formed by the streams themselves in alluvial-filled valleys.

A comparison of many streams will show that the differences just referred to, depend on their age, or, more accurately, on the stage of development they have reached.

Young streams, or such as have not cut down their channels so as to produce a uniform gradient, are the ones supplied in part by lakes, and are broken by places of rapid descent; while older streams have removed the inequalities from their channels, and the lakes that may formerly have existed along their courses have been drained. It thus becomes evident that the degree to which variations in the hardness of the rocks influence the scenery of streams is greatest in youth and gradually beomes less and less, but seldom, if ever, entirely vanishes.

All stages in development, from extreme youth to sluggish old age, may be recognised in the streams of North America, and among the most marked characteristics of this slow change is the presence of cataracts and rapids in the courses of the streams which have not yet made a decided advance in their appointed tasks.

Waterfalls.—Young streams are obliged to accept inherited conditions of slope, and may discover that their courses are broken by places of deep descent, and rapids and cascades result. If, for example, a stream originates on a tableland, with an irregular surface, or is perhaps bounded by an escarpment, it will have an uneven channel, at least for a time, and be broken by places of steep descent. Again, streams coming into existence on the withdrawal of an ice-sheet, or the draining of a lake, will usually find inequalities in their channels which will cause waterfalls. In such instances the conditions producing the falls are an inheritance from pre-existing topographic conditions. As stream development progresses, however, the cascades resulting from inherited conditions disappear; but others due to inequalities in rock texture, to the more rapid rates at which a trunk stream may deepen its channel than its branches, to the loads sometimes deposited in sluggish streams by swifter tributaries, and still other causes, make their appearance.

In illustration of the processes by which cascades originate through the action of the streams themselves, it is evident that when a stream flows across alternating hard and soft beds, the soft beds will be removed more easily than those of greater resistance, and when the streams leave a hard bed, a rapid, cascade, or waterfall may be produced. The refer-

FIG. 2. A Young Valley being Cut in Shale Rock, Central New York. (After R. S. Tarr.)

ences just made to a trunk stream cutting more rapidly than its tributaries, and the deposition of debris in a sluggish stream at the mouth of a high-grade tributary, need no special explanation.

All of the conditions just referred to, including inherited

inequalities of channel and the production of places of steep descent during stream development, pertain principally to young streams. As a stream advances in its task of cutting down to baselevel and acquires the gradient best adapted to its work, inequalities in the slope of its channel disappear. Cataracts, of whatever character, are usually an index of immature stream development. The development of a stream progresses, however, from its mouth towards its source, and the feeding brooks of even well-developed river systems are young, and may have cascades, while the lower portions of the same drainage system may have reached perfect adjustment. The streams draining the southern Appalachians have been allowed to progress with the execution of their tasks without serious interruption for a long period of time, all lakes and waterfalls resulting from inherited conditions, and practically all cascades produced by irregularities in rock texture, have long since disappeared throughout their lower courses, but their head branches are still young and are yet being extended. On these young twigs of the drainage system cascades are common. An illustration of a cascade of this nature is presented in Plate IV.

An exception to the rule that cascades are not developed in the courses of mature streams, is sometimes found in limestone regions where surface drainage enters underground channels. The breaking of the roof of a cavern may lead to the production of a cascade at any stage in the life of a stream, but the chances of such an accident, as it may be termed, become less and less as baselevel conditions are approached.

In addition to the causes just considered, there are changes produced by movements in the earth's crust, as when the rocks are folded or faulted; the birth and growth of glaciers; volcanic eruptions; the deposition of rock material from solution, as when a spring precipitates travertine, siliceous sinter, etc., in the course of a stream; the work of animals, as when beavers build their dams; the stranding of driftwood so as to block drainage, etc., which may interrupt the even flow of water, and give origin to rapids, cascades, and waterfalls.

The tens of thousands of waterfalls in North America may be arranged principally in two classes: those resulting from the excavation of alternating hard and soft layers, and occurring mostly on the head branches of well-developed streams, as in the southern Appalachians; and those due to previous glacial conditions. Of these two classes the second is by far the more numerous, and furnishes the most magnificent examples of waterfall of all grades.

As already stated, the northern half of North America was formerly covered by ice-sheets. Local centres of snow accumulation and of glaciers also existed on the Rocky and Cascade Mountains, and the Sierra Nevada, far to the south of the southern limit of the former continental glaciers. Throughout nearly all of the vast regions which were formerly ice-covered, the melting of the glaciers left the land encumbered with debris. The surface inherited by the post-glacial streams was essentially a new-land area, and the streams have not progressed far enough in their development to have removed the inequalities in their channels. and waterfalls are common.

Illustrations of this class of cascades are furnished by those in the picturesque streams of the Catskills, Trenton Falls, the many beautiful cataracts near Ithaca, the well-known instances in Watkins Glen, and numberless others of the same general character in New York. Still more numerous instances might be cited in Canada, as, for example, the leap made by the water at the Falls of Montmorenci, near Quebec, the Great Falls in Labrador. In fact, scarcely a stream can be ascended in all of the eastern and northern portion of the formerly glacier-covered region, without discovering that it has recently been turned from its former channel, or exhibits the characteristics of youth from mouth to source.

On the headwater of the Mississippi, and about the upper Great Lakes, the drift sheet is thicker than farther eastward, and the streams have less frequently cut down to the hard rocks beneath, so as to develop cascades. It is only the stronger rivers in this more thoroughly drift-covered country that have progressed far enough with their recently added task, to lay bare the solid rock beneath the superficial covering.

A far-reaching result of the disturbance produced in stream development by the glacial epoch is seen in the distribution of water power produced by it. In New England, manufacturing industries were soon established after the coming of Europeans, and a decided impression made on the character of the people by this circumstance. South of the glacial boundary, water power was far less abundant, and mostly within the more inaccessible portions of the mountains; the development of manufacturing industries was hence delayed, and attention given more largely to agriculture, for which climatic and other conditions were more favourable. When steam was introduced as a motive power, the waterfalls at the north declined in importance as sources of energy, but in this budding age of electricity they are again coming into demand.

In all of the various phases of stream development and of the diversity in the relief of the land produced by stream erosion, thus far considered, a marked feature has been that changes are continually in progress. To this rule, the waterfalls furnish no exception. They have their periods of growth and decline, and in many instances shift their positions, or migrate.

In the case of waterfalls resulting from inherited topographic conditions, they may spring into existence all at once, and at the very start be grander than ever after. Niagara, when it first leaped from the summit of the escarpment near the present site of Lewiston, was higher than at any subsequent period of its history.[1]

When falls result from the wearing away of soft rocks so as to make adjacent hard beds prominent, there is usually at first a small difference in relief, producing a rapid, and then greater changes resulting in a cascade the height of which is increased by reason of the increased energy of the waters as they plunge into the pool below, but there comes a time when the stream channel below the fall can be lowered no farther. The cascade, or waterfall, as we may choose to call it, then reaches its greatest development, or

[1] G. K. Gilbert, " Niagara Falls and their History," in *National Geographic Monographs*, vol. i., pp. 203–236. American Book Co., 1895.

its majority.   But the lowering of the stream channel above the fall continues, and its height gradually decreases.   Such a sequence in the life of a waterfall originating from unequal stream corrasion in soft and hard rocks, would result when the fall did not migrate up stream but remained in one place.   But most waterfalls are subject to a process of migration.

The Migration of Waterfalls.—When a hard layer causing a waterfall is horizontal, or but slightly inclined, the escarpment over which the waters plunge recedes, owing, in most instances, to the removal of softer rocks beneath, by the friction of stones washed about by the swirling waters, and the fall migrates up stream, leaving a more or less canyon-like valley to mark the path along which it travelled.   Thus, below Niagara Falls there is a canyon about seven miles long, and approximately two hundred feet deep, which has been left by the migration of the cataract.

FIG. 3.   Profile and Section at Middle of Horseshoe Fall, Niagara, Showing Hard Limestone above Soft Shale, and Probable Depth of the Pool into which the Waters Plunge.   Scale : 1 inch = 384 feet. (After G. K. Gilbert.)

If the hard bed cut through by a stream so as to produce a cascade has a sharp downward slope in the direction opposite to the flow of the stream, the fall will become lower and lower as corrasion progresses, and when the hard layer is passed, the life of the cataract will come to an end.   If, however, as may happen, the hard layer dips downstream, the rapid or fall produced will manifestly increase in magni-

PLATE IV.

FIG. A.   Fall on Black Creek near Gadsden, Alabama.

A young branch of Coosa River, at the south end of Lookout Mountain; hard sandstone above shale.

FIG. B.   Echo River in Mammoth Cave, Kentucky.

(Copyrighted photograph by H. C. Ganter.)

tude until the locality where the outcropping edge of the hard bed comes to the surface is cut through, and then a comparatively sudden lowering and adjustment of grade will follow. When the hard layer which a stream has to cut through is horizontal instead of being inclined either with or against the current, it presents a greater task to a stream cutting through it than in any other position, because the mass of rocks necessary for the stream to remove in order to reduce the grade of its channel is greater than if the bed is inclined. When the rocks are horizontal, the life of a cataract may be immensely prolonged.

The only cases in which waterfalls produced by hard adjacent to soft rocks do not migrate, are when the hard layer is vertical. In such a case the change in the position is limited to the thickness of the resistant bed. In the Cascade Mountains there are numerous rapids and cascades due to vertical dikes of basalt. These dikes are harder than the adjacent rock, and cause inequalities in the beds of the streams crossing them, but the positions of the falls produced remain essentially the same throughout their lives.

In the streams flowing eastward from the Appalachians, falls and rapids occur where they leave the hard crystalline rocks forming the Piedmont Plateau and enter the soft rocks of the Coastal Plain. As these falls recede up stream, they leave canyons to mark the paths they follow.

Many of the falls in the drift-covered region of North America are due to the turning of streams from pre-glacial valleys in such a way as to cause them to flow over what were formerly divides or rocky spurs between adjacent streams and plunge into valleys. In some instances, also, they have cut through a covering of drift and been lowered upon harder rocks beneath.   In either case falls may result. Cascades are also produced where these streams leave a region of hard rock and enter areas of drift which is more easily removed.

Niagara Falls came into existence when a large lake, which formerly flooded both the Ontario and Erie basins, was lowered so as to be divided into two water bodies by a ridge trending east and west, formed by the summit of the Lewiston escarpment.

The Falls of St. Anthony are due to the Mississippi having been turned from its pre-glacial course by deposits of drift, and made to flow over the surface of a comparatively thin horizontal sheet of limestone resting on soft sandstone.   A cataract about one hundred feet high was produced where the river left the edge of the limestone layer and plunged into a pre-glacial valley.   From this escarpment the fall has receded about eight miles, leaving a steep-sided canyon, as in the case of Niagara.

Shoshone Falls, Idaho, were produced by a hard sheet of trachyte which Snake River discovered as it sank its channel in nearly horizontal layers of basalt.   The falls have migrated up stream, leaving a narrow canyon as a record of the work already performed.

Many beautiful cascades in the Rocky and Cascade Mountains, and others no less picturesque in the Sierra Nevada, are due to changes produced by a former period of glaciation.   In some instances in the Sierra Nevada, large Alpine glaciers flowed down the main valleys, and blocked the streams in lateral gorges so as to cause them to cease

corrading. The glaciers deepened the main valleys, however, during the time the development of their tributary
streams was arrested, and when the ice melted and water
drainage was once more established, the branches of the
main streams were compelled to descend steep precipices
and in many instances form fine cascades, in order to reach
the bottoms of the glacier-deepened main valleys.

The ancient glaciers, to which so many references have
been made, brought destruction in their paths as they advanced and left fields of desolation as they retreated, but in
many ways the beauty of the region they occupied was enhanced by the changes they made. Our greatest debt to
the vanished glaciers, so far as the revolutions they wrought
appeal to our artistic sense, is for the tens of thousands of
placid lakes they left strewn over the land, and the tens
of thousands of leaping waterfalls which sprang into existence on their retreat. The former are emblems of rest, the
latter of ceaseless activity.

Bluffs Bordering Aged Streams.—As previously stated,
the influence of the unequal yielding of hard and soft rocks
is most marked in the case of streams that are still young,
and decreases as they advance in development, but seldom
entirely disappears.

Topography being largely the result of the action of
streams, it follows that the various features in the relief
of the land must be due, to a marked extent, to the unequal waste of hard and soft rocks. The hard rocks stand
as bluffs, ridges, and peaks, while the soft rocks are worn
away more rapidly,. and dells and valleys appear. The
various stages from youth to old age, so characteristic of

streams, find a counterpart in the general changes in form
and expression experienced by the surfaces of land areas.
A new land area may have a generally even surface, but as
time passes, and topographic maturity is reached, it becomes
roughened, and if the elevation has been great, and marked
inequalities in the hardness of the rocks occur, exceedingly
rugged topographic forms will be developed.   When a land
area has been long exposed, the inequalities of surface due
to differential weathering gradually decrease, but except in
the rare instances of nearly complete baselevelling, do not
disappear.

Throughout the courses of streams that have passed their
periods of maturity, and even after having developed a
gentle gradient characteristic of old age, their valley walls
frequently retain evidences of the great topographic diversity that characterised them during youth.   Rivers flowing
through lands having in general all the characteristics of
topographic old-age may yet be bordered in places by steep
bluffs and overshadowed by towering precipices.

The Highlands of the Hudson, where the river valley is
narrow and bordered on each side by rugged mountains, in
contrast with the wider portions above and below, where the
bordering uplands are less precipitous, reveal the influence
of hard rocks on the scenery of an ancient river.   The
picturesque " coves " in the Southern Appalachians, as
along the upper course of the Hiawassee, have been hol-
lowed out in soft beds, and are surrounded by precipitous
mountains of hard rock.

Many bold headlands in the upper Mississippi valley are
remnants of ancient eminences, rounded and worn by long

.xposure, which in several instances rise directly from the border of the river that sweeps about them and has long since passed its period of youth.

Much of the wonderfully impressive scenery of the Columbia is due to great bluffs of basalt which rise directly from the river's brink, and on account of their hardness, in contrast with softer beds adjacent, remained prominent even after the river had cut down its channel to an even grade and become navigable.

The same sequence of events was noted by the writer in many instances while ascending the Yukon. That noble river, although well adjusted to the various rock conditions it discovered as it deepened its channel, and flowing with such an even grade that it can be ascended by steamboats for over fifteen hundred miles, is bordered in places, as shown in Plate II., by magnificent bluffs of hard rock which intervene between long reaches where the valley is several miles broad, and has been excavated in softer beds.

While the persistence of the topographic forms on the borders of river valleys is conspicuous, and accounts for many of the more prominent features adjacent to aged rivers, yet the lives of many streams have been so greatly prolonged that movements in the earth's crust have produced changes simulating those just considered. The rocks crossed by a great river may be upraised so as to form ridges, or even mountain ranges, athwart its course, and dam its waters or turn them aside. When such changes occur, however, with sufficient slowness to allow the river to deepen its channel as fast as the rocks rise, it will maintain its right of way, and excavate a gorge or canyon through the obstruction.

In such instances a portion of the stream will have the characteristics of youth, while adjacent portions above and below,
whose development was unchecked, present all the features
of old age.   Rivers which maintain their right of way in
the manner just cited, and carve gorges and canyons through
newly elevated lands, have been termed *antecedent rivers* by
Powell, in recognition of the fact that they are antecedent
to the movement which causes the rocks to be elevated.

CHAPTER IV

MATERIAL CARRIED BY STREAMS IN SUSPEN-SION AND IN SOLUTION

THE waters flowing from the land back to the sea, whence they came as vapour, carry material with them, as is well known, in two distinct ways: namely, in suspension and in solution. The debris carried in suspension and rolled along the bottom, or the *visible load*, as it may be termed, sooner or later finds its way to the sea and forms stratified deposits. The material dissolved by the waters during their excursion through the air and over the land, or their *invisible load*, goes to increase the salinity of the sea and to supply marine plants and animals with substances necessary for their growth.

THE VISIBLE LOADS OF STREAMS

The material transported mechanically by streams may be divided into two classes: 1st, the portion rolled and pushed along the bottom; and, 2d, the portion lifted well above the bottom and carried forward in suspension. The dividing plane between these two classes is indefinite, as much of the material moved along the bottom makes short upward excursions, and the fine particles normally carried forward in suspension from time to time rest on the bottom.

Bottom Load.—Concerning the manner in which the *bot-om load*, as it may be termed, is moved, and the amount of such transportation in a given stream, but little information is available.

If we watch a clear stream supplied with sand or gravel of such size that the current has power to move it, it will be seen that the debris does not advance as a continuous sheet, but rather as a succession of wave-like forms. The action of the water-current in this respect is similar to the behaviour of air-currents when moving over dry sand. The ripple-like ridges on the bottom of streams are frequently and probably always broad in reference to their height. The up-stream slope of each ridge is gentle and its down-stream border short and precipitous. Grains of sand are moved over the broad gently ascending surface and rolled down its steep down-stream margin. At the base of the steep border of each ripple-like sheet, there are secondary currents caused by the plunging of the water, and the particles forming the bottom are there disturbed and carried onward and the process repeated. When the material at the bottom is in excess of the transporting power of the stream, sedimentation takes place, and cross-stratified or current-bedded accumulations result ; but if the bottom current is under-loaded, the material is carried forward by being removed from the up-stream margin of a broad ripple-like sheet, and re-deposited on its steep down-stream margin.

The process just described goes on at the bottom of clear streams, and illustrates the fact that such streams, contrary to what is sometimes stated, have power to corrade. It is only when their bottoms are swept clean of all grains of such size as are within the capacity of the stream to sweep away, that mechanical corrasion ceases.

These statements concerning the bottom loads of streams may be said to be qualitative, inasmuch as measures of the amount of material thus transported are lacking. It is difficult and at present seemingly impossible to ascertain how much material a large river is moving in the manner just considered. Bottom transportation will evidently vary with changes in conditions, being favoured by swiftness of current and the character of the debris available for transportation. Variations probably also occur in reference to the amount of material a stream carries in suspension. If a stream is heavily charged with silt, the friction of flow will be increased, and as this friction is greatest in proportion to rate of flow, near the bottom, it is to be expected that bottom transportation will be checked while transportation in suspension is still actively progressing. It would seem, therefore, as if bottom transportation is favoured by decrease of material in suspension; or, other conditions being the same, clear streams have a greater power to move bottom loads than muddy streams. I must confess, however, that this is theory rather than a deduction from observations and experiments, and the reader is invited to test the conclusion for himself.

It is evident that the principal conditions favouring bottom transportation are velocity and volume of water. As velocity increases with declivity, we should expect that high-grade streams would move proportionately heavier loads along their bottoms than low-grade streams, other conditions being the same. The ratio of bottom load to total transportation should be greater during floods than during low-water stages. Observation seems to confirm these conclusions.

The proportion of bottom load to the amount of material carried by a stream in suspension is dependent largely on the character of the debris within the reach of the stream— that is, whether it is fine or coarse; but in general it seems true, as just stated, that the bottom load in swift streams is greater in proportion to the amount of material in suspension, than is the case in slower streams under similar secondary conditions.

Although the manner in which bottom loads are carried is not thoroughly understood, and the amount of such transportation difficult to determine, the fact remains that much of the energy of streams is consumed in rolling debris along their bottoms. In many measures of the rate at which streams are removing rock debris from their drainage basins, the quantity moved along their bottoms is not considered. For this reason most estimates of the rate at which land areas are being lowered by denudation require important modifications.

Measures of Material in Suspension.—The methods employed for ascertaining the amount of sediment carried by a stream in suspension are illustrated by the careful work done in this connection by Professor Forshey, during the survey of the Mississippi by the United States Topographic Engineer Corps.[1] Stations were selected near Carrollton, a short distance above New Orleans, one about three hundred

[1] Humphreys and Abbot, *Report upon the Physics and Hydraulics of the Mississippi River*, p. 137, 1861.

feet from the east bank of the river, the next in mid-stream, and a third about four hundred feet from the west bank. The high-water depths at these stations were 100, 100, and 40 feet respectively. Samples of water were collected daily at surface, mid-depth, and bottom at the first two stations; and at surface and bottom at the third station for a period of one year. During the succeeding year, the ratio between the sediment contained in the water at any one station and that contained in the entire cross-section of the river having been ascertained, one sample was taken each day from the surface at the station near the east bank.

The samples from below the surface were secured by means of a small keg heavily weighted at the bottom and provided at each of its ends with a large valve opening upward. These valves allowed a free passage to the water while the keg was sinking to the required depth, but prevented its escape while being drawn up. When the keg reached the surface, the water contained in it was thoroughly stirred and a bottle filled from it. The sediment contained in the water samples was subsequently filtered out and weighed after drying.

From the tabulated results of the first year's work referred to, it was found that the greatest amount of sediment was carried in June, during the annual high-water stage of the river, the weight of sediment then being $\frac{1}{681}$ of the weight of the river water containing it; the minimum was obtained during the low-water stage late in October, the ratio of weight of sediment to weight of water then being as 1 to 6383. The mean for the year was $\frac{1}{1808}$, or one ton of sediment to 1808 tons of water.

A discussion of a still larger number of observations, made under the direction of Humphreys and Abbot, gave the ratio of 1 of sediment to 1500 of water by weight, and of about 1 to 2900 by volume.

The variation in the amount of sediment with positions in the stream is indicated in the following table of the weekly means for the two months of highest and lowest water respectively:

SEDIMENT IN THE MISSISSIPPI AT CARROLLTON

NUMBER OF WEEK.	FIRST POSITION.			SECOND POSITION.			THIRD POSITION.		
	Surface.	Mid-depth.	Bottom.	Surface.	Mid-depth.	Bottom.	Surface.	Mid-depth.	Bottom.
First in June, 1851.....	0.345	0.407	0.187	0.365	0.415	0.410	0.285	0.390	0.365
Second " " "	0.456	0.507	0.510	0.477	0.515	0.517	0.365	0.457	0.442
Third " " "	0.917	0.960	0.940	0.731	0.981	1.105	0.666	1.046	0.447
Fourth " " "	0.498	0.570	0.557	0.528	0.597	0.601	0.427	0.536	0.452
Mean for June........	0.559	0.611	0.548	0.525	0.627	0.658	0.436	0.607	0.426
First in October, 1851..	0.137	0.187	0.220	0.125	0.215	0.235	0.096	0.265	0.170
Second " " " ..	0.120	0.169	0.170	0.109	0.193	0.220	0.107	0.235	0.092
Third " " " ..	0.100	0.132	0.136	0.097	0.146	0.159	0.089	0.195	0.071
Fourth " " " ..	0.068	0.096	0.106	0.059	0.115	0.116	0.061	0.136	0.081
Mean for October......	0.106	0.146	0.158	0.096	0.172	0.182	0.088	0.208	0.104

The figures denote the number of grammes of dry sediment contained in 600 grammes of river water.

Knowing the amount of water discharged annually by the Mississippi and the proportion of sediment contained in it, the amount of material carried by the stream each year in suspension may be readily computed. The mean annual discharge, as determined by the survey in charge of Humphreys and Abbot,[1] is 19,500,000,000,000 cubic feet, and the amount of solid matter carried in suspension 812,500,000,-000 pounds.[2] The average specific gravity of this material is about 1.9; with this density, the sediment carried annually would occupy 6,718,694,400 cubic feet, or sufficient to cover one square mile to the depth of 241 feet.

In addition to the silt carried in suspension, it has been estimated by the engineers cited above, that the amount of sand and gravel rolled along the bottom and contributed each year to the filling of the Gulf of Mexico is about 750,000,000 cubic feet; making the total visible load carried by the river each year about 7,468,694,400 cubic feet, or sufficient to cover one square mile to a depth of 268 feet.

The Mississippi has been more carefully studied than any other river in North America, but it is well known that other streams are doing a similar work. In many streams the proportion of material in suspension to the amount of water is greater than in the lower Mississippi; while rivers might be selected, as, for example, the St. Lawrence, in which the percentage of sediment is much less. An inspec-

[1] *Report on the Mississippi River*, p. 149. If I understand this portion of Humphreys and Abbot's report correctly, the above measures do not include the three outlet bayous, which leave the main river above New Orleans. It is stated on page 93 of the report, that, including these bayous, the annual discharge is 21,300,000,000,000 cubic feet of water.

[2] Taking the specific gravity of water as 1, the relative weight of coarse river-sand is 1.88; fine sand, 1.52; clay, 1.90; alluvial matter, from 1.92 to 2.72. A cubic foot of water weighs 62.5 lbs.; of coarse sand, 117.5 lbs.; fine sand, 95 lbs.; clay, 118.75 lbs.; alluvial matter, 120 to 170 lbs.; silt, 103 lbs. W. H. Wheeler, *Tidal Rivers*, p. 62. Published by Longmans, Green, & Co., 1893.

tion of the following table, compiled by C. C. Babb,[1] in which data concerning the amount of material that is being carried by several large rivers are presented, shows that the Mississippi, although commonly recognised as a muddy stream, holds a smaller percentage of silt in suspension than several other rivers with which it may be compared.

DISCHARGE AND SEDIMENT OF LARGE RIVERS

RIVER.	DRAINAGE AREA IN SQUARE MILES.	MEAN ANNUAL DISCHARGE IN CUBIC FEET PER SECOND.	SEDIMENT.			
			Total annual tons.	Ratio of sediment to water by weight.	Height of column, one sq. mile base. Feet.	Depth over drainage area. Inches.
Potomac	11,043	20,160	5,557,250	1: 3,575	4.0	.00433
Mississippi	1,244,000	610,000	406,250,000	1: 1,500	241.4	.00223
Rio Grande.	30,000	1,700	3,830,000	1: 291	2.8	.00116
Uruguay.	150,000	150,000	14,782,500	1:10,000	10.6	.00085
Rhone.	34,800	65,850	36,000,000	1: 1,775	31.1	.01075
Po	27,100	62,200	67,000,000	1: 900	59.0	.01139
Danube.	320,300	315,200	108,000,000	1: 2,880	93.2	.00354
Nile	1,100,000	113,000	54,000,000	1: 2,050	38.8	.00042
Irrawaddy.	125,000	475,000	291,430,000	1: 1,610	209.0	.02005
Mean	334,693	201,468	109,649,972	1: 2,731	76.65	.00614

Estimates similar to those given in the above table have been published by several geologists. One series of these, probably as reliable as any, by Archibald Geikie,[2] is here copied for the purpose in part of showing that the observations now available concerning the work of streams are defective. Even the areas of hydrographic basins are stated differently by different writers, and with perhaps a few

[1] *Science*, vol. xxi., p. 343, June, 1893.
[2] *Text-Book of Geology*, 2d edition, p. 428. Macmillan & Co., 1885.

exceptions the measures given of the annual discharge of large rivers, the amount of sediment they carry, etc., should be considered as subject to corrections.

SEDIMENT OF RIVERS

RIVER.	AREA OF BASIN IN SQUARE MILES.	ANNUAL DISCHARGE OF SEDIMENT IN CUBIC FEET.	FRACTION OF FOOT OF ROCK BY WHICH THE AREA DRAINED IS LOWERED IN ONE YEAR.
Mississippi.	1,147,000	7,459,267,200	$\frac{1}{6000}$
Ganges (Upper).	143,000	6,368,077,440	$\frac{1}{N\frac{1}{2}6}$
Hoang Ho.	700,000	17,520,000,000(?)	$\frac{1}{1464}$
Rhone.	25,000	600,381,800	$\frac{1}{1628}$
Danube.	234,000	1,253,738,600	$\frac{1}{6848}$
Po.	30,000	1,510,137,000	$\frac{1}{725}$

A brief discussion of the rate at which land areas are being lowered by the removal of material by streams will be given after the measures of mineral matter in solution have been considered.

THE INVISIBLE LOADS OF STREAMS

Water as it reaches the land as rain, snow, dew, etc., is never chemically pure, but contains both organic and inorganic matter in solution and dust particles in suspension. The substances most commonly occurring in solution in rain-water are shown by the following analysis of a sample collected near London, England[1]:

Organic carbon.	.99 part in 1,000,000 of water.	
Organic nitrogen.	.22 " " "
Ammonia.	.50 " " "
Nitrogen as nitrates and nitrites. .	.07 " " "
Chlorine.	6.30 parts in " "
Total solids.	39.50 " " "

[1] Quoted by W. P. Mason, *Water Supply*, p. 204. John Wiley & Sons, 1896.

Examinations for chlorine in water samples representing the average condition of the rain-water at Troy, New York, for one year, gave a mean of 1.64 parts in a million. That is, each million pounds of rain-water contained 1.64 pounds of chlorine in solution.[1]

The impurities in rain-water vary in character and amount in different localities. In general they are greatest near cities, and least in the open country at a distance from volcanoes, gas springs, etc. They also vary with climatic conditions, being greatest in arid and least in humid regions, and greater in dry than in wet seasons. The amount of common salt is large near the sea, and normally decreases inland, but probably reaches a maximum in the neighbourhood of saline lakes and over salt deserts. Rain-water, then, comes to the earth with its solvent power increased by the presence of various substances washed out of the air, but its ability to take up mineral matter in solution is greatly increased as it flows over the land.

The soil usually contains organic matter which is easily dissolved. The most common substances thus added to the water, which enhance its chemical activity, are carbonic acid or carbon dioxide (CO_2), and a large group of organic acids, known as the humus acids; these, however, are unstable, and soon change to carbon dioxide. The organic acids are derived mainly from the decay of vegetation, but in part are of animal origin.[2]

The percentage of the organic acids taken in solution by

[1] W. P. Mason, *Water Supply*, p. 205.
[2] A. A. Julien, "On the Geological Action of the Humus Acids," in *American Association for the Advancement of Science, Proceedings*, vol. xxviii., pp. 311–410, 1870.

a given quantity of water percolating through the soil varies with different localities, being greatest when decaying vegetation is most abundant and where the temperature is high. In all portions of the earth's surface, however, the water, on coming in contact with the soil or with solid rocks, has the power to dissolve portions of them. The water which runs over the surface and is gathered quickly into streams has less opportunity to take up mineral matter in solution than that which percolates through the soil and in many instances descends into the hard rocks beneath and comes to the surface again as springs. The water flowing quickly over the surface and that following more or less extensive underground courses are commingled in the streams, and send their combined tribute of dissolved matter to the sea. Chemical denudation thus assists the mechanical action of flowing water in lowering the land, and is an important factor in the process.

The rate at which rocks are dissolved varies not only with the rain-fall, with the amount of organic acids in surface and subterranean water, and with temperature, but is influenced especially by the nature of the rocks in various regions. The solution of mineral matter in general is greater, other conditions remaining the same, the higher the temperature, although this does not apply to limestone, and is greatest where the rocks are composed of easily soluble minerals. For these reasons the chemical composition of river-water varies, but the departure from a mean, as shown by a large number of analyses, is less than might at first be expected.

By the time the surface waters have united to form rills they contain sufficient mineral and organic matter to give them a complex chemical composition. Throughout their journeys to the ocean, as they form brooks, creeks and rivers, and especially when travelling underground, they become more and more highly charged with dissolved mineral matter. The longer the waters are in contact with soil and rocks, and with the finely divided material held by them in suspension, temperature conditions, etc., remaining the same, the more highly charged they become with substances in solution. Evaporation also tends to concentration, but this process, particularly in humid regions, is more or less completely counteracted by direct precipitation.

River-waters, filtered of all material in suspension, and evaporated to dryness, leave a solid residue, which is the principal portion (the more volatile substances escaping) of the foreign matter previously held in solution. These waters are fresh in the every-day use of the term, but in fact owe their agreeable taste and, to a certain extent, their health-giving qualities, to the mineral salts and gases contained in them. In Table A, analyses are given of the waters of a number of American rivers, which show that the principal substances in solution are calcium and carbonic acid, probably combined as calcium bicarbonate. In some instances, however, as in the case of Jordan River, Utah, calcium sulphate is in excess of all other salts.

From a large number of analyses of water samples obtained from the rivers of Canada and the United States, it has been found that the average amount of total solids in solution is 0.15044 part in a thousand by weight; of this material, 0.056416 part in a thousand is calcium carbonate. In a table of forty-eight analyses of European river-waters

[Reduced to parts per million by Dr. H. J. Von Homeyer.]

given by Bischof,[1] the average of total solids in solution is 0.2127, and the average of calcium carbonate 0.1139 part per thousand. From the analyses of thirty-six European river-waters, published by Roth,[2] including some of those tabulated by Bischof, the average of total solids is 0.2033, and of calcium carbonate 0.09598 part per thousand.

In both American and European river-waters, so far as can be determined from the data in hand, the average of total solids is 0.1888, and of calcium carbonate 0.088765 part per thousand. These figures may be assumed to represent the average of the solids in solution in the waters of normal rivers. It will be noticed that the average for calcium carbonate is nearly one-half the average for total solids.

Knowing the annual discharge of a river and the percentage of mineral matter carried in solution, we can ascertain the amount of dissolved matter that the river contributes annually to the ocean, or enclosed lake into which it flows. To one unfamiliar with studies of this nature, the amount of rock-forming material thus annually transported by a large river in an invisible state is astonishing. The following table, showing the total amounts of solids in solution carried by certain rivers, has been compiled from various sources:

Rhine.......................	5,816,805 tons per year.
Rhone	8,290,464 " "
Danube	22,521,434 " "
Thames.....................	613,930 " "
Nile........................	16,950,000 " "
Croton......................	66,795 " "
Hudson.....................	438,000 " "
Mississippi..................	112,832,171 " "

[1] *Chemical Geology*, vol. i., pp. 76, 77. English edition, London, 1854.
[2] *Allgemein und chemische Geologie*, vol. i., pp. 456, 457. Berlin, 1879.

The fact that streams transport great quantities of dissolved mineral matter, derived from the rocks in the basins they drain, may be shown by computing the numbers of tons of material in solution in a cubic mile of river-water. This has been done by John Murray,[1] and the result, based on the average composition of the waters of nineteen of the principal rivers of the world, is given below:

MATERIAL IN SOLUTION IN ONE CUBIC MILE OF AVERAGE RIVER-WATER[2]

CONSTITUENTS.	TONS IN CUBIC MILE.
Calcium carbonate (CaCO$_3$)........................	326,710
Magnesium carbonate (MgCO$_3$)....................	112,870
Calcium phosphate (Ca$_3$P$_2$O$_8$)....................	2,913
Calcium sulphate (CaSO$_4$)........................	34,361
Sodium sulphate (Na$_2$SO$_4$).......................	31,805
Potassium sulphate (K$_2$SO$_4$).....................	20,358
Sodium nitrate (NaNO$_3$)..........................	26,800
Sodium chloride (NaCl)...........................	16,657
Lithium chloride (LiCl)..........................	2,462
Ammonium chloride (NH$_4$Cl)	1,030
Silica (SiO$_2$)........	74,577
Ferric oxide (Fe$_2$O$_3$)	13,006
Alumina (Al$_2$O$_3$)...............................	14,315
Manganese oxide (Mn$_3$O$_3$)......................	5,703
Organic matter..................................	79,020
Total dissolved matter......................	762,587

It has also been computed by Murray, and published in the article just cited, that the volume of water flowing to the sea in one year, including all the land areas of the earth, is about 6524 cubic miles. From the average chemical composition of river-water, it follows that about 4,975,117,588 tons of mineral matter in solution are being removed annu-

[1] *Scottish Geographical Magazine*, vol. iii., p. 76, 1887.
[2] Acids and bases combined according to the principles indicated by Bunsen.

ally from the land area of the earth. This process of removing material of the land in solution has, very properly, been termed *chemical denudation*.

It is instructive to follow the history of the material carried in solution by rivers, and to see what changes occur, especially in inland seas where ordinary river-waters are concentrated by evaporation, and in many instances the salts they contain precipitated in a crystalline form, and to extend such studies to the ocean. Another fruitful line of investigation in this connection is the manner in which mineral matter in solution is eliminated. This occurs in part, as just mentioned, by chemical precipitation, but is effected to an equally great extent, and from dilute solutions, through the action of plant and animal life. These interesting studies, however, lie beyond the scope of our present thesis.

RATE OF LAND DEGRADATION

Measures of the amount of material carried by streams both mechanically and in solution furnish a means of approximately determining the rate at which the surface of the land is being degraded.

Mechanical Degradation.—As shown in the table on page 74, the amount of silt carried annually by the Mississippi, if taken uniformly from the area it drains, would lower it $\frac{1}{5376}$ of a foot. That is, considering only the material carried in suspension, the basin is now being lowered at the rate of one foot in 5376 years. If we take into account also the material rolled along the bottom, computed to be 750,000,-

000 cubic feet per year,[1] we find that the basin is being lowered at the rate of one foot in 4638 years.

Studies of the Potomac River, conducted by the United States Geological Survey, have determined the fact concerning that river presented in the table on page 74. Assuming that one cubic foot of the silt carried by the Potomac weighs 100 pounds, the average annual amount transported would cover one square mile to a depth of 3.98 feet. If this amount should be taken uniformly from all parts of the area drained, it would be lowered 0.0043 of an inch, or $\frac{1}{2772}$ of a foot. In other words, the Potomac is lowering its hydrographic basin at the rate of one foot in 2772 years. Other similar estimates are given in the table on page 75, which, if approximately correct, might be taken as indicating the work that the rivers of the world are doing. It is probable, however, that except in the case of the Mississippi, in the table compiled by Geikie, the bottom loads of the rivers are not included. I am also inclined to doubt the accuracy of some of the other measures referred to. The average for the nine rivers tabulated is one foot of denudation in about 9000 years.

Chemical Degradation.—The importance of the slowly acting and invisible process by which the surface of the land is being lowered by solution, has only recently been recognised. The earliest definite discussion of the rate of chemical degradation now in progress, so far as I am aware, is in a series of three papers by T. Mellard Reade.[2] In these

[1] A comparatively slight discrepancy comes in here, since the specific gravity of the bottom load and of the silt in suspension is not the same.

[2] Republished with the title, *Chemical Denudation in Relation to Geological Time.* Daniel Dogue, London, 1879.

instructive essays it is estimated that the amount of material removed in a century by the streams of England and Wales in solution, if spread evenly over the land from which it is derived, would have a thickness of .0077 of a foot. That is, it will take 12,987 years to denude the surface of England and Wales of one foot of solid matter by the process here considered, under the supposition that the material is taken evenly from all parts of the surface.

The Mississippi, as previously stated, carries annually about 112,832,171 tons of mineral matter in solution. This amount of material may be considered as about equivalent to 1,350,000,000 cubic feet of limestone, and if spread evenly over the Mississippi basin would cover it to the depth of about $\frac{1}{25000}$ of one foot; or, in other words, chemical degradation is lowering that area at the rate of one foot in 25,000 years.[1]

Rate of Both Mechanical and Chemical Degradation.—The best and in fact the only approximately reliable measures we have of the rate of the combined mechanical and chemical degradation by the rivers of North America, is in the case of the Mississippi. On account of the large size of the drainage area of that river and the variety of rocks forming its surface, as well as the diversity of climate included within its border, it may be reasonably assumed to represent about the average rate of degradation which is being performed by rivers in general.

[1] The material in solution is taken in part from the surface and in part from below the surface. While an estimate of the average lowering of the surface by degradation during a single year need not perhaps include the material removed in solution from below the surface, yet this should certainly be taken into account in estimates of average degradation.

As we have seen, the Mississippi is lowering its basin by the process of mechanical degradation at the rate of one foot in 4638 years, and by solution at the rate of one foot in 25,000 years. The average rate of general degradation is therefore about one foot in 3912, or, in round numbers, 4000 years.

This estimate of the rate at which the Mississippi is lowering its drainage basin is somewhat greater than is given in several text-books of geology, but in these the amount of material carried in solution and the bottom load of the river do not seem to have been taken into account. An inspection of the tables on pages 74 and 75, shows that the Mississippi is removing material from the land at a less rate than is the case with several other rivers, and at even a less rate than the average of the rivers tabulated.

UNDERGROUND STREAMS

The water which finds its way below the surface of the land for the most part percolates through the rocks without forming definite streams. When the rocks are readily soluble, however, as when limestone is present in thick layers, underground channels are frequently dissolved out, and subterranean streams occur of sufficient size to be classed as rivers. During the underground flow of water, whether percolating through porous rocks or forming streams in caverns, it is brought into contact with the material forming the earth's crust, thus facilitating solution. One marked difference between surface and subterranean streams is that the former perform the task of eroding the land mainly by mechanical means, while the latter carry on a similar work principally by solution. Underground streams, in part, occupy ready-made galleries or caverns, like the opening along fractures and faults, or the tunnels in lava streams formed by the flowing out of the still molten parts after a crust formed. More frequently, however, subterranean streams make passageways for themselves. This process is analogous to the excavation of the valleys by surface streams. We may carry this analogy a step farther, and say that the underground streams flowing through previously made channels are subterranean consequent-streams, and those which dissolve out their own galleries are subterranean subsequent-streams. But there is little, if any, advantage in such a nomenclature.

The conditions most favourable for the beginning and growth of subterranean streams are that the rocks should be of comparatively easy solubility, and also in thick, nearly horizontal, and unbroken layers, situated at a greater elevation than the adjacent surface valleys. The rocks most easily dissolved by cold water, and the ones, too, which frequently occur in thick, nearly horizontal layers, are the limestones. For this reason most caverns are in such beds. If the soluble layer has a bed of less soluble rock in contact with it both above and below, the conditions for the production of large caverns are still more favourable.

The advantage of having the soluble layer elevated above adjacent surface drainage is that the water flowing through the galleries opened in it may readily escape and flow rapidly. A roof of rock which does not yield readily to the solvent action of percolating water admits of the dissolving out of broad galleries beneath and decreases the liability of their roofs to fall. A roof to a natural cavern is as essential as a roof to a mine.

Subterranean, like surface streams are dependent on rainfall for their water supply. They are also influenced by other climatic conditions. A humid climate not only insures an abundant water supply, but favours the growth of vegetation, which contributes organic acids to the descending waters, thus increasing their power to dissolve mineral substances. A dry climate not only decreases the water supply of subterranean streams, but, as will be shown later, favours the precipitation of mineral matter, principally calcium carbonate, in pre-existing rock-openings.

The temperature element of climate also plays a part in the history of underground drainage. A warm climate, if humid, insures a luxuriant vegetation, and hence an abundant supply of organic acids, while a dry climate has a reverse influence. A cold climate, by leading to the freezing of the water in soils, checks percolation, and in other ways exerts an unfavourable influence on the tendencies of sub-surface waters to enlarge the galleries they flow through.

Underground passages in many instances owe their inception to joints and fractures of small width which are enlarged by solution. The percolating of water through porous rocks, however, on account of inequalities in rock texture or composition, might be freer along certain courses than along others, and thus lead to unequal waste by solution, and to the making of cavities and galleries. When once a beginning is made, from whatever cause, the flowing waters tend to enlarge the galleries they pass through by dissolving their walls. The water which finds its way through such galleries eventually emerges as springs, or again reaches the surface by percolation. The springs supplied from caverns usually come to the light in the sides or bottoms of valleys, and contribute their water to the surface drainage; but not infrequently they emerge at the bottoms of lakes, or even beneath the sea.

Subterranean, like surface streams remove rock material both by mechanical and chemical means, but the relative importance of the two processes is reversed. Caverns are enlarged principally by solution, but mechanical wear is frequently and sometimes an important part of the process. The flow of water through small or tortuous passages, the beginning of caverns, is probably sluggish in most instances, thus favouring solution, but retarding mechanical corrasion. Water, in descending to small underground passages, mostly percolates through soil or rock debris, and is thus filtered. This, again, is unfavourable for mechanical abrasion, since solid particles, the tools with which flowing water performs the greater part of its mechanical work, are removed. As underground galleries become larger, and especially when the surface of the country is lowered by denudation, openings in their roofs are frequently made, into which surface streams plunge with all of their freight of material in suspension. The waters in the underground courses of such streams are more or less heavily charged with sediment, and mechanical corrasion assists in the enlargement of the passageways they flow through. The rocks removed in order to make subterranean galleries frequently contain sand grains, chert nodules, silicified fossils, etc., of diffi-

cult solubility. Such bodies are separated by the removal of the more soluble material enclosing them, and,
being swept along by the streams, assist the debris
brought from above in abrading the rocks with which the
waters are brought in contact. The behaviour of underground streams is thus seen to be similar in many ways to
surface streams. As will appear as we proceed, cavern
streams not only remove rock material, but also make both
mechanical and chemical deposits, thus still further bearing
out their similarity to ordinary brooks and rivers.

The features of subterranean streams just enumerated,
and of the results they bring about, are illustrated in the
well-known instance of Mammoth Cave, Kentucky. The
surface rocks in that region are mainly horizontally bedded
limestones, about 350 feet thick. Above the limestone
there is a sheet of sandstone, which forms the roof of the
higher series of galleries. The ground above the cavern,
over an area of thousands of acres, is elevated from 300 to
350 feet above the adjacent valley of Green River, and is
mostly without surface streams. The rain-water is largely
absorbed by the deep residual soil left by the solution of
hundreds of feet of limestone, and percolates slowly downward to the galleries beneath. During summer, all of the
water entering the cavern probably gains access in this manner, but during heavy rains, surface rills and brooks are
formed which plunge into openings or " sink-holes " and
enter the underground galleries directly as heavily silt-
laden streams. After rains, as the writer has observed,
the streams within the cavern are muddy, flow swiftly in
many places, and are actively engaged in mechanical as well

as chemical corrasion. The manner in which Echo River, the largest stream in Mammoth Cave, is now enlarging its channel is much the same as in the case of many surface streams, except that, owing to the irregularities and especially the numerous constrictions in the passages it follows, its waters, when in flood, come in contact with the roofs of the galleries in some localities, and corrasion occurs above as well as at the bottom and sides. Like many surface streams, Echo River has its rapids, cascades, and quiet reaches, and in places, also, is ponded and forms lakelets. A photograph of this remarkable river is reproduced in Plate IV.

Applying the criteria to be described later, by means of which young surface streams may be distinguished from mature or well-adjusted streams, to this example of subterranean drainage, we find it to be but imperfectly adjusted to its environment, and, therefore, it may be designated as an immature subterranean river. It has not deepened its channel throughout to the level of Green River into which it discharges, and which determines the baselevel of subterranean drainage in the rocks forming the adjacent uplands. As is the rule with surface streams, the adjustment of Echo River to baselevel has progressed most rapidly in its lower course. Near where it comes to the light as a huge spring on the border of Green River, it is about on a level with that stream. Farther within the cavern, it has many high-grade reaches, and is fed by torrent-like tributaries. A farther advance in its life history, the present local baselevel being maintained, should be characterised by the development of features analogous to those of a broad valley. A great gallery, corresponding with the valley of a surface stream, should be formed with its floor about on a level with the adjacent portion of Green River.

The lowering of Green River has led to the deepening of the channels of tributary underground streams, and the abandonment, as avenues of drainage, of many galleries that were formerly waterways. The occurrence of one series of galleries above another, or the origin of the several stories in the cavern-house, as Mammoth Cave may be termed, can be accounted for, in part at least, on the principle just referred to: the highest series of galleries having been formed at a time when Green River flowed at the level of their place of discharge, and each lower series dissolved out during subsequent stages in the deepening of master rivers.

A different explanation from that just suggested has been advanced by N. S. Shaler,[1] who states that the floors of the various stories in the great cavern are formed of resistant layers, each of which gave a lateral direction to the flowing water, until an opening was found leading to the next layer of limestone below, when the process of lateral excavation was repeated. Hard layers, or layers less pervious than those above and below, have had an important influence in the development of the cavern, but rather, it seems to me, in the direction of modifying the action of the streams in response to a lowering of the place of discharge, than in furnishing the main control. The adjustment of underground streams to rock texture is analogous to the adjustment of surface streams to the conditions furnished by hard and soft rocks.

[1] *Aspects of the Earth*, p. 109.   Scribner's Sons, 1889.

A surface stream, as the reader has learned, when carrying debris but not overloaded, corrades its channels; but if its velocity is checked, will deposit a part or all of its load. These same features characterise subterranean streams. When subterranean waters run swiftly they flow over bare rock, but when their velocities are checked, sediment is deposited. Many of the galleries in Mammoth Cave and other similar caverns have long since been abandoned as avenues of drainage, and are deeply filled with what is termed " cave earth." In part, this material has been brought into the cavern by streams from the surface, but to some extent, certainly, it is the residue left by the solution of limestone. Ordinary grey limestone contains about one per cent. of insoluble material which remains when the calcium carbonate is removed, and forms a reddish clay. The sedimentary deposits in caverns are frequently terraced; showing that the streams after dropping their burden of silt have been able to again resume the work of transportation and to cut channels through it. Conditions favouring sedimentation are frequently brought about during high-water stages when the water in certain galleries is ponded, owing to constriction lower down their course. Subsequently, during low-water stages, the streams are not held in check, and resume the task of deepening their channels.

In dwelling on the similarity between the mechanical action of surface and of sub-surface streams, I do not wish to be understood as advocating the view that caverns are enlarged principally by the friction of the debris in the water flowing through them; the main agency in their growth in most, and possibly all, instances is solution.

There is a process in the chemical action of subterranean
streams analogous to the manner in which they mechanically
corrade and deposit alternately. When the waters are
abundant and flow freely, they carry away all of the material
contributed to them in solution, and passageways are enlarged. When, however, the water supply is greatly diminished, and water falls from the cavern roofs mainly in
drops, or descends their sides and flows over their floors
in thin sheets, evaporation leads to an increase in the percentage of mineral matter in solution and to the precipitation
of certain salts.

In addition to the evaporation, when the mineral-charged
waters fall in drops, or are spread out in thin sheets, and of
more importance in the history of caverns, is the fact that
these conditions lead to the escape of carbonic acid. Lime
(calcium carbonate), the most abundant substance dissolved
by both surface and cavern waters, is held in solution owing
to the presence of carbonic acid, and is precipitated when it is
removed.[1] The calcium carbonate precipitated on the roofs
of caverns frequently takes pendent or icicle-like forms,
termed stalactites. After the water falls to the floor of the
caverns precipitation is continued, and sheets and pillars of
calcium carbonate, termed stalagmites, are formed.

Calcium carbonate is by far the most abundant, and, in
fact, in most caverns, seems to be the only precipitate
thrown down. The roofs of caverns, however, are some-

---

[1] Pure water when cold dissolves calcium carbonate in the proportion of one
part of the salt to 10,800 parts of water, and 8875 parts if the water is boiling
(Fresenius); but if charged with carbon dioxide cold water will dissolve one
part in about 1000 : the calcium when in solution is in the condition of a
bicarbonate.

times beautified by rosettes and star-like brilliants of gypsum (calcium sulphate) and by other and more soluble salts which appear as crystalline efflorescences.

It is this process of lining caverns with crystalline incrustations, the forming of pendants of many shapes and tints from their roofs, as well as of no less beautiful and frequently grotesque stalagmite columns, that gives to those silent galleries of the nether world much of their fascination and beauty. One of the very finest examples of subterranean galleries, partially filled by calcareous precipitates from percolating waters, is furnished by the beautiful Luray Cavern, Virginia. Other remarkable illustrations of the same occurrence may be seen in the justly celebrated Wyandotte Cavern, Indiana.

The process of infiltration, just noticed, if allowed to continue, will, in time, fill the cavern previously excavated when the water supply was abundant. In many caverns galleries occur which have been nearly closed by this method, and in other instances it is evident that the filling has been completed. Checks in the process of refilling may evidently occur from an increase in water supply or from its nearly complete cessation. Surface changes, such as the removal of vegetation, would also influence the conditions favouring enlargement, or refilling, in the caverns beneath.

Many peculiarities in the surface features, particularly of limestone regions where caverns occur, have an intimate relation to the galleries beneath. The holes through which surface water descends are enlarged by solution or by the falling of portions of the roofs of the caves, and become basins termed " sink-holes." Should the openings in the bottom of these depressions become filled, lakelets may be formed. Such basins and lakelets are a characteristic feature of many limestone regions, as, for example, in the Great Appalachian valley, Western Kentucky, and much of Tennessee. Some of the basins near Mammoth Cave, caused by the solution of the rocks beneath and the falling of the roofs of caverns, occupy an area of about 2000 acres.[1]

The subsidence of the roofs of caverns also gives origin to trench-like depressions in the surface above, which become avenues of drainage. The course of Green River near Mammoth Cave, is through a depression of this character which has been modified by surface erosion. When portions of a cavern roof fall, leaving other portions in position, natural bridges and tunnels result. The most striking example of this nature is the justly famous Natural Bridge of Virginia.

Another but minor influence of subterranean drainage on the relief of the region above, is brought about when the caverns by conducting away the surface waters decrease the rate of surface erosion. When this occurs and the lowering of the adjacent land continues, the rocks traversed by galleries are left in relief and form a mound or perhaps a series of hills, while the surrounding country, without sub-drainage, sinks into valleys. An illustration of this is furnished by the low hills in which Luray Cavern is located.

Subterranean drainage goes on with the greatest freedom and produces the most conspicuous results above the level of adjacent surface streams. This assertion needs, perhaps,

---

[1] Hovey and Call, *The Mammoth Cave of Kentucky*, p. 4.　Morton & Co., Louisville, 1897.

to be qualified, as only such caverns as are above the level
of neighbouring valleys are ordinarily open to inspection,
while the size and extent of the galleries below the level of
surface drainage can only be judged from indirect evidence.
The flow of water through caverns above the level of the
surface streams into which they discharge, except in part
during high-water stages, is due directly to gravity—that is,
the waters flow as through ordinary open channels; but the
flow through lower galleries is produced by hydraulic pressure, and is similar to the movement of water through pipes,
as in the case of the water-mains of a city.[1] There is a
marked difference in these two methods in reference especially to mechanical corrasion. The work of subterranean
streams in galleries not completely filled is, in most instances, mainly in the direction of solution, but is aided also
by the friction of particles in suspension or rolled along the
bottom. In such instances, also, the conditions are normally unfavourable for sedimentation. When water is
forced through galleries by hydraulic pressure, they are
completely filled up to the level of the surface of the re-
servoir, friction is greatly increased, and the rate of flow is
normally not rapid. This is an incomplete statement, to be

---

[1] The possible influence of heat in causing water to flow through subterranean
galleries has recently been discussed by F. W. Crosby and W. O. Crosby
(*Technology Quarterly*, vol. ix., pp. 6–23, Boston, 1896) in connection with a
study of what are known as the Sea Mills of Cephalonia, in Greece. In this
instance fresh water at the ordinary surface temperature enters openings at
sea-level and is supposed to emerge below sea-level and against the pressure
of the denser sea-water. In explanation of this exceptional occurrence, it is
suggested that the descending water traverses a more or less U-shaped system
of galleries, and is heated in the ascending portion of its course and thus rendered lighter than the inflowing and colder water.

sure, but sufficient, I think, to show that below surface
drainage the conditions are less favourable for cavern-mak-
ing than in similar rocks situated at higher levels. In
galleries below surface drainage, it may be reasonably presumed, mechanical corrasion is retarded and the conditions
favouring sedimentation are augmented.

Deep within the earth's crust the conditions differ from
those near the surface. The tendency of pressure to
close cavities increases with depth. The limit below which
openings of such size as to be classed as caverns can
exist, must be at a very moderate depth,—possibly not
more than a few thousand feet. With increasing depth,
also, there is a progressive rise of temperature (so far within
the earth as man has ever penetrated), which exerts a
marked influence on the solvent power of water. A rise
of temperature, at least until excessive heat is reached, increases the solvent power of water for all common minerals
except calcium carbonate. With the increase of temperature
and of pressure, in subterranean waters, there is an increase
in the variety and abundance of mineral substances which
are taken into solution, and also increased chemical reac-
tions, some of which lead to precipitation and to the filling
of openings. These and still other reasons favour the belief
that caverns, and consequently underground streams, do
not exist below an extremely superficial portion of the
earth's crust.[1]

[1] To the books of reference concerning American caverns already mentioned,
I would add the following :

H. C. HOVEY. *Celebrated American Caverns.* R. Clarke, Cincinnati, 1882.

W. S. BLATCHLEY. " Indiana Caves and their Fauna," in *Geological Survey of Indiana, Twenty-first Annual Report,* pp. 121–212, 1896.

CHAPTER V

STREAM DEPOSITS

THE ability of a stream to carry detritus in suspension, as we have seen, varies as the sixth power of its velocity. The velocity depends mainly on the steepness of the stream channel and on the volume of water. It is a familiar fact that streams vary in velocity throughout their courses. In general, mainly as a result of development, their channels are steepest and their waters swiftest near their sources, and become less steep and more sluggish as they near the sea; but throughout their length they are commonly broken into alternate swift and quiet reaches or sections. Evidently a stream may be able to transport all of the debris brought to it in certain portions of its course, and to corrade its channel, while in other portions it may be overloaded and consequently forced to drop a portion or even all of the material previously held in suspension. Evidently, then, streams both transport and deposit material as a part of their normal work. It is to the manner in which streams lay down their burdens and to the character and histories of the deposits thus formed that attention is now invited.

Many streams, and especially large rivers, rise in mount-

ains and flow across broad plains to the sea. It is convenient to divide such streams into three sections in
accordance with their velocities and with reference also to
the topography of their borders. Although these divisions
are really determined by the stage of development each
stream has reached in various portions of its course, they
are somewhat definite for such periods of time as man may
have been acquainted with them. The three divisions referred to are the *mountain tract*, where the waters usually
flow impetuously in narrow, trench-like depressions; the
valley tract, where a stream widens and is bordered by narrow flood-plains; and the *plains tract*, where the grade is
still more gentle, and the stream meanders in broad curves
through alluvial lands of its own making.

In the mountains the streams, as a rule, are swift, and
able to bear along not only fine debris in suspension, but
to roll great boulders down their channels, especially during
high-water stages. In the valleys through which the streams
leave the mountains, the current slackens, and the coarser
material brought from above is dropped. In the plains tract
velocity is again diminished, and again a selection is made,
the coarser portions of the burdens brought from above
being deposited, and only the finest silt and sand ordinarily
carried forward.

The dropping of material in the valley and plains tracts
of a stream leads to the filling in, or *aggrading*, of its
channel in those parts. This means an increase in the general gradient of the stream channel below the mountain
tract and consequently a swifter flow and an increase in the
transporting power of the current. Coarse material is then

PLATE V.

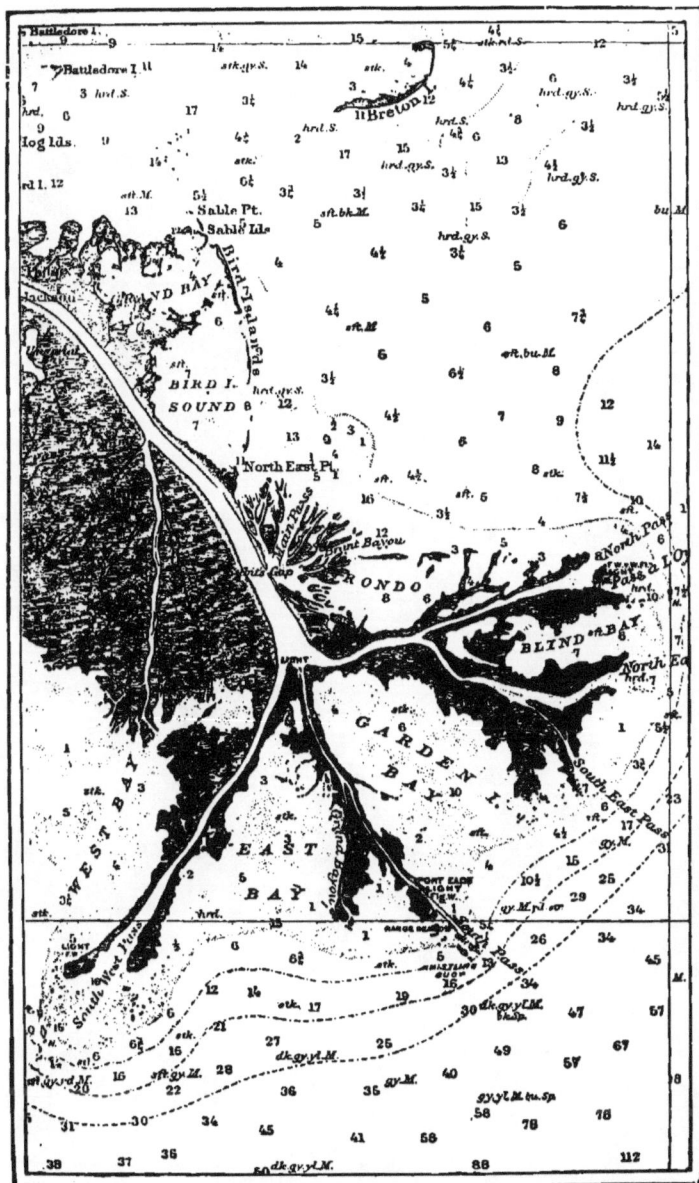

Delta of the Mississippi ; by U. S. Coast Survey.

Soundings on dotted areas in feet, all others in fathoms.

carried farther than before the stream bed was raised, and a new adjustment is made throughout the valley and plains tract. This process of aggrading will continue as long as the material brought by the swift head-waters of a stream is in excess of the transporting power of the current lower down. As will be shown later, a stream throughout much of its life deepens its channel in its mountain tract and deposits all but the finest of the material thus removed in the lower and less swift portion of its course.

The action of a stream in corrading its channel in one portion of its course and aggrading it in another portion, is carried on at the same time, and is a highly complex process. This complexity is again increased especially by variations in the volumes of the streams. During high-water stages a stream moves more material and carries it farther than during low-water stages. The result of these varying conditions may be seen in any stream that rises in high lands, and flows through a valley and across a plain. In the hill or mountain tract the stream channel is narrow with steep sides, and its bed comparatively free of fine debris, except in crevices and holes, although perhaps clogged with great stones too large for the water to move except during times of unusual flood. In the valley tract, where, for reasons to be considered later, the gorge through which the stream flows becomes wider, the stream bed is occupied by coarse gravel and small boulders, and much fine material may be found in the more sluggish reaches. Where the stream emerges into a plain, its bed is lined with fine sand and silt, except in the swifter reaches, where gravel occurs.

This general decrease in the size of the debris dropped

by streams between their sources and their mouths would be much more regular than one ordinarily finds it, if it were not for the fact that velocity increases with volume, other conditions remaining the same, so that coarser material is carried during floods to localities where only fine material is normally dropped. As a rule, streams increase in volume from their sources to their mouths, but the increase in velocity due to this cause is, in most cases, more than counterbalanced by loss of grade.

The debris that starts from the mountains on its journey down a stream channel to the sea makes many halts, and is gradually reduced in size both by mechanical wear and by solution. The periods of rest are due largely to variations in the volume of the stream, and also to its general decrease in grade from source to mouth. The larger stones are delayed until finer debris washed against them and the solvent power of the water reduce their size so that the stream is competent to move them. The material laid aside is constantly undergoing chemical changes which decrease the size of the fragments by solution and tend to make them friable, so that they are more easily broken or worn when next exposed to mechanical agencies. Even during the more continuous portions of the journey of stream-carried debris, its onward movement is irregular, since particles carried upward by ascending currents are pulled down by gravity, and reaching the bottom may rest for a time until disturbed and again carried upward so as to feel the influence of the general onward flow. For these and other reasons, the journeys of the debris transported by rivers are varied and usually long delayed. The removal of a given rock fragment from the mountains to the sea may require tens of thousands and even millions of years. The dropping of debris by streams, or its lying aside until conditions for transportation are more favourable, leads to the origin of several varieties of deposits.

ALLUVIAL CONES

The influence of a decrease of slope in a stream's bed is revealed by deposits of debris in nearly every stream, but finds its greatest expression when sudden and excessive changes from high to low grade occur. When a stream descends a precipitous gorge in a mountain-side and emerges into a valley, there is an abrupt loss of power, and the greater part or perhaps all of the load that the swift waters in the mountain tract swept along, is deposited. A conical pile of debris is thus formed, the base of which is in the valley and the apex at the mouth of the high-grade gorge through which it was swept out of the mountains. (See Plate VI.) In America such piles of debris are termed *alluvial cones*. In India[1] and in Europe they are generally known as *alluvial fans*, in reference to their fan-like forms when seen from above. As suggested by Gilbert, there is an advantage to be gained by retaining both of these terms, employing cone when the angle of slope is high, and fan when it is low.

The best example of alluvial cones occurs in arid regions where precipitous mountains border desert valleys. They

[1] An excellent account of alluvial fans in India, by Frederick Drew, may be found in the *Quarterly Journal of the Geological Society of London*, vol. xxix., pp. 441-471, 1873.

are a common and characteristic feature in the scenery of the arid portions of the United States and Mexico, and are especially well displayed in Utah, Nevada, and Southern California. In that region the intermittent streams from the mountains are swollen during the infrequent storms and sweep along large quantities of debris. When the waters reach a valley and the grade of the stream abruptly decreases, they lose velocity and much of their loads is dropped. In many instances, the waters on leaving the mountains where their channels are in solid rock and entering alluvial-filled valleys are absorbed and percolate away. When this occurs, all of the debris brought from the mountain is deposited. Piles of debris are thus formed which are of all sizes up to one or two thousand feet or more in height, and with bases frequently three to five miles in radius. The slope of the surfaces of these piles varies with their size, the grade of the stream that deposited them, the nature of the material of which they are composed, and possibly other conditions. Their profiles along lines radiating from their apexes are gently convex to the sky. The material of which they are composed varies in size from fine silt to boulders six or eight feet or more in diameter and weighing hundreds of tons, but in general they are composed of gravel and sub-angular stones and fine yellowish silt-like material. As the piles increase in size their bases expand and their apexes are extended farther and farther up the feeding gorges.

In the arid portions of North America referred to, alluvial cones have been formed in such abundance and of such great size at the mouths of canyons on the borders of desert

PLATE VI.

FIG. A.   Sketch of Alluvial Cones.

FIG. B.   Indian Creek, near Taylorsville, California.

The creek meanders through a flood-plain; cut bank on the left in the foreground, and a sloping deposit of gravel on the opposite side of the stream; these conditions are reversed at the second bend.

ranges, that they unite laterally in the valleys so as to form a fringe about the bases of the mountains. The contrast between these smooth, sloping pediments and the angular crags and peaks rising above them is frequently very marked, and adds an interesting feature to the peculiar scenery of the regions where they are best developed. The bases of the united alluvial cones are lobed, the greatest expansions being opposite the mouths of the larger canyons, thus giving to the bases of the desert ranges when seen from above a scalloped outline. Where the curving margins of the alluvial cones are drawn in toward the mountains surrounded by them, they meet projecting spurs and ridges from which there is but little drainage, and talus slopes frequently occur. The length and size of the gorges in the mountains may thus be judged by the extent and height of the alluvial deposits at their mouths.

The streams reaching the alluvial cones, when not at once absorbed, build up their sides and channels, and thus become unstable. The waters break through the ridges formed along their margins, and branch or bifurcate in various directions, and are thus led from time to time over all portions of the surfaces of the cones, and distribute their burdens evenly upon them. This tendency of the supplying streams to bifurcate and send off *distributaries* is of the same nature, as will be noted later, as occurs on deltas. In fact, the upper portion or cap of a delta built by a high-grade stream, is an alluvial cone, having all of the characteristic features of the example under discussion. The abandoned courses of distributaries on the surfaces of alluvial cones are frequently marked by parallel ridges with a stream bed between. The branching of the streams is also frequently well mapped in this manner during the long intervals between storms, when no water reaches the alluvial deposits. Sometimes huge boulders occur on the surfaces of the alluvial cones of the Far West, two or three miles from the mouths of the gorges from which they came, and remain as records of the violence of the streams during storms.

Normally the surface of the alluvial cones, in the region just referred to, is bare of all vegetation except desert shrubs and grasses, while at their heads and in the mouths of the feeding gorges there are frequently clumps of willows, alders, and other less familiar shrubs. Occasionally the slight perennial drainage from the mountains, which is concealed by the debris in the bottoms of the gorges, comes to the surface at the head of an alluvial cone, and forms a spring towards which the cattle and game trails in the valleys converge.

During the rainy season each year the gorges in the mountains are occupied by streams which bring down debris and make additions to the alluvial deposits, but in summer all contributions cease, except during occasional heavy rainfalls. The growth of the alluvial cones is thus markedly spasmodic. When the heavy rains, usually termed cloudbursts, occur, torrents rush down the mountain gorges and carry with them vast quantities of debris which had been slowly accumulating in their channels, possibly for scores of years, and marked additions are made to the alluvial cones in the valley below. Between these occasional catastrophes, disintegration of the rocks goes on, and the gorges again become charged with rock fragments. During the intervals between floods, the winter streams frequently remove some of the material previously deposited, and a notch is cut in the apex of the alluvial cone. Many alluvial cones in Utah, Nevada, and adjacent regions, are thus notched at their summits, so that in ascending them in order to gain the gorge above, one passes through a trench in alluvium, possibly a hundred feet or more in depth. The sides of these gorges reveal sections of the alluvial deposit, and show that the material is rudely stratified. The strata are not horizontal, but inclined in conformity with the surface slopes of the cones, and show cross-bedding and many other irregularities. In general, the material composing an alluvial cone is coarse near the entrance to the gorge to which it leads, and fine on its outskirts in the valley, but even on the lower borders coarse gravel and stones may occur.

Within the gorges cut in the summit portions of these conical piles there are frequently terraces, which record various stages in the down-cutting performed by the streams. The reason why a small stream fed by winter rain and melting snow is able to excavate a channel in the apex of an alluvial cone that has been built up during occasional heavy storms, seems to be because during the normal winter flow the streams are less heavily charged with debris than at the time of the occasional floods, and can expend a portion of their energy in corrading. The light loads of the normal winter streams can, in some instances, be accounted for by the fact that the canyons have been cleared of available debris by a previous great storm. Another condition that may favour the cutting of the channel referred to, is that during times of slack drainage the waters are absorbed by the alluvium, and the silt brought by them is left in the interstices in the coarser debris, and the filling the interspaces causes the waters to be retained at the surface, thus allowing them to corrade. Yet another change in conditions which leads to the cutting of the chan-nels referred to, and one which occurs also, as will be con-sidered later, in the history of flood-plains, is a result of normal stream development. The removal of material from a mountain gorge when corrasion is in excess of weathering, causes a lowering of the gradient above the apex of the alluvial cone at its mouth, and necessitates a readjustment of grade in the lower course of the stream where deposition was previously in progress; this is accomplished by the cutting of a channel through the apex of the alluvial cone and the re-deposition of the material removed lower down on its surface. In such an instance a second cone is built on the surface of the first one formed, with its apex in the notch excavated in the summit of the earlier accumulation. Many alluvial cones are for this reason compound structures. Still greater complexity of the same character occurs in the flood-plain deposits of large rivers, as will be shown later.

The fact that alluvial cones are more common and more conspicuous in arid than in humid regions depends on a variety of circumstances. One of the controlling conditions favouring their growth is an abrupt change in the grade of a stream bed. In humid regions, the grade of streams is more quickly adjusted than when the climate is arid and the streams intermittent. In humid regions, also, the streams are more constant, and, instead of terminating in desert valleys, flow on and carry their loads to lakes or to lower regions instead of dropping them at one locality. Then, too, in humid regions, there are usually streams in the valleys bordering the mountains, to which the torrents are tributary. The valley streams tend to cut away and remove the alluvial deposit on their border, and thus prevent great accumulation of debris at the mouths of lateral gorges. Abundant rain-fall and vegetation also have an important influence on the deposits that may be formed. The rocks decay more rapidly, and sub-aërial deposits of debris are usually more quickly removed, in humid than in arid climates, even when the mean annual temperature is the same. Vegetation not only masks the deposits of the nature here considered, but assists in various ways in their removal.

The principal conditions favouring the origin and growth of alluvial cones are high-grade gorges leading to adjacent valleys in which there are no streams, and climatic conditions favourable to great fluctuations in the flow of the mountain torrents and also to rock disintegration rather than rock decay.

As the rocks forming a mountain in an arid region are shattered and disintegrated by changes of temperature and other similar agencies, the loosened material is washed down the gorges and deposited in alluvial cones, in the manner just considered. As the alluvial cones about the base of a mountain gradually increase, their apexes progress farther and farther up the gorge, and should the favourable climatic conditions prevail sufficiently long, the alluvial deposits begun on opposite sides of a range may grow until they meet on the divide at the crest of the mountain. The disintegration of the still exposed peaks and ridges will continue, and not only will the main valleys become choked with rock fragments, but each lateral gorge will also contain an extension of an alluvial cone.   In time the exposed pinnacles and ledges of rock will become covered with loosened fragments and the entire range assume subdued and flowing outlines.   The core of still solid rock will then be covered and concealed by a sheet of disintegrated fragments, which will be thickest in the former gorges.   There are mountains in the arid regions referred to above which have become buried in this manner in their own debris.

The life histories of alluvial cones are long and remarkably unvaried.   The chief episodes in their lives are the sudden and severe storms which increase their rate of growth in a striking manner.   They continue to increase in all of their dimensions as long as there is high land to furnish debris, unless climatic conditions change and the streams which supply them become perennial.   If the climate remains arid, however, they gradually expand, perhaps with the engrafting of secondary or parasitic cones on their sides, until the mountain about which they began to form is buried, and then, owing to decay and the removal of material in solution, flatten out and become hills with gracefully flowing outlines, which in time slowly fade away.

The reader will no doubt fancy that I have given too much space to the consideration of this special phase of stream deposition, and one which is of minor importance when all of the accumulations made by streams are considered, but the study of alluvial cones assists in an important way in understanding the nature of all other stream-

PLATE VII.

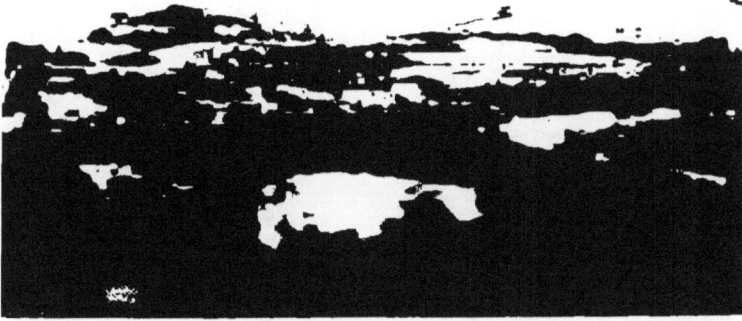

FIG. A.   Valley of Big Goose River, Wyoming.
An old, alluvial-filled valley with a meandering stream.   (Photograph by W. H. Jackson.)

FIG. B.   New River, Tennessee.
A young valley excavated in a peneplain.   (Photograph by M. R. Campbell.)

made deposits. The upper portions of deltas, for example, are simply alluvial cones. Even the flood-plains of rivers are imperfectly developed, or, perhaps more properly, composite, alluvial cones with greatly extended sides and low surface slopes. The alluvial cones of arid regions and the alluvial caps of deltas are usually allowed to expand symmetrically, but flood-plains, as will be shown later, are confined by the sides of the valleys in which they are formed, and may be considered as long, narrow, longitudinal sections of deposits of a similar origin.

TALUS SLOPES

Alluvial cones frequently unite with or merge into the accumulations of debris which form at the bases of cliffs and are supplied directly by rock fragments falling from the precipices above them. These *talus slopes*, or *screes*, as they are sometimes termed, are composed of angular fragments of rocks, although frequently rounded by weathering, of all sizes up to many cubic feet, and have surface slopes frequently as great as thirty or thirty-five degrees. Unless cut away at the base, as by a stream, the surface slopes represent the angle of repose of the material of which the apron-like piles are composed.

Talus slopes are not stream deposits, but are frequently associated with alluvial cones, and may be mistaken for them. They differ from alluvial cones, however, in their mode of origin, and in the fact that they are not composed of water-worn material, unless the cliffs above them contain conglomerate, and usually have much higher surface slopes.

The spaces between the large blocks are not usually filled, and the material of which they are composed is not stratified. These differences, and the fact that talus slopes occur at the base of precipices, while alluvial cones are built at the mouth of gorges, enable one to·readily discriminate between them.

FLOOD-PLAINS

It is well known that streams, whether rills or rivers, seldom follow a straight course for any considerable distance, unless held in a definite channel for a time by walls of solid rock. The path of a stream is a series of curves. Owing to the deflection of the thread of swiftest current, the banks on the concave or outer curves are eaten away, while those bordering the convex or inner curves are added to. As has been described in considering the meandering of streams, any inequality in their bottoms or banks may lead to a deflection of the current. If we imagine a stream flowing through a broad valley, even if of constant volume, this process of meandering from side to side in a tortuous course will go on. As the stream bed is shifted, deposits are laid down on the border of the convex curves, and new land formed. The first deposits made are of coarse material, usually well-rounded gravel or stones, next above this layer finer material is deposited, and last of all, fine silt. If the stream migrates from one side of its valley to the other, one bank is progressively cut away and the material thus removed in part re-deposited lower down on the other side, and at the same time assorted. In this manner a plain is formed, having an even surface of fine rich soil which changes towards its base into coarser and coarser material. When the meandering of the stream is reversed and it swings back again across the valley, the material it previously deposited is again cut away and again carried lower down and re-deposited on the slack-water sides of lower curves, and is again assorted during the process. In this manner the material flooring a river valley is worked over and over many times.

The manner in which streams cut away the land on the outer sides of stream-curves so as to produce steep banks, and deposit material on their inner or convex sides so as to form gentle slopes, is illustrated by the view of Indian Creek, California, presented on Plate VI. Other characteristic examples of meandering streams are shown on Plate III.

In the case of a stream without marked variations in volume, flood-plain building goes on slowly, or rather, perhaps, an approximate equilibrium is first reached and then the change is slow, but is probably always in progress, although varying in different instances according as the stream is clear or more or less charged with sediment. In nature the process just outlined is almost always assisted by variation in the volume of a stream. During periods of decreased rain-fall, as, for example, in the summer season in most regions, the streams are low and confined to their immediate channels; when storms come, however, or the snow melts, the streams are swollen and more than fill their summer channels. It is during floods that the greater amount of corrasion on the concave curves and of deposition on the convex curves takes place.

There are certain limitations to the extent a stream may

meander to the right and left of its general course, inherent in the process by which curves are formed, which determine the width of the belt of country it works over. In studying these limitations, however, a distinction should be borne in mind between the comparatively small curves originating in the manner just described, and the much greater sweeps, made up of many small curves, which I have termed migrations, as, for example, the great swings of the Mississippi from side to side of its broad alluvial valley below the mouth of the Ohio. The checks mentioned below on the tendency of a stream to meander in small, sharp curves do not seem to be operative, or at least do not act in the same manner, in the case of the broad migrations.

When a stream forms an oxbow curve, it is plain that its course is lengthened, and that aggrading must take place in order to allow the waters to carry their burden over the extended course. The bed of the stream at the beginning of a curve will thus be raised higher and higher, as the curve increases in length. During times of flood when the stream overspreads its banks, the waters cross the narrow neck of the oxbow curve and begin to excavate a channel. Once a start is made the entire river soon takes the shorter and steeper course, and the curve is cut off. The entrance and exit of the abandoned curve are soon silted up, on account of the deposition of debris in the slack water in the embayments on the side of the straightened stream, and an " oxbow lake " is the result.

As cited by C. R. Keyes,[1] the difference in elevation on

[1] *Missouri Geological Survey*, vol. x., p. 97, 1896.

the two sides of the neck of an oxbow curve is frequently sufficient for a small ravine to be cut backward from the lower side so as to make a slight rent in the narrow strip of land, thus directing and facilitating the work of the overflowing waters when a flood occurs.

There is thought to be a definite limit established in this manner on the extent to which a stream may meander, but on account of the numerous varying conditions entering into the problem,—such as the volume of a stream, its velocity, its fluctuations, the influence of vegetation, the nature of its banks, and in many regions the influence of ice,—it has not been found possible to determine how widely any given stream may meander.

The broad migrations referred to above depend on conditions still more complex than those limiting a stream's meanderings, and as they have not been carefully studied, it is perhaps best not to attempt to discuss them at this time.

During floods, also, a stream frequently inundates the plains formed during previous meanderings. The region thus submerged is for this reason termed a *flood-plain.* The waters on spreading from the main channel lose velocity, and the silt they hold in suspension is, to a great extent precipitated. A layer of fine material is thus spread over the plain and raises it by the addition of a layer of rich soil.

The debris brought from the upper portion of a stream course, where, on account of the high grade, corrasion is in progress, is thus dropped in the valley and plain tracts, and not only raises the bed of the stream but is built into flood-plains.

8

Flood-plains of the character just described border practically all the streams of North America, below the region of active corrasion, and furnish some of the richest and most easily cultivated lands the continent possesses. The flood-plains of the Mississippi, for example, are from ten to fifty or sixty miles broad, and in the neighbourhood of fifty thousand square miles in area. In the settlement of a new country the flood-plains are usually the first areas occupied, not only on account of their fertility, but because of their ready access. The main obstacle met with by early settlers is usually the heavy growth of timber that has to be cleared away in order to admit of the cultivation of the soil. Another difficulty arises from the fact that the flood-plains are subject to inundation at times of high water, as is well known in the case of the lower Mississippi. After the floods have subsided, the moist lowlands are in many instances unhealthy and malarial fevers are apt to be prevalent.

It is of interest to note that flood-plains begin to form where a stream loses grade and is no longer able to transport the debris brought down its higher-grade upper course. Usually they first appear as one descends a river, at the lower end of its mountain tract, and extend from that locality to the sea. Their similarity to alluvial cones is thus made apparent. An alluvial cone is in fact a flood-plain, formed under special conditions. The surface slopes of alluvial cones are high in comparison with what may be termed normal flood-plains, because the gorges of the short streams supplying them are of higher grade than the larger streams which build long flood-plains. The purpose, as we may say, of the alluvial cone is to grade up the lower course of a stream to conform with its slope in its upper portion, and thus furnish an even grade down which the stream may carry its burdens. The same is true of flood-plains; the river has more material delivered to it at the head of its valley tract than it can continue to carry with the current necessitated by the lower slope farther downstream, and at once begins to raise its grade. The aggrading progresses all the way from the locality where the stream begins to be overloaded, throughout its lower course to the sea, unless rapids break its course. When rapids occur, each separate portion of the stream behaves like an independent river, and each section deepens its channel or fills it in, as the case may be.

In an alluvial cone the greatest depth of the deposit is near its head, and probably at the locality where deposition first began. In a flood-plain, in general, the greatest depth of the deposit is near the lower end of the mountain tract and decreases all the way to the sea. The locality of greatest depth of filling, however, will migrate up stream as the flood-plain increases in length. Unless the stream is building a delta and thus lengthening its course, the flood-plain at its mouth cannot be raised. Hence deposition on a flood-plain at sea-level is practically nil.

If the changes experienced by a stream from youth to old age are followed, it will be found that its valley, plains, and mountain tracts are mutually extended up stream. The plains tract especially increases in length, while the mountain tract becomes shorter and shorter unless it is so situated that it can extend its branches headward. With the lengthening of the portion of the stream characterised by low gradients—that is, of the plains and valley tracts,—there is an up-stream migration of the locality where flood-plains begin. These normal phases of stream development, however, will be more readily understood after the adjustment of streams to the structure of the rocks corraded by them has been considered. The fact that a stream under certain conditions, already noted, cuts a channel through the upper portion of an alluvial cone and forms terraces in the gorge thus produced, will assist us later in understanding the manner in which streams may cut channels through their flood-plains, and form terraces on the side of such channels.

NATURAL LEVEES

On visiting a stream that is subject to floods, and carries a heavy load of silt especially during high-water stages, one will usually find that its immediate banks are higher than the general level of the surface of the adjacent flood-plain, and form ridges. In the case of creeks and small rivers, the ridges may be a hundred feet across, and their crests five to six feet or more above the surface of the flood-plain or back country, as it is frequently termed. In many instances, too, the back country between the river and the bluffs bordering the valley, is imperfectly drained and in a swampy condition. The region referred to is frequently densely covered with alders and other swamp-loving plants, and may support great cottonwoods and other forest growths. Through the forests one frequently finds open, park-like passages, clear of vegetation, which mark secondary channels, occupied by branches of the main stream during high-water stages. The embankments referred to on each border of a stream, where it flows through a flood-plain, are built up by the river. As the waters rise during floods, and spread beyond the border of the low-water channel, the current is checked, and they drop all but the very finest of the material held in suspension. It thus happens that the thickest deposits are made on the immediate border of the channel, and ridges which follow all the meanderings of the stream are built up. These embankments resemble the levees built by man in attempting to confine a stream to its immediate channel, and are hence known as *natural levees.*

When the waters of a rising river pass the natural levees, they are still charged with silt, much of which is precipitated on the inundated country and adds to the layer of fine material found on the surface of all low-grade flood-plains. It is to the addition of this thin layer of exceedingly fine mud, mingled in many instances with organic matter, derived from the working away of soil farther upstream, that the wonderful fertility of flood-plains is largely due. The decay of the rank vegetation on many flood-plains, especially during the time previous to the clearing of the land for cultivation, also adds to the fertility of " river bottoms,'' as the flood-plains are frequently termed.

While natural levees are a protection to the back country during moderate floods, serving as they do to retain the waters in a definite channel, yet, as has been found, especially in the case of the Mississippi, they are also a source of danger. During unusually high floods, the rivers break the embankment confining them, and branching streams **are**

formed, which carry destruction in their paths and sweep
away the fields and whatever else obstructs their flow.

The typical cross-profile of a river valley in which levees
occur, as has been shown by Hicks,[1] does not present a
straight line from the stream's channel to the bordering
bluffs, but a double curve. If no terraces are present on
the sides of the valley, each half presents a weather-curve
at the top of the bluff, and two other curves of opposite
character, one concave due to erosion, and the other convex
due to deposition. At the intersection of the water-curves
there is usually a swamp. These features, somewhat exaggerated in the vertical scale, are shown in the following
diagram.

FIG. 4.   Cross-Profile of a Valley Occupied by a Constructive River.   After
L. E. Hicks.)

a b. Weather-Curve at Crest of Bluffs ; *b c.* Water-Curve of Corrasion ; *c d.* Swamp; *d e.*
Water-Curve of Deposition ; *s.* Stream Channel.

The water which covers a flood-plain between the levees
and the uplands bordering a valley during flood, finds its
way back to the river again at some locality lower down-
stream, usually by entering a tributary. In the lower Mississippi, much of the water that escapes in this manner
from the main channel is carried to the Gulf of Mexico by
distributaries from the main stream.

Where natural levees are built, the bed of a stream is

[1] L. E. Hicks, "Some Elements of Land Sculpture," in *Bulletin of the Geological Society of America*, vol. iv., p. 143, 1893.

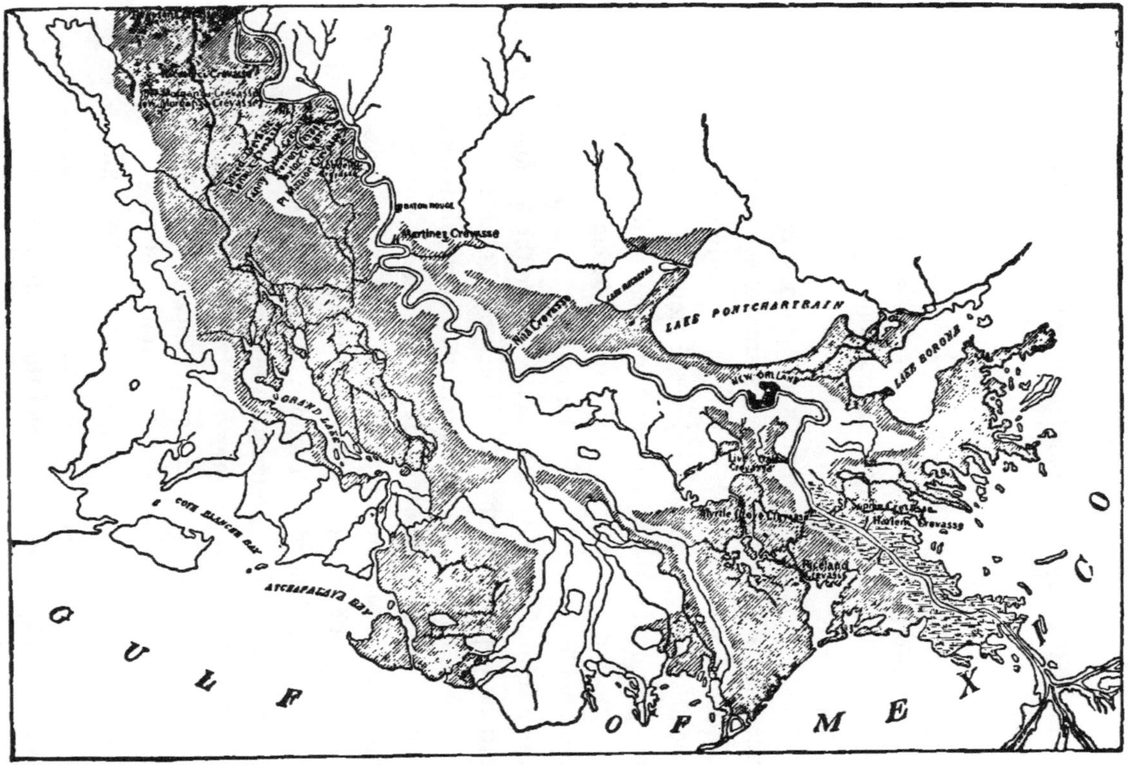

FIG. 5. Overflowed Areas and Crevasses of the Lower Mississippi, March, April, and May, 1890. (After L. C. Johnson.)

119

usually raised by deposits made in its bottom.   In this way it happens that a stream sometimes flows in a trench on the top of a ridge more elevated than the back country, and is thus in an unstable position, and liable to shift its channel when breaks in the levees occur.   This is one method by which streams are led over all portions of the valleys they occupy.

Illustrations of the manner in which a river subject to floods breaks through its levees from time to time and inundates its flood-plain are furnished nearly every year by the Mississippi, especially below the mouth of the Ohio.   In the case of this river, however, the extent of the inundation is increased in many instances by the attempts that have been made to confine it to its main channel by adding to the height of the natural levees.   Under the artificial conditions imposed on the river, when breaks, or *crevasses*, as they are termed, in the levees do occur, plantations are ruined, buildings swept away, and in some instances the mollusks, fishes, and other animals in the bays and sounds bordering the deltas are destroyed by the vast quantities of fresh water, charged with mud, poured into them.

The extent of the inundation in the lower Mississippi, in the spring of 1890, is shown on the accompanying map. The shaded portion of the map indicates the regions that were covered by the overflowing waters, while the unshaded portion reveals the distribution of the land too high to be reached by the flood.   It is instructive to note that the unsubmerged land lies close along the borders of the streams, and indicates the position of their embankments.   At the time of the inundations referred to, the water broke through the left embankment of the river at what is known as the Nita crevasse, about twenty miles above New Orleans, and formed a current of fifteen miles an hour, which carried destruction in its path. The escaping water, joining that from another break known as the Martinez crevasse, approximately twelve miles in a straight line higher up the stream, flowed eastward and caused Lake Maurepas and Lake Pontchartrain (six hundred square miles in area) to overspread their banks. The water flowed over the country eastward to Lake Borgne and entered Mobile Bay, with such volume as to cause a current eastward and destroy for a time the important oyster and fish industries of that arm of the sea.[1]

The study of flood-plains and the manner in which streams divide near their mouths when aggrading, or delta-building, is in progress, illustrates a natural method by which inundations of the country bordering the lower course of an alluvial river are lessened or prevented. When a distributary leaves a trunk stream, the volume of water below the place of escape is lessened, and the tendency to break across the levees decreased. The practice of building artificial levees, so frequently resorted to in the vain attempt to control large rivers subject to high-water stages, checks this natural tendency. If, for example, instead of attempting to confine the Mississippi to a single channel in its lower course, the natural distributaries could be cleared

[1] L. C. Johnson, "The Nita Crevasse," in *Bulletin of the Geological Society of America*, vol. ii., pp. 20–25, 1891.

The areas overflowed by the Mississippi in 1897 are shown on an excellent map forming Plate II. of Park Morrill's report on the "Floods of the Mississippi River." Published by the Weather Bureau, Washington, 1897.

of driftwood or other obstructions and enlarged, the excess of water during floods might be drawn off, thus lessening the danger to the levees farther seaward.

The influence of natural levees on the geography of a valley where aggrading is in progress, receives additional illustration from the manner in which tributaries of the main stream are deflected from what would otherwise be their natural courses. The building up of the borders of the main stream necessitates important changes in its tributaries. If the main stream increases the height of its levees at a greater rate than its tributaries can aggrade their channels, evidently their waters must either rise so as to discharge across the dam thus formed, or be turned aside and flow more or less nearly parallel with the main stream until conditions favour a junction with it. The most common cause for such a union lies in the fact that each stream is meandering, and sooner or later one or the other will cut into the embankment built by its neighbour. The origin of lakes along Red River, Louisiana, owing to the raising of the levees on its margins faster than its tributary streams are able to aggrade their channels, has been described by Davis.[1] An examination of a good map[2] of the lower Mississippi will show that its tributaries below the mouth of the Ohio frequently exhibit an abrupt change in direction after entering the broad valley of the main river, and flow parallel with it for many miles before being able to effect a junction. The various

[1] W. M. Davis, *Science*, vol. x., pp. 142, 143, 1887.

[2] An excellent map of the lower Mississippi valley in eight sheets, scale five miles to in inch, has been published by the U. S. Mississippi River Commission, price forty cents. This can be obtained by applying to the Secretary, Mississippi River Commission, St. Louis, Mo.

branches of the Yazoo, for example, after entering the valley of the Mississippi, flow nearly parallel with that river for about two hundred miles, but join it at Vicksburg, where the main river curves eastward and washes the base of the bordering bluffs, leaving no room for a secondary · and parallel stream.

DELTAS [1]

When streams deliver their loads of detritus to bodies of still water, either lakes or the ocean, deposition takes place in much the same way as when alluvial cones are formed, but the structure and shape of the deposit are influenced in an important manner by the presence of the still water into which the stream discharges. These deposits, when seen from above, as represented on a map, have the shape of an open fan. The curved margin of the fan faces the open water, and the sharp apex, or handle, is situated at the mouth of the feeding stream or well up its valley. The deposits laid down in the Mediterranean by the Nile have the characteristic form referred to, except that the fan is not fully open; that is, the outline of the delta is a triangle and resembles the Greek letter Δ, as was long since noted; hence the generic name still in use. All deltas do not exhibit the characteristic form of the type example, however, but may be markedly semicircular on their outer margin, or variously lobed or indented, as is shown by the compound

[1] The account of deltas here presented is essentially the same as may be found in the author's book entitled *Lakes of North America*, one of the series of reading-lessons to which the present volume belongs, but this repetition is thought desirable in order to make each book as nearly complete in itself as practicable.

delta of the Mississippi.   An inversion of the Δ form in the case of certain small deltas in Seneca Lake has been described by the writer.[1]

The conditions governing the formation of deltas are mainly that a stream shall bring detritus to a body of water which is unaffected by strong currents.   If currents exist in the receiving water-body where the stream enters, capable of bearing away the debris delivered to it, the plan of the delta will be modified, and if the currents are sufficiently strong, all of the material is carried away and deposited over the bottom or built into bars and embankments of various forms along the margin of the lake or ocean.   It is sometimes stated that deltas are not formed in water bodies affected by a tide, but this is an indirect explanation.   To be sure, deltas are seldom found along the shores of the ocean where the rise and fall of the tides are well marked, but this is for the reason that the tides usually cause currents which bear away the debris brought by streams as fast as delivered.   Water bodies sufficiently quiet to favour the growth of deltas are not necessarily tideless.   Currents in water bodies are also produced by the wind, and may influence delta-building in a similar way to tidal currents. For these reasons, sheltered bays and estuaries, where the fluctuations of level due to winds and tides are not excessive, are among the most favourable places for the growth of deltas.

In the study of deltas, it is convenient to divide them into two classes, namely, those made by high-grade and consequently rapid streams, and those made by low-grade

[1] I. C. Russell, *Lakes of North America*, pp. 48–51.   Ginn & Co., 1895.

and therefore comparatively sluggish streams. These distinctions apply of course only to the lower courses of the delta-making streams. Between the two types referred to, a complete gradation may be found.

Deltas of High-Grade Streams.—Typical examples of deltas of this class occur in Utah about the borders of ancient Lake Bonneville,[1] and have had gorges cut through them since the lake surface was lowered. A radial section of a delta of this type, such as would be exposed in the walls of a trench cut through it from apex to outer margin, is shown in Fig. 6, page 126, which will assist the reader in understanding the leading characteristics of such deposits. A swift stream is able to bring to the still waters of a lake, or of the sea, a heterogeneous load of detritus. On entering the receiving water-body, this detritus is more or less perfectly assorted. The coarser or heavier portions, namely, the boulders, gravel, and coarse sand, fall to the bottom, while the lighter and finer particles, that is, the fine sand and silt, are carried farther. The very fine silt is floated away from the mouth of the feeding stream, and slowly settling to the bottom forms an addition to the sheet of mud which is being laid down in nearly every water-body.

The coarse material referred to, dropped at the mouth of the stream so as to form a delta, makes an addition to the land and the stream channel is lengthened. The outer border of this deposit is steep for the reason that the debris as it is dropped tends to form a pile much the same as when similar material is heaped up on the land, the supply being

[1] G. K. Gilbert, " Lake Bonneville," *U. S. Geological Survey, Monographs,* vol. i., pp. 65-70, 1890.

from the top. The angle of repose, that is, the surface slope of material deposited under water, is steeper than would be assumed by the same material accumulated in a similar manner on land, and some assorting takes place. Additional material brought by the stream is carried to the top of the steep submerged slope referred to, and rolls down it so as to form an addition to the inclined layers. As a delta grows in all directions from the mouth of the feeding stream in which the water has freedom to flow, and invades deeper and deeper portions of the receiving water-body, the accumulation of inclined layers becomes broader and broader at the same time that its outer slope or under-water escarpment increases in height. The angle which the escarpment makes with a horizontal plane varies with the size and shape of the material composing it, but in most instances is in the neighbourhood of thirty-five degrees.

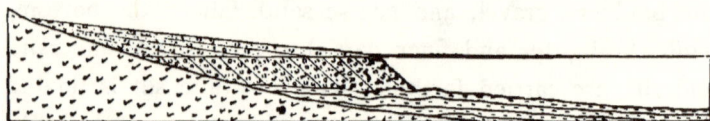

FIG. 6.   Radial Section of a Delta Built by a High-Grade Stream.

The inclined layers, as indicated in Fig. 6, terminate upward in a horizontal plane, which coincides with the surface of the receiving water-body. As is indicated in the diagram, a delta built by a high-grade stream has three well-defined portions; the middle member of the series being the debris laid down in inclined layers, in the manner just described.

The fine material delivered by the feeding stream is carried beyond the outer margin of the system of inclined beds forming the medial member of the delta, and subsides to the bottom. This material is also assorted. The coarser and heavier portions reach the bottom at the immediate base of the escarpment formed by the inclined layers, while the finer portions are carried farther before coming to rest. In this manner a conical deposit of fine material with a low surface slope is made about the base of the accumulation of inclined layers. As the delta grows, the medial member, that is, the system of inclined beds of coarse material, advances over the finer deposits accumulated about its base, and in many instances causes them to be pressed outward and variously disturbed. The layers of fine material are frequently folded or broken by the weight of the body of coarse debris as it advances upon them.

The third or superior portion of the delta, or the *delta cap*, as it may be called, is an alluvial cone which is built on the plane formed by the truncated edges of the inclined layers in the medial portion. The apex of the cone is well up the feeding stream from the locality where the delta first began, and as the delta increases in size, migrates up stream at the same time that the alluvial cone increases in all of its dimensions.

The feeding stream in flowing down the surface of the delta cap is deflected, or caused to divide, from time to time, on account of the deposits made on its bottom and sides, and sends off branches in the same manner as has been explained in the case of alluvial cones, and at one time or another flows over all portions of the surface of the delta and discharges at all points about its outer border. The delta cap is thus built up, and the periphery of its base extended by the addition of material to its surface. As in the case of alluvial cones, the surface slope of the delta cap is controlled by the grade of the feeding stream, but becomes less and less steep as the area of its base increases. The more or less definite layers of which it is composed are inclined and slope downward towards the receiving waterbody. As each layer was added to its surface at a certain stage in its growth, the inclination of those first formed is somewhat greater than the slope of those deposited later. An inclination of three to five degrees with a horizontal plane is common in deltas of the class here considered. If we visit a growing delta in process of construction by a high-grade stream, it will be found that the stream is bringing both coarse and fine material to the apex of the delta cap. The coarser portions of this load are dropped on the exposed surface of the delta, together with much fine material which serves to fill the interspaces between the boulders and larger stones and tends to prevent loss of water by percolation. This building up or aggrading serves to adjust the grade of the feeding stream as its length increases owing to the outward extension of the delta. Both coarse and fine material is carried down the slope of the delta cap and delivered to the receiving water-body, where it is assorted, the larger and heavier debris falling at once and adding to the series of inclined layers previously deposited, while the finer material is carried beyond the periphery of the delta and distributed over the adjacent bottom or floated away, as already stated, and finally brought to rest with other fine sediment on the floor of the basin occupied by the still waters.

In the passage of the debris down the surface of the delta cap an assorting in reference to form may frequently be recognised. The flat and angular stones come to rest under conditions that allow rounded and well-worn stones of similar size and density to be rolled along. The highly inclined layers in a delta are usually composed of well-rounded stones.

Referring once more to the radial section of a delta given above, it will be understood that the upper portion or delta cap consists of gently sloping, cross-stratified, and irregular beds of both coarse and fine material, the larger stones being frequently angular; the medial member is composed of steeply inclined layers, usually of well-rounded stones, mainly gravel and sand; the basal member is of fine sand and clay, deposited originally in nearly horizontal sheets which decreased in thickness in a direction opposite to the source of supply, but later were pressed into folds, or broken and displaced, owing to the heavy weight imposed upon them.

It should be noted that the growth of a delta increases the length of the supplying stream, and in order that it may carry debris to its advancing terminus, the newly occupied territory must be built up or aggraded. This process of filling in causes the apex of the alluvial cap to migrate up stream.

At an advanced stage in the building of a delta, the lengthening of the course of the feeding stream would decrease its rate of flow, and at the same time the deepening of the stream's channel above the delta, owing to corrasion, would tend in the same direction. These changes would necessitate a readjustment of grade which might lead to the

9

cutting of a channel through the apex of the delta in the same manner that the apexes of alluvial cones are sometimes notched.

Deltas of Low-Grade Streams.—Typical examples of the deltas of this class are furnished by the deposits now being laid down at the mouth of the Mississippi, Yukon, Mackenzie, Nile, Ganges, and many other streams that have a low grade for a long distance near their mouths and de- liver only fine sediment to the still waters into which they flow.   In these deltas the three divisions so characteristic of the similar deposits of high-grade streams cannot be recognised. All of the material delivered by low-grade streams is fine, mostly of the nature of fine sand and silt, and no marked assorting takes place and no distinctions between gently and steeply inclined layers can be distin- guished. The tendency of low-grade and mud-charged streams is to make broad deposits with indefinite borders rather than thick, well-defined accumulations.

The debris brought to still waters by the class of streams here considered, is dropped as in the case of high-grade streams, but, being fine, a larger proportion is carried to a distance from the shore.   Much debris is dropped as the incoming stream meets still water, but the angle of repose for fine sand and silt is much less than for coarse gravel, and the outer slope of the deposit is not well defined.   More- over, fine material is easily disturbed by currents in the re- ceiving water-body, which again is unfavourable for the formation of sharply defined delta margins.   Low-grade, muddy streams shoal the still water at their mouths and gradually form new land, which, however, is but slightly raised above the surface. The length of the stream is thus increased, which necessitates a new adjustment of the grade for a long distance up its course. Owing to the gentle grade of the stream, the changes produced in this manner are not pronounced. As the length of the stream is extended, the natural levees are also prolonged. When floods occur, breaches are made in the levees, and the stream divides, and sends off distributaries which discharge independently. Each distributary builds a pair of embankments or levees, and also an independent delta. The results of this process of subdivision are well illustrated at the mouth of the Mississippi, as may be seen from the accompanying map (Plate V.). Each of the finger-like extensions of the delta is due to the prolongation of a pair of embankments into the Gulf, by each distributary, and the growth of a secondary delta at its mouth. The Mississippi is thus building a compound delta, composed of the secondary deltas formed at the mouths of the several distributaries of the main river. The fact that each distributary is forming a delta of its own is best illustrated perhaps at the mouth of what is known as Cubit's Gap, a break in the left levee, about four miles upstream from where the main " passes " or distributaries diverge.

The branches of the secondary deltas, with their levees, frequently join, and the low spaces between them become transformed into lakes. Delta lakes, like Pontchartrain to the north of New Orleans, are thus formed. Several lakes of this type are shown on the accompanying maps (Fig. 5 and Plate V.), as well as a number of bays, which will evidently be shut off from the sea in time and become lakes.

The surface of the delta of a low-grade stream is in reality an alluvial cone, but of such a low slope that the eye cannot usually distinguish it from a horizontal plane. The exposed portion of such a delta, with its many levees, corresponds, both in the manner of its formation and in the alluvial nature of its material, with the delta cap of a high-grade stream. As in the type of delta first considered, the extension of the delta increases the length of the feeding stream, and necessitates a grading up of the extended portion of the river channel so as to furnish the requisite slope for the transportation of debris to the advancing extremity. The surface of the delta is also raised, and its apex migrates up stream.

The apex of a low-grade delta is usually indefinite, and its position difficult to determine. For this reason in part, such a delta is usually considered as beginning when the first distributary having an independent course to the receiving water-body is given off. Under this definition, the head of the delta of the Mississippi is near the mouth of Red River, or about two hundred miles in a direct line from its extreme southern end. In reality, the apex of the delta cap is much farther upstream. The area of the Mississippi delta, as determined by Humphreys and Abbot, is one thousand two hundred and thirty square miles. The depth of the deposit, as shown by recent borings at New Orleans, is over one thousand feet,[1] but, as will be seen later, this great depth is due to subsidence and the superposing of one delta on another.

---

[1] E. L. Corthell, " The Delta of the Mississippi River," in *The National Geographic Magazine*, vol. viii., p. 351, 1897.

A delta, comparable in many ways with that of the Mississippi, has been formed by the Yukon in Bering Sea; the distance in this instance from where the first distributary is given off to the periphery of the delta, is about one hundred miles. The outer or seaward margin of the deposit measures about seventy miles. The land between the several distributaries is swampy, and natural levees are less conspicuous than in the case of the Mississippi. The surface of the delta, a glimpse of which is given in Fig. A, Plate II., is treeless, but covered with a luxuriant growth of grasses, rushes, and low flowering annuals, and is a luxuriant garden of flowers in early summer, but at a depth of a few feet the soil, as has previously been mentioned, is always frozen. The delta in fact is a part of the extensive frozen marshes, or *tundra*, which border the shores of Bering Sea and the Arctic Ocean. No survey of this delta has been made, but a most instructive example of the nature of the deposit formed by a heavily loaded river, subjected to great inundation, there invites the student of geography.

A great delta is also being extended into the Arctic Ocean by the Mackenzie. The Colorado is filling in the Gulf of California, and many smaller streams are making delta deposits in the lakes of North America. In each of these instances some phase of delta-building is apt to be more prominent than others, but in almost any example that can be chosen the general laws governing the deposition of material brought by loaded streams when their currents are checked by still water may be observed.

An abnormal delta, and one of interest on account of its novelty, is being made in Lake St. Clair by the St. Clair

River. The river referred to is the outlet of Lake Huron, and as lakes act on settling basins, it would be expected that the stream draining it would be clear and therefore incapable of forming a delta. The shore currents in Lake Huron, however, bring debris to the place of outlet, and deliver it to the draining stream. This material is carried to Lake St. Clair and there deposited in a broad delta, with several distributaries, similar in some of its features to the delta of the Mississippi.'

Many of the large streams of North America are not making conspicuous deltas for various reasons. The St. Lawrence, for example, is a clear stream, and therefore has but little material to deposit when its current is checked. Like a large number of rivers flowing to the Atlantic, the St. Lawrence, as already stated, has been greatly affected at a comparatively recent date by a subsidence of the land, which has allowed the ocean to extend far up its valley, and to submerge the deltas it may have previously formed. Other streams on the Atlantic border of the continent, like the Hudson, Delaware, Susquehanna, Potomac, and James, also enter estuaries, but are not clear streams. The absence of conspicuous deltas about their mouths is due to currents in the receiving water-bodies, and to the recency of the drowning of their lower courses.

Effects of Changes in the Elevation of the Land on the Growth of Deltas.—A rise or a subsidence of the land along the ocean's shore where deltas are being formed, has the same effect on their growth as the lowering or raising of

---

[1] I. C. Russell, *Lakes of North America*, p. 40. Ginn & Co., Boston, 1895.

the surface of a lake where similar additions to the land are being made.

If the surface of a lake rises after the building of a delta on its borders is well under way, the deposit may be partially or wholly submerged and a new structure of similar character formed above it. If the waters of a lake subside after a tributary stream has built a delta, its outer or sublacustral escarpment will be more or less completely exposed. The waters of the stream will descend this slope with accelerated velocity and corrade. Of the two or more subdivisions into which the stream may be divided on the delta cap, previous to the change just assumed, some one branch, either by being shorter than the others, or by having a greater volume, will deepen its channel more rapidly than its competitor and draw off its water, so that but one trench will be cut in the emerged delta. If the surface of the lake is depressed below the level of the base of the delta it will be completely cut through so as to expose a section of the deposit and a portion of the material on which it rests. The material removed during the cutting of the gorge, together with fresh debris brought by the feeding stream from above the old delta, will be again deposited and a new delta built at a lower level. The apex of the second delta will be in the gorge cut through its predecessor or below the base of the old delta according to the extent principally to which the lake surface is lowered.

Variations in the stages of delta-building, owing to changes in the elevation of the land, or of the level of a lake, as well as modifications of the process which would follow a change in grade, or in the volume or load of the feeding stream, may be readily determined.

VARIATIONS IN NORMAL STREAM DEPOSITIONS

In the preceding portion of this chapter we have con-sidered, for the most part, the various processes by which streams lay aside their burdens when not influenced by dis-turbing conditions. Let us glance at what may be termed the accidents that sometimes modify or interrupt the normal processes of stream deposition.

Influence of Elevation and Depression of the Land on Stream Deposition.—The velocity of a stream, as we have seen, has a controlling influence on the amount of debris it can transport. A change in conditions which will increase the velocity of a stream, other conditions remaining the same, will increase its transporting power. The reverse of this proposition is also true.

Movements of the land both of the nature of elevation and depression are known to be in progress in many regions and, we have good reasons for believing, have at one time or another affected every portion of the earth's surface. These movements, due to changes in the interior of the earth, in many instances affect the surface in such a manner as to tilt broad areas. Such tilting furnishes an example of the simplest movements of the earth's crust, so far as the changes here considered affect the flow of streams.

When the land is tilted downward in the direction in which a stream flows, the velocity of the stream will evi-dently be increased and its energy available for corrasion and transportation also increased. If, however, the rocks underlying the hydrographic basin of a river are tilted downward in a direction opposite to the flow of the stream, its velocity will be decreased, and its corrading and transporting power lessened.

It is thus evident that when the land is tilted so as to favour corrasion, stream channels will be deepened at a more rapid rate than previous to the change; and when the tilting is in such a direction as to check the flow of streams, other conditions remaining the same, corrasion will decrease and deposition may take place and the stream valleys be aggraded. Areas in the course of a stream which are depressed with reference to adjacent areas will receive deposits and be filled until the normal relation of stream bed to current has been re-established. An illustration of this process is furnished in Southern Washington, at the west base of the Blue Mountains, where movements in blocks of the earth's crust are producing a depression of an area some twenty miles in diameter, with reference to adjacent areas. The streams from the Blue Mountains descend steep declivities, are swift, and bring large quantities of debris to the depressed area. Deposition is there in progress and a gravel plain is in process of formation. The streams in crossing the area where aggrading is under way, bifurcate much the same as on a delta, but the waters unite to form a single stream, Walla Walla River, where the area of relative depression is passed.[1]

Influence of Variations in Load on Stream Deposition.—It has been demonstrated that a stream of given velocity and

[1] I. C. Russell, " Reconnoissance in Southeastern Washington," *U. S. Geological Survey, Water Supply and Irrigation Papers*, No. 4, pp. 23, 24, 1897.

of stated volume has a certain competency to transport debris. If the quantity of debris delivered to a stream exceeds its competency, a part is dropped and a part carried on. Under such conditions, a selective power is manifest, the stream dropping the larger and heavier debris and carrying on the smaller or lighter. Changes in velocity, as from swift to sluggish reaches in a stream, lead to the dropping of debris when the current slackens, and a consequent aggrading, which tends to give the stream channel a uniform slope. If debris is added to a stream already partially loaded, the result is much the same as if its velocity was checked. If the debris added is in excess of the competency of the stream, the coarser material is dropped and the finer, up to a certain grade, carried on.

The principal results of this law are seen where high-grade and consequently swift tributaries join a low-grade trunk stream. The tributaries may under such conditions bring more debris to the main stream than it is competent to carry on, and a deposit is made. The result is that an obstruction is formed in the main stream at the mouth of each high-grade tributary and the waters above are more or less completely ponded. Lakes are sometimes formed in trunk streams for this cause. Lake Pepin, for example, is held in check by debris brought to the Mississippi by Chippewa River, in excess of the amount the receiving stream is able to remove. In the Colorado, as described by Powell, rapids due to a similar cause occur just below the mouths of several of its tributaries.

The rate at which streams corrade varies, other conditions being the same, with the resistance of the rocks over which they flow. When the rocks are soft and easily corraded, the loads of the streams are increased and their velocities checked. In such regions, also, vertical corrasion is frequently retarded by the occurrence of harder beds farther down the streams, while lateral corrasion is still possible; the streams then expand in the areas of soft rock and may form broad flood-plains.

The loads of streams are also increased, as previously stated, by the action of the wind in bringing sand and dust to them. When this occurs, the tendency is much the same as when a high-grade tributary delivers more debris than the stream can bear away. Trains of sand dunes travel over many regions in the direction of the prevailing wind. If a train of dunes reaches a river, the load of the stream is increased, and may exceed its capacity to transport and a dam be formed. The waters may rise above such a dam and an increase of velocity be secured which will lead to the removal of the obstruction either wholly or in part. In many instances, a struggle ensues between the winds bringing debris to a stream, and the water striving to remove it. If the supply of wind-borne debris is sufficient, a dam is formed, and may be raised high above the level of the lake that it holds in check. The waters of the lake may then rise until a balance between inflow and loss by evaporation is established, and an enclosed lake, that is, one without an outlet, is formed. An example of a water body held in check by sand dunes is furnished by Moses Lake in the central part of Washington. In this instance the waters of the lake escape in part by percolating through the sand dunes retaining them. The influence of drifting sand on the flow of streams is more pronounced in arid than in humid regions, for many reasons which will suggest themselves to the reader.

Another way in which the loads of streams are varied, is by glacial action. The streams flowing from the ends of alpine glaciers, frequently receive greater contributions of both coarse and fine material than they are able to bear away, and consequently are engaged in filling in their valleys. This is true of every one of the hundreds of glaciers in the valleys of the Cordilleran region that have come under the writer's notice. Should these glaciers melt, the streams flowing from them and now aggrading their valleys, would be able to resume the work of excavation, and channels would be cut through the deposits of debris over which they now meander.

During the Glacial epoch, when half of North America was covered by ice-sheets, the streams fed by the melting of the ice were greatly overloaded and their valleys consequently deeply filled. Now that the ice-sheets have melted, the streams are at work in removing the loads they previously laid aside.

Influence of Changes of Climate on Stream Deposition.—The elements of climate which exert the most direct and important influences on stream deposition are precipitation, evaporation, and temperature.

Of these, precipitation is by far the most important. Any change in the amount of rain-fall, or in its distribution throughout the year, is at once felt by the streams in the region affected.

Evaporation depends on temperature and on the strength

of the wind, and tends to diminish the volume of streams throughout their entire length.

Temperature exerts a varied influence. A high mean annual temperature favours evaporation from the ocean, especially, and except under certain local conditions insures abundant rain-fall and favours also the growth of vegetation, thereby increasing the supply of organic acid available for surface water. Warm water charged with organic acid promotes rock decay and thus favours the preparation of debris for transportation. A low temperature, on the other hand, not only reverses the conditions just named, but when the decrease is sufficient to cause the freezing of water, rain changes to snow, the ground is frozen, and percolation ceases. The storing of the winter's precipitation in the form of snow and ice, however, favours stream work and the general degradation of the land, by concentrating the energy of the streams at the time the snow melts. The freezing of water in the interstices of rock, as previously mentioned, is one of the most powerful agencies tending toward rock disintegration. In these and still other ways climatic conditions exert an influence either directly or indirectly on stream deposition, but at present it will be most profitable to confine attention to variations in volume due to changes in supply.

In general, as is well known, a decrease in the rain-fall of a given region is accompanied by a decrease in the volume of the draining streams, and consequently a loss in their transporting power. The behaviour of streams under such conditions is materially influenced by the rate at which they are supplied with debris. During heavy rains a stream may be overloaded and caused to deposit, in spite of its increased velocity due to greater volume, and the amount of work done in a given time is far in excess of that accomplished during an equal time when the precipitation is less.

The influence of variations in precipitation is illustrated by the annual change in streams during rainy and dry seasons. During rainy seasons, more especially in spring in temperate latitudes, when the rain causes the melting of previously accumulated snow, the streams are swollen and heavily charged with debris. They overspread their banks and deposit material on their flood-plains. It is during the time the streams overflow their banks that the greater amount of material is deposited. Much debris is also laid down at such times, however, in the stream beds, even when the current is swift, and in some instances the less heavily loaded water, when much decreased in volume, corrades channels through deposits made during high-water stage. This may be seen in many wayside rills, which spread out in sheets, heavily charged with debris, during storms, and make deposits through which the shrunken and less heavily charged rills at a later stage excavate channels.

THE GENERAL PROCESS OF STREAM CORRASION AND DEPOSITION

The action of streams in corrading, transporting, and depositing debris is such a complex process that it is convenient to consider the different phases of their work separately. For this reason, an effort has been made in this chapter to direct special attention to the manner in which streams lay aside their loads during the process of development that they pass through. The behaviour of streams is much like the action of a complex piece of machinery, as a watch, for example; changes cannot be made in one portion of the mechanism without affecting the action of the whole, and necessitating adjustments throughout. Considering deposition alone, we find that streams in general, in passing from a high to a low grade, make deposits, as where a river leaves its mountain tract and enters a valley tract, or passes from a swift to a more quiet reach. Streams subject to floods make deposits over the lands they inundate during high-water stages, and spread out floodplains. At such times, also, the heaviest deposit is in the immediate border of the low-water channel, and natural levees are built. A high-grade stream, tributary to a low-grade and consequently less swift stream, unless the difference in grade is more than counterbalanced by the volume of the receiving stream, makes deposits and the waters of the main stream are more or less completely ponded. Local overloading from the action of the wind or of glaciers produces similar results.

The debris carried in suspension by streams or rolled along their beds is also deposited in lakes as deltas, or distributed over their bottom. As lakes in many instances are of the nature of expansions of streams, the filling of their basins may be considered as a part of the general process of stream deposition by which stream channels are aggraded. In discussing corrasion it was shown that a stream, at least in humid climates, cuts down its channel to baselevel most quickly at its mouth, and that the process of deepening progresses up stream. The head-waters of a well-developed stream are steeper than the lower portion of its trunk. A general view of stream deposition shows that a similar order is followed in the process of stream deposition. When the seaward portion of the trunk of a stream has been lowered to baselevel, the stream continues to corrade laterally, and thus makes it possible for flood-plains to form. As a stream continues to widen its channel farther and farther from its mouth, the flood-plain follows. If a stream is making a delta, its length of flow is increased, and its flood-plains and channel are raised by deposition in order to furnish the necessary slope. When a stream reaches maturity, its plains tract and valley tract are greatly lengthened at the expense of the high-grade portions of its course in the uplands. The high-grade branches, then, bring more material than the trunk stream can bear away, and the flood-plains along its sides are raised by the deposition of material laid aside. During the upbuilding of the flood-plains the stream channel is also raised. Hence, for a long time after a normal river has cut down its channel in its lower course practically to baselevel, building is in progress and the valley becomes filled in with abandoned debris. There comes a time, however, when the highlands from which the river flows have been lowered so that the branches of the main stream are not as swift as previously, and the stream is enabled to devote a portion of its energy not consumed in the friction of flow to the re-excavation of its channel farther seaward. As this process is continued, the highest flood-plain is abandoned and new ones formed at lower levels, thus giving origin to terraces, as will be shown in the next chapter. During this stage of a stream's development, as in the preceding stages, changes occur, also, in the longitudinal profile of the stream throughout its length.

The manner in which flood-plains are formed and advance up stream as the down cutting of the upper portion of a stream channel progresses, shows that only an approximation to baselevelling is reached during the earlier stages of a stream's development. It is after a stream has lowered its head-water channels so as to permit of the removal of the flood-plains built lower downstream, that what may be termed a second approximation to baselevel is normally reached.

PROFILES OF STREAMS

In a discussion of the succession of changes experienced by a stream during its life, consideration should be given to the orderly variations in shape that occur in the valley it excavates.

The shape of a valley may be illustrated by two classes of profiles; one longitudinal and the other transverse. A generalised longitudinal profile of a stream would be what is understood as a projection on a vertical plane; that is, it is approximately the profile which the stream would have if it flowed in a perfectly straight course from source to mouth. Such a profile, together with a sufficient number of cross-profiles, would enable one to construct a model of a valley showing the actual relations and proportions of its several parts.

The Longitudinal Profile.—A young stream flowing down the surface of a tilted plain, we will assume, will necessarily
10

have the same gradient as the land which gave direction to its current. As such a stream entrenches itself by corrading the bottom of its channel, and during the process of cutting down to baselevel spreads out flood-plains, which are subsequently dissected, it will develop a series of profiles to suit the various stages of its development.

An ideal example of the succession of longitudinal profiles which a stream makes, may be had by assuming that it works in homogeneous rocks throughout its course and is not disturbed by changes of climate, the formation of glaciers, or other modifying conditions. When the typical profile of a young stream and the changes it passes through as the stream advances in its appointed task is understood, the modifications due to climatic and other disturbances, or accidents, as they may be termed, can be readily recognised.

As has been shown with exceptional clearness by Hicks,[1] corrading streams have curved profiles, the curvature being concave upward, while deposits laid down by currents, such as alluvial cones, have a reverse curvature, that is, they are convex to the sky. The longitudinal profile of a stream which is corrading in its mountain tract and spreading out a flood-plain farther down its course, must therefore have a double curvature—that is, it will be concave in its upper course but convex in its lower course. The concave portion of the curve is much more conspicuous than the more gentle curve due to deposition, and it is frequently stated that the profile of a stream is a concave curve throughout its length. This, however, can only be strictly true when a

[1] L. E. Hicks, " Some Elements of Land Sculpture," in *Bulletin of the Geological Society of America*, vol. iv., pp. 133–146, 1893.

stream is engaged in corrading its channel from source to mouth.

A generalised profile of a stream which is corrading its channel throughout is shown approximately in the following diagram. It will be noticed that the curvature is compara-

FIG. 7. Longitudinal Profile of a Young Stream.

tively great near the source of the stream, but decreases and becomes nearly horizontal on approaching its mouth. There is a suggestive resemblance between such a profile and cycloid curves. As is well known, a cycloid curve is the curve of quickest descent for a body moving from a given point to a lower one not in the same vertical line. Should accurate survey show that streams corrading homogeneous rocks actually produce cycloid curves, or the curves of quickest descent for their debris-charged waters, it will furnish another illustration of the wonderful harmony that prevails in nature. A stream in cutting down its channel to baselevel must evidently reach that limit first at its mouth, and will then continue to deepen its bed progressively up stream. If this operation should be allowed to go on without deposition and the formation of flood-plains, the result would evidently be the flattening of the curved profile from the mouth of the stream to its source at the same time that the elevation of the stream channel above sea-level was lowered progressively and in an increasing ratio from mouth to source. Corrasion, however, is accompanied by sedimentation. In young streams, corrasion may occur through-out their courses, but as soon as their mouths are lowered to baselevel, deposition begins and progressively advances up stream. The longitudinal profiles of most streams result from both corrasion and sedimentation, and have a double curvature. Corrasion is more active in the mountain tract than in the valley and plains tracts, and until these divisions are obliterated by advancing age, the profile of a stream is, in part, due to corrasion and in part to sedimentation. With advancing age the portion of the curve due to deposi-tion advances up stream at the expense of the steeper portions of the profile where corrasion is still in progress. There comes a time in the development of a stream, how-ever, when this advance is checked, and when the flood-plain deposits begin to be dissected; the swing is then the other way, and the portion of the profile due to corrasion is lengthened and progresses toward the mouth of the stream.

In old age the profiles of streams become flattened and ap-proach more and more nearly a straight line, but probably never reach that condition.

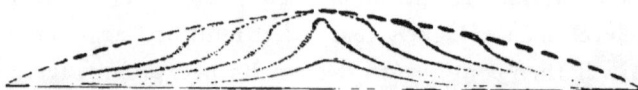

FIG. 8.   Successive Changes in the Profile of a Divide Owing to Corrasion and Weathering: Vertical Scale Exaggerated.

The heavy broken line indicates the profile of an uplift as it might appear had there been no erosion; the smaller broken lines show weather-curves; the dotted lines, successive cor-rasion curves; and the solid curved line below, the profile of the resulting old-land surface.

In the above diagram an attempt is made to show quali-tatively the successive changes that the profiles of streams pass through from youth to old age. In the case assumed, two streams flow in opposite directions from a common divide, and are so nicely balanced against each other that the divide has been lowered in a single vertical plane. The concave curvature of the profiles in their upper courses increases during early youth, reaches its maximum when the streams are mature, and then decreases with advancing age. On account of the exceedingly gentle concave curves due to deposition, it is impossible to represent them on the scale here used.

When the profiles of oppositely flowing streams meet at the crest of a mountain range, there should be, if no modifying conditions intervene, a sharp divide, as is indicated in Fig. 9. On some mountain crests this condition is very nearly reached. As one follows up a stream and approaches

FIG. 9. Ideal Profile of a Divide between the Head-Waters of Two Opposite-Flowing Streams: Vertical Scale Exaggerated.

its ultimate source, the rate of corrasion progressively diminishes, for the reason that the water supply becomes smaller and smaller. The rocks, however, are everywhere exposed to the denuding agencies of the air, namely, rain, wind, frost, etc., and at the heads of drainage lines the action of these agencies is in excess of stream corrasion, and convex curves due to weathering modify or replace the concave curves due to stream action. Unless the rocks on a divide between two drainage systems which head against each other are unusually resistant, and maintain angular forms as they weather, the concave profile leading up to the divide from either side changes to convex curves before uniting.[1] The usual profile in such instances is shown in the lower curves in Fig. 8.

Cross-Profiles.—The cross-profiles of stream-cut valleys change in the same locality with the age of the stream, and are modified by the weathering of the valley sides, the texture of the rocks, etc. If, as above, we conceive of a valley being cut out of homogeneous rocks and ascertain what changes in its cross-profile at a given locality will result from stream action and weathering, the modifications due to other causes may be more easily recognised.

A young and rapidly corrading stream working in moderately hard rocks produces a gorge or canyon with steep sides. The cross-profile of such a gorge is markedly V-shaped, except that the bottom of the V is slightly rounded. The width of the concave bottom of the trench varies with the size of the stream. If the stream is working in hard rocks the sides of the trench cut by it may be vertical.

As a stream advances with its task of cutting down its channel to baselevel, its energy available for corrasion is more largely exerted in the direction of broadening its valley. The cross-profiles of the valleys of old streams become broadly U-shaped. The valleys of streams where an approximation to baselevel has been reached, or when flood-plains are being formed, generally have flat bottoms with more or less flaring sides. The cross-profiles then resemble more or less closely the figure which would be obtained by

[1] L. E. Hicks, " Some Elements of Land Sculpture," in *Bulletin of the Geological Society of America*, vol. iv., pp. 133–146, 1893.

breaking a plate straight across. That is, the bottom is a horizontal line bordered by ascending lines. The graceful double curves in the profile on each side of an aggrading stream have already been referred to.

As a stream advances in age, the cross-profile at a given locality gradually changes from a V-shape to a U-shape, and then to a ﹀-shape. In extreme old age the bottom becomes greatly broadened with reference to the height of the sides.

The slope of the sides of a valley, whatever its age, depends on the texture of the rocks and on weathering. In hard rocks the slopes are steeper than in soft rocks. If the rate at which a stream deepens or widens its valley is rapid in reference to the rate of weathering, the sides will be steep, but if the reverse is the case the slopes will be gentle. It is thus evident that the character of the cross-profile of a stream-cut valley depends largely on climate, on rock texture and rock structure, on relative rate of corrasion and weathering, and on the stage in development that the stream has reached.

CHAPTER VI

STREAM TERRACES

A TERRACE may be defined as a step-like area with a nearly even and approximately level surface, bounded on one margin by an ascending and on the other by a descending slope. A stairway may be considered as an example of a series of terraces bounded by vertical escarpments. In nature there are many departures from the regularity in form implied in the above statements, due in part to the conditions under which they were made, but more commonly to subsequent changes. The surface of a terrace is frequently uneven, and cut across by rill-channels and gullies, or talus slopes and landslides may encumber it. The bounding slopes may be steep, or depart but slightly from the horizontal. A cross-profile of a river valley with terraces on each side is shown in the following diagram.

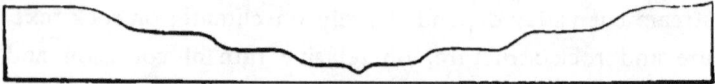

FIG. 10.   Ideal Cross-Profile of a Terraced Valley.

This figure is intended simply to illustrate the general characteristics of stream terraces, and not to indicate the precise conditions which the student may expect to find when he supplements his reading by cross-country tramps.

Terraces of this general character, from a few feet to several rods broad, may frequently be traced for many miles on each border of a river valley. In numerous instances several terraces one above another with various intervals between may be recognised on the same slope. They follow all of the windings of the valleys, sweeping about prominent bluffs and into adjacent embayments in broad, beautiful curves. Much of the charm alike of sheltered dells and of broad valleys is frequently due to the symmetrically curving lines formed by the terraces on the bordering slopes of the adjacent uplands. This is true more especially of the valleys of the Northern Appalachians and New England and thence westward through the vast areas formerly occupied by glaciers. Many of the valleys in the mountains of the Cordilleran region are also terraced in a remarkable manner.

River valleys, as we know, have been excavated by the streams flowing through them, and it is at once evident that the terraces beautifying their sloping sides must, in most instances, be due to the same agency. Another observation confirming this conclusion, is that the terraces are not horizontal when followed in the direction of their lengths, but have a gradient similar to that of the stream flowing through the bottom of the valley in which they occur, but not precisely coinciding with it.

The fact that stream terraces are not horizontal in the direction of their lengths serves to distinguish them from similar topographic forms made by the waves and currents of lakes or of the ocean. The surfaces of standing water-bodies are horizontal in the every-day sense of the term,

and the terraces made by such water bodies on the land
confining them are also horizontal.

The presence of terraces on the borders of stream-cut
valleys suggests that they owe their origin to the processes
of corrasion or of deposition which characterise the work of
streams. The study of the topographic forms under consideration has shown that they may be due to either of these
processes, or to their combined action. Certain stream terraces have been formed by excavation, others are the result
of deposition, while still others owe their existence to a
combination of the two processes. We might classify them
as cut terraces, built terraces, and cut-and-built, or compound, terraces. Such a classification has but little significance, however, unless the relation of the terraces to the life
histories of the streams which gave them origin is understood.

When the life histories of streams are reviewed, and the
modifications in their normal development due to climatic
changes and to secular movements in the earth's crust are
considered, it will be found that there are three principal
causes which lead to the origin of terraces. These are: 1st.
the normal changes in a stream valley due to the successive
processes of corrasion, flood-plain building, and re-excavation; 2d. climatic changes which cause variations in the
volumes of streams or lead to excessive deposition for a
time, and the re-excavation of the partially filled valleys;
and 3d. oscillations in the land which vary the rate of corrasion and of deposition. Let us consider these three
methods in the order named.

Origin of Terraces during the Process of Normal Stream

PLATE VIII.

FIG. A.   Terraces on Fraser River, British Columbia.
Showing post-glacial re-excavation.   (Photograph by Geological Survey of Canada.)

FIG. B.   Terraces in Connecticut Valley, near Bellows Falls, Vermont.
(Photograph by C. H. Hitchcock.)

Development.—In discussing the combined process of stream corrasion and deposition, when not seriously modified by climatic changes or movements in the crust of the earth, it was found that a river in flowing from highlands to the sea first cuts down its channel to baselevel at its mouth and then lowers it progressively up stream, but during its early life makes only an approximate adjustment to the level of the receiving water-body. Succeeding the first stage of excavation and following it progressively up stream, the valley is aggraded. This combined process is checked when the head branches of the river no longer supply more debris than the trunk stream can carry away, or, less commonly, when the course of the river is lengthened by the formation of a delta. The stream then begins to excavate a channel through the flood-plain previously formed. When this process of re-excavation begins the stream is usually meandering in broad curves over a flood-plain. As the stream deepens its channel and sinks below the level of the flood-plain, it retains its windings; although the accelerated velocity of the stream may tend appreciably to straighten its course. When the stream lowers its channel, portions of the original flood-plain are left as terraces on the sides of the valley. At the time a stream begins to deepen its channel, it may, in one portion of its course, be in the centre of its flood-plain, and will then leave a terrace on each side, or may flow on one side or the other of its valley, and therefore leave a terrace only on one border of its course. The stream may then broaden its channel, and spread out a second flood-plain in the valley excavated through the previously formed deposit.

A stream in flowing down a flood-plain, it will be remembered, makes not only short bends, but broad sweeps which carry it from one side of its valley to the other.   The short bends are made during periods of time measured by tens or hundreds of years, while the great migrations from side to side of a broad valley require thousands of years to complete a single swing.   The short bends which combine to make much greater curves have been referred to in the case of the Mississippi, and may be readily recognised on any good map of that river.   While a stream is deepening its channel in a broad alluvial plain and building a second flood-plain at a lower level, the down-cutting, between the time it leaves one border of its valley, migrates to the other side, and returns, may be so great that on its return it will be flowing at a sufficiently lower level to prevent its re-flooding its previously formed flood-plain.   When this happens, and the stream in its migrations does not swing back to its previous position, a portion of the flood-plain is left and forms a terrace.   Successive terraces may be left at lower and lower levels by a continuance of this process.

A cross-section of a valley terraced in the manner just described would present the features shown in the following diagram.   Each terrace is a portion of a flood-plain deposit,

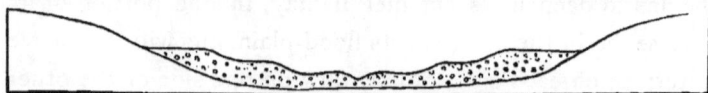

Fig. 11.   Ideal Cross-Section of a Partially Filled Valley with **Terraces Left** during Re-Excavation.

and the highest in the series is the oldest.   The material forming the superficial portion of the second terrace from the top has been removed by the stream, and re-deposited as a portion of the second-formed flood-plain, and this process has been repeated also in the case of the third terrace.

In the normal development of a stream after the stage in a certain portion of its course, indicated in Fig. 11, is reached, the stream will continue to deepen its channel, and may cut into the rock below the flood-plain deposits. This stage in the process is illustrated by the cross-section shown below. Should subaërial erosion remove the alluvial material indicated by dots in the diagram, a rock terrace would be left. If stream development progresses and a second

FIG. 12. Ideal Cross-Profile of a Partially Alluvial-Filled Valley Re-Excavated to below its Original Depth.

approximation to baselevel is made, all of the alluvial material and a portion of the rocky floor on which it rests may be removed.

Other ways in which normal alluvial terraces might be formed have been cited by Dodge.[1] Suppose that a stream whose load is slightly in excess of its carrying power acquires by capture the head-waters of another stream, as will be considered later. In the district thus acquired there might be an excess of carrying power over load; if such was the case, the capturing stream would have its carrying power increased without a corresponding increase in load, and

[1] R. E. Dodge, " The Geographical Development of Alluvial Terraces," in *Boston Society of Natural History, Proceedings*, vol. xxvi., p. 263, 1894.

therefore be able to deepen its channel in previously deposited alluvium, and terrace it.

Again, as cited by Dodge, a stream which had been working in soft rocks might cut down into hard rocks underneath the soft ones. The effect of such a change on the headwaters of a stream would be to decrease its load and enable it to corrade in its alluvial tract. Hence, without varying in volume a stream might be able to terrace an alluvial plain formed while it was previously removing soft rock.

Thus in several ways, or as a result of the combined influence of two or three normal variations in streams, alluvial terraces might result. These processes of terrace-making, however, are slow, and the topographic forms resulting may be greatly modified or even obliterated by subaërial denudation as fast as they appear. These processes, also, are a part of a larger process, *i. e.*, cutting to baselevel, which insures the ultimate destruction of the topographic features referred to. For these reasons the methods of terrace-making just considered have received but little attention, and their results are difficult to recognise. And, besides, other methods of terrace-forming are apt to produce such conspicuous results that the terraces due to what has been termed the normal stream development are usually masked or obliterated.

Terraces Due to Climatic Changes.—In considering the various influences of changes of climate on stream deposition, it was shown that heavy rains may cause the tributaries of a stream to bring to the main channel more debris than can be removed, and deposition takes place. In a similar way a secular change of climate producing an increase in precipitation, might lead to the filling, especially of low-grade river-valleys, and the raising of the flood-plains throughout all of their lower courses.

A climatic change which would admit of the birth and growth of glaciers on the higher portions of a mountain range, previously deeply stream-sculptured, would lead to the overloading of the streams below the glaciers and the thickening and broadening of the flood-plains throughout their lower courses.

Climatic conditions favourable for the birth and growth of glaciers are usually, and probably always, accompanied by increased precipitation and decreased evaporation. Thus for several reasons the occurrence of a glacial epoch like that in late geological time, when one-half of North America was occupied by ice-sheets, would favour the filling of pre-existing valleys with debris. When the climate experienced a reverse change and the glaciers melted, the draining streams would for a time be still more deeply flooded, and additional quantities of debris carried from high to low regions. If a warmer and drier climate should succeed a glacial epoch, the streams, no longer heavily loaded, would begin the task of removing the debris deposited in their valleys during the preceding time of overloading. As the streams deepened their channels in the alluvium previously deposited, portions of the flood-plains left intact would appear as terraces, and the elevation of their surfaces would record the depth to which the valleys had been filled with debris.

This process of removing the accumulations of debris clogging a valley might be accompanied by the formation of terraces at lower levels, according to the laws, cited above, governing the normal development of streams. As will be shown later, however, a still more potent agency in the formation of the lower terraces would be climatic changes and periodic elevation of the land.

Should several glacial stages occur with intervals of milder and less humid climatic conditions intervening, it is evident that the terraces resulting from the trenching of the first-formed flood-plains might be obliterated by subsequent deposition, and the surface of the debris in the valleys be carried higher than during the first ice invasion; or the valleys, cut in the first-formed flood-plain, might be only partially refilled, and when excavation was renewed, lower terraces would be formed.

The conclusion that glacial conditions would lead to the filling of pre-existing valleys downstream from alpine glaciers or about the margins of piedmonts and continental ice-sheets, and portions of these deposits be left as terraces when corrasion was resumed, is sustained by an abundance of examples throughout the northern portion of the United States and Canada. In the valleys in this region terraces excavated in material deposits by glacial streams are magnificently displayed. On the head-waters of Columbia River in Washington and Idaho, terraces of the nature here considered are perhaps as well developed, and their history as easily read, as in any other portion of the continent. The great canyon of Snake River, the principal tributary of the Columbia, was excavated to its present depth,—four thousand feet throughout a considerable portion of its course,— previous to the Glacial epoch. During that epoch, glaciers existed in the more elevated valleys and about the summits of the mountains of Idaho. The branches of the Snake were flooded, and brought such quantities of debris to the canyon of the main stream that throughout hundreds of miles of its course it became filled to a depth of three hundred and sixty feet. When the glaciers passed away and the streams were no longer supplied with debris by them, and still more effectually when a mild and but moderately humid climate prevailed, the streams were enabled to attack their flood-plains and cut valleys and canyons through them. Snake River has now removed by far the greater portion of the coarse gravel and boulders that formerly occupied its canyon, and has resumed the task of deepening its channel in the hard rock beneath. Episodes similar to that just referred to in the history of Snake River, but with various minor modifications, occurred in the lives of tens of thousands of streams not only in the northern part of North America, but as far south as the Gulf of Mexico and also in the Rocky Mountains and Sierra Nevada, as a result of the climatic change to which the Glacial epoch was due.

In studying the effects of changes in climate on the behaviour of streams, the fact should be borne in mind that such changes, although by reason of the comparatively brief time during which man has taken account of secular variations in atmospheric phenomena they are commonly considered as exceedingly slow in their occurrence and embracing but a moderate range, appear relatively rapid and of well-marked amplitude when such periods of time as are involved in geographic cycles are studied. Many of our rivers, as, for example, the Susquehanna, Mississippi, and Columbia, were far advanced in their development before the beginning of the Glacial epoch. The time that has elapsed since the melting of the continental glaciers on the head-waters of these rivers is but a small fraction of the current geographic cycles. Many annual climatic changes, as is well known to everyone, occur while even a meadow brook undergoes but slight modifications; in a similar way, as is well known to geographers, many secular changes in climatic conditions may take place during the life history of a great river.

Terraces Due to Elevation of the Land.—The manner in which a stream carries on its work, it will be remembered, is controlled in an important way by declivity. Consequently, changes in the elevation of the land must have a direct bearing on the history of the streams draining an area thus affected. The movements in the earth's crust referred to are known to have modified the surface slopes throughout large areas, and frequently to be of the nature of a tilting of the land. Other movements occur, but at present let us consider simply the effects of the tilting of a region drained by a large river on the problem of terrace-making.

A tilting of the rocks which decreases the gradient, and consequently the velocity, of a stream, other conditions remaining the same, will favour deposition, and may lead to the partial or complete filling of its previously formed valley. The flood-plain deposits would then increase in thickness and become broader at the surface. In other words, a decrease in velocity favours the process of aggrading.

If the region drained by the Connecticut, for example, be considered as a plane gently inclined southward, and to be affected by a movement in the earth's crust which decreases the gradient of the river, the depression of the land being least at the south and progressively increasing north-ward,—that is, the hinge-line, so to speak, on which the tilted block of the earth's crust moves, being situated near its southern margin,—the main trunk of the river would have its current slackened, and its transporting power diminished, while the gradients of the branches of the river coming in from the east or west would be but slightly affected. The direct result of such a change would be to favour deposition in the main valley and to a less extent in its branches.

If, after such a change of grade as has been postulated, when the valley of the Connecticut has become deeply filled and a broad flood-plain spread out, we imagine the land to remain stationary, the branches of the main river would cut down their channels, thus decreasing their velocities and diminishing the amount of debris carried annually to the main valley. When this stage had been reached, the Connecticut would begin to cut a channel through its previously formed flood-plain, as in the case of normal stream development already considered.

In case the inclined plane drained by the Connecticut should experience a reverse movement after its valley had become deeply filled—that is, if elevation should occur, the hinge-line retaining its former position,—the gradient of the main stream and of all its branches flowing southward would be increased, while the lateral branches would be but little affected. The increased gradient of the main stream would give its waters greater velocity, thus favouring corrasion at the expense of deposition, and a channel would be cut through the previously formed flood-plain. Portions of the flood-plain not removed would remain as terraces. Imagine the re-elevation at the northern border of the tilted area to be one hundred feet, and to decrease to zero at the hinge-line at the south. The result would be acceleration of velocity in the extreme head branches flowing southward; this might cause them to bring more debris to the main stream than it could transport, but the branches from the east and west being but slightly affected, the more probable result would be the deepening of the bed of the main stream throughout. The river would excavate a channel through its previously formed flood-plain, leaving portions of it on either side of the valley as terraces. When the river, after adjusting itself to the new conditions, began to broaden its channel and spread out a second flood-plain, it would be flowing a hundred feet below its former bed in the upper portion of its course, but this difference would gradually decrease downstream and become zero where the hinge-line was crossed. The southward or down-stream slope of the surface of the old flood-plain, portions of which remain for a time as terraces, would therefore be greater than the slope or gradient of the readjusted stream. This postulated case thus furnishes an explanation of the fact that when a number of stream terraces occur on the border of a valley, they are not only not horizontal, but have different gradients. The gradient of every stream terrace is determined by the gradient of the parent stream at the time it was formed.

The terraces originating in the several ways thus far considered consist of alluvium, which was deposited in a previously formed river valley, and the surface of each terrace is a portion of a flood-plain. In cross-section, such terraces would have the characteristics shown by the diagram on page 156, introduced in connection with the discussion of what are termed normal terraces, and would be cut through or finally removed during subsequent stream development in the manner already described, unless subsidence carried them below baselevel. In the discussion just presented, we have assumed a river valley to have been deeply filled with alluvium previous to the elevation of the land which enabled the stream to deepen its channel. This assumption is not

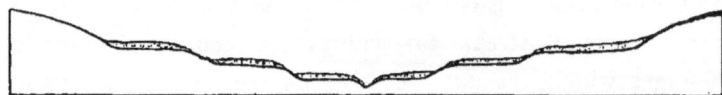

FIG. 13. Ideal Cross-Section of a Valley with Terraces Cut in Solid Rock and Covered with Alluvium.

necessary, however, and numerous instances might be cited where terraces in solid rock have resulted from accelerated corrasion due to periodic uplifts. Imagine a stream like the Connecticut to have broadened its valley and spread out a flood-plain, and then an elevation to take place as before. Accelerated velocity may enable the stream to lower its bed so as to cut through the flood-plain deposits and into the rocks beneath. A broadening of the new channel may then occur, and renewed elevation allow the process to be repeated. With each upheaval the stream cuts deeper into the rocks, leaving each time a terrace of solid rock with a sheet of alluvium on its surface. The characteristic features of a cross-section of such a terraced valley are shown in the ideal diagram, Fig. 13. As the excavation of solid rock is normally a slow process, the sheet of alluvium covering the terraces would be apt to be removed by rain, rills, etc., and rock terraces but scantily covered or without debris be exposed.

The formation of terraces during what has been termed the normal development of a stream—that is, when changes of level have not occurred, and climatic variations, etc., have not materially affected its volume, velocity, or load—is an extremely slow process, and, as previously stated, it is probable that atmospheric agencies under most climatic conditions would destroy the terraces as fast as formed. For this and other reasons it is believed that most of the terraces on the borders of stream-cut valleys are records of climatic changes which caused excessive deposition in low-grade valleys followed by a period of erosion; or are due to land oscillation.

Bottom Terraces.—Still another variety of terraces is formed by streams by deposition when their bottom loads are small. When their bottom currents are underloaded, as we may term the condition here referred to, the material is carried forward like a wave, in the manner in which a ripple in sand is produced under the influence of a wind- or water-current, and deposited with a steep escarpment facing downstream. These *bottom terraces* have broad, gently ascending surfaces in the direction of the flow of the current, and steep escarpments, facing downstream, and trend in general at right angles to the flow of the water, but are usually lobed on their lower margins. Such terraces or broad ripples may be seen in process of growth in many clear streams which have moderate bottom-loads of coarse sand and gravel. They are frequently several feet or even yards broad, with escarpments from a few inches to a few feet high. Although of minor importance when considered in connection with associated stream-made topographic forms, yet under special conditions, as when a broad stream is moving debris over a gentle slope, they might become relatively conspicuous if the stream should be diverted. There is a gradation between bottom terraces of the nature just considered and delta terraces which would repay investigation.

Delta Terraces and Current Terraces.—In the discussion of deltas in a previous chapter, it was shown that they are formed where streams deposit their loads on entering still water. Now, streams sometimes expand and have sluggish currents so as to simulate lakes. When this happens a tributary stream freighted with debris may drop a portion of its load and build up a delta-like deposit at its mouth.

The most favourable conditions for this process are when low-grade, sluggish rivers extend into embayments on their borders, as the mouths of tributary valleys, and a stream from the tributary valley brings in sediment. A lowering of the main stream after such a delta has been formed would leave it as a terrace. Such structures have been termed *delta terraces* by Edward Hitchcock.[1] A section of a delta terrace would reveal a series of inclined beds, as shown in the diagram on page 126, and possibly the upper

[1] " Illustrations of the Earth's Surface," *Smithsonian Contributions to Knowledge*, vol. ix., pp. 32-34, 1857.

and lower members of a typical delta built by a high-grade stream as well. The surface of such a delta terrace would have a slope corresponding with the grade of the supplying stream.

The current of a river washes its banks in much the same way as the currents in lakes wash their shores. The study of the action of lake currents has shown that they bear along debris, and drop it in part so as to form what are known as built terraces. The current, especially of a broad river, behaves in much the same manner. Debris brought by tributary streams, or derived from localities where the river is corrading its banks, is carried down stream and may be deposited adjacent to the shore, so as to form a built terrace. A subsidence of the waters would leave the terrace exposed. Its surface would slope gently toward the stream, and, as in the case of all river terraces, would have a gradient, when followed along the valley on the side of which it was formed, corresponding with the surface gradient of the building stream. In cross-section such a terrace would reveal the structure characteristic of built lake-terraces, the general features of which are shown in the following ideal diagram. The slope rising above such a

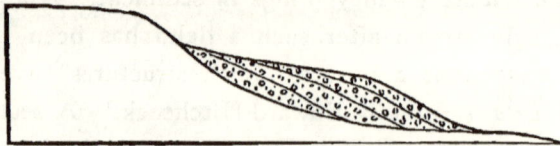

FIG. 14.   Ideal Cross-Section of a Current-Built Terrace.

terrace may be the valley side, produced by stream corrasion and weathering, or be a steeper slope due to lateral corra-

sion of the current and correspond more nearly with the
" sea-cliff " above a lake terrace.

The waves and currents of a broad river may lead to corrasion along its shores in the same manner as in a lake, and
cut terraces result. A miniature example of this is shown
in Fig. F, Plate II.

So far as the present knowledge of stream terraces allows
one to judge, it does not appear that those built after the
manner of lake terraces, as just described, are common. In
fact, delta terraces and current terraces, as they may be
termed, depend for their origin on a delicate balancing of
conditions which apparently is seldom reached.

Delta terraces and current terraces formed on the sides of
streams are of interest, as they constitute a group, although
small and of minor importance, which may be designated as
built terraces in distinction from other stream terraces which
are due to both deposition and excavation, or to excavation
alone. The downward slope bordering the nearly flat surface of a built terrace is due to deposition; in the other
varieties, this slope is produced by excavation.

Glacial Terraces.—The terraces built by streams con-
jointly with glaciers need not claim much attention at this
time, since they derive their greatest interest from their
connection with the ice-bodies about which they are formed.
When a glacier, however, or perhaps more frequently a stag-
nant ice-mass, occupies a valley, streams sometimes bring
gravel, sand, etc., and deposit it along the margin of the ice
so as to give a level floor to the space intervening between
the ice and the valley border. After this space has been filled
to a greater or less depth and the ice melts, the deposit re-

mains as a terrace.[1] Such terraces have approximately level surfaces, are composed of current-bedded gravel and sand, and perhaps certain occasional boulders or angular rock-masses, but do not exhibit the arrangement of coarse and fine material characteristic of flood-plains; and, besides, their down-stream gradients are markedly different from those of true stream-terraces.

Relative Age of Terraces.—When stream terraces occur one above another on the side of a valley, the highest in the series is usually the oldest. But exceptions to this rule may occur, as when changes of level lead to the build-ing of delta or current terraces on the surface of previously formed terraces. Again, a valley in which a terrace has been cut in solid rock might become filled with alluvium so as to bury the terrace, and re-excavation again bring it to light, and form another terrace at a higher level; the lower terrace would then be older than the one above it.

In a series of alluvial terraces in which the highest is the oldest, each one or each pair, if fragments of the same flood-plain are left on each side of the valley, is a remnant of a flood-plain, and the material in the highest terrace is younger than the main portion of each lower terrace; but the surface portion of each terrace was worked over and re-distributed at the time the flood-plain of which it is a part was formed, and hence may be said to be younger than the material in each higher terrace.

---

[1] The terraces here referred to have been termed "kame terraces" by R. D. Salisbury, *Geological Survey of New Jersey, Annual Report for 1893*, pp. 155, 156. Similar topographic forms were previously termed "moraine ter-races" by G. K. Gilbert, *U. S. Geological Survey, Monographs*, vol. i., p. 81, 1890.

Other Terraces.—Terraces similar to those formed by streams originate in other ways, and it is important that the student of geography and geology should be able to distinguish those which owe their origin to one series of agencies from those belonging to other categories.

Cut terraces in rock or in loose material are a characteristic feature of lake and ocean shores, as are also delta and current terraces. In nearly all of their main features, these terraces are similar to stream terraces except that they are essentially horizontal when traced in the direction of their length. Movements in the earth's crust, however, may tilt a previously horizontal terrace so as to give it a gradient closely approximating to the normal slope of a stream terrace. A similar tilting of the land might affect a river terrace so as to alter its gradient and perhaps make it horizontal. In cases of this sort associated topographic features would usually furnish the best clue to the true history. River terraces are formed in comparatively narrow valleys, while lakes may occupy valleys of any shape. Lake terraces are usually accompanied by escarpments which rise above them, termed " sea-cliffs "; these may or may not be characteristically different from the corresponding slopes above river terraces. The normal lake-terrace is either cut-and-built—that is, it is a shelf made by excavation with a current-built covering on its surface,—or may be entirely a deposit formed by construction. Stream terraces do not usually have this structure, but yet may have it. As may be judged, the tests just suggested might not lead to definite conclusions. In fact, in the case of abandoned stream- and **lake-terraces, that is, when a former lake basin has been** emptied and perhaps has a stream flowing through it, or when a former stream valley is no longer a line of drainage, it is frequently difficult to satisfactorily determine their origin. In such an instance, if the former topography is not greatly altered, it may be possible to work out the history of the changes that have occurred and to construct a map of the country as it existed when the terraces were formed, and thus be able to decide whether flowing water or bodies of still water were responsible for the terraces.

River terraces frequently make a direct connection with lake terraces so that the place of junction may be difficult to determine. The main difference to be looked for in such an instance would be a change from horizontality to an inclination in the surfaces of the terraces where it passed from the lake valley into the stream valley. In a tilted or otherwise disturbed region, where both lake and stream terraces occur, a difference in their gradients may still be recognisable, and assist in their discrimination.

Instances occur, however, in disturbed and eroded regions, where only fragments of terraces remain, when it is practically impossible to tell whether they record lacustral or stream conditions. River terraces also pass into terraces made about the borders of estuaries and on ocean shores. Here, again, when disturbances occur and the estuaries are emptied of their water and the streams have been diverted, difficulties in interpreting the records might arise. The sedimentary deposits made on the floor of the estuaries and the evidences of life buried in them, as well as the fossils in the terraces themselves, might here furnish assistance. The shells in river terraces will be fresh-water or land species;

while those in the estuary sediment and terraces will be, in part at least, such as inhabit brackish or saline water.

Terraces also result from the weathering of the outcrops of alternating hard and soft strata. When the strata are horizontal or but slightly inclined, the hard beds may stand out as shelves or terraces, as, for example, in the sides of a valley cut in stratified rocks. The downward slope of such a terrace is the exposed edges of hard layers, and may be steep or gentle according to climatic and other conditions; the slope rising above the terrace is formed of the edge of the weak strata above the terrace-making layer, and is usually a gentle slope unless the layer is thin and another hard terrace-making layer occurs just above. The arrangement of resistant and weak strata in the case of these terraces of *differential erosion* usually makes it easy to distinguish them from river terraces. There is an absence, also, on the terraces of this nature, of stream deposits, and this negative evidence might assist in the diagnosis. Weathered debris falling on the surface of a terrace of differential erosion may simulate stream deposits, however, and lead to erroneous conclusions.

Fractures in the rocks along which differential movement of the sides has taken place, producing what are known as faults, may also give origin to topographic forms of a terrace-like character, but these are usually irregular, with reference to both horizontal and vertical planes, and in most instances are easily distinguishable from stream or other terraces.

Landslides also produce terrace-like forms, but these are seldom continuous for considerable distances, and are usually so irregular and bear such relations to the slopes from which the fallen blocks descended, that their origin may usually be readily determined. When a landslide occurs it frequently happens that the displaced material acquires a surface slope toward the place from which it came. This backward slope frequently produces basins in which lakes and swamps occur, thus furnishing additional evidences bearing on the origin of the terrace-like forms produced.[1]

Terraces due to still other causes might be enumerated and the means for their discrimination indicated, but I believe those most nearly simulating stream terraces have been referred to. The reader who may desire to follow this subject farther will find assistance in the treatises named below.[2]

General Distribution of Stream Terraces.—In North America stream terraces may be said to occur on the borders of nearly every river valley north of the central part of the United States, but are less conspicuous in the more south-eastern States and about the Gulf of Mexico: the reason being that the northern half of the continent was occupied by glaciers in late geological time, and has also undergone movements of the nature of elevation and depression throughout broad areas; while in the southern half of the continent there are no records of glaciation except on high mountains in the south-west, and evidences of recent changes of level are seldom pronounced.

Stream terraces extend far southward from the formerly glaciated region, for the reason that the glaciers drained by

---

[1] I. C. Russell, "Topographic Changes Due to Landslides," *Popular Science Monthly*, vol. liii., 1898, in press.

[2] G. K. Gilbert, *U. S. Geological Survey, Monographs*, vol. i., pp. 78–86, 1890. W J McGee, *U. S. Geological Survey, 11th Annual Report*, part i., pp. 256–273, 1889–90.

southward-flowing streams furnished more debris than the streams could remove, and they became overloaded and consequently filled in their previously excavated valleys. When the glaciers disappeared and the streams were no longer overloaded, they cut channels through their previously formed flood-plains, and left portions of them as terraces on their sides. This process was aided also by a general depression at the north, due to some extent, it is believed, to the weight of the ice, and in part to the effect of the lowering of the temperature to a considerable depth in the earth's crust and a consequent contraction and depression of the surface, and a partial re-elevation when the glaciers vanished.

Many of the beautiful river-valleys of New England owe much of their attractiveness to the gracefully bending curves traced on their borders. Numerous towns and villages in that region are indebted for their sightly locations to the terraces on which they are built. Present flood-plains and abandoned portions of former flood-plains afford rich agricultural lands. These were among the first areas to be cleared and cultivated after European immigration began. A direct relation between the effects of distant and far-reaching changes in geography and the advance and growth of civilisation is here abundantly illustrated.

What has been said of the terraced valleys of New England is true in varying degrees of a great area to the north embraced in the south-eastern provinces of Canada, and of a still broader region to the west including New York, Pennsylvania, Ohio, and thence north-westward to the Pacific.

The valleys of the Ohio and of many of its tributaries are noted for their terraces. In this region and also in the valleys tributary to the upper Mississippi, the numerous terraces are due principally to the re-excavation of pre-glacial valleys, in which overloaded glacial streams dropped the burdens too heavy for them to carry. The effects of the changes in drainage accompanying the great ice invasion at the north may be traced throughout the length of the Mississippi, but become less and less conspicuous towards its mouth.

The borders of the streams flowing to the Gulf of Mexico (other than the Mississippi), including the larger rivers of the Texas region and those draining the eastern slope of the Appalachians south of Maryland, are mostly without conspicuous terraces. The streams in this region did not feel the direct influence of the glaciers at the north and have passed their period of youth, except on their extreme headwaters. The terraces they may have formed as a part of their normal aggrading and re-excavation have been removed principally by weathering, and the comparatively gentle slopes of their valleys show vertical scorings due to the action of rills and not the nearly horizontal lines which record higher water stages. Such terraces as do occur along the sides of southern rivers are in part remnants of ancient baselevel plains, or, in some instances, the result of local changes in elevation. These statements are intentionally made general, as it is only the more marked differences between the characteristics of southern and northern valleys to which attention is here sought to be directed.

The rivers flowing eastward from the Rocky Mountains, like the Platte, Missouri, Arkansas, etc., are bordered by terraced slopes in a portion of their valley tracts, and for many miles in the plains tracts after leaving the mountains, but well out on the Great Plains they are in part, and perhaps mostly, engaged at the present time in aggrading previously formed valleys, and terraces are not conspicuous.

One reason for the presence of conspicuous terraces adjacent to the mountains and in the valleys eroded in them previous to the great extension of the glaciers, is that the streams dropped the coarser and heavier portions of their loads at those localities, and bore on only fine material to their low-grade plains tracts. Subsequently, when the floodplains thus formed were terraced, the escarpments in coarse and in part cemented gravel and boulders retained their slopes for a longer period than the similar escarpments in fine material a hundred miles or more downstream. In addition to this, it is to be noted that the gradients of the highest terraces are greater than the gradients of the streams as they flow at the present day. For this reason the vertical interval between the terraces and the present streams which they follow—that is, the height of the downward-sloping escarpments bordering them on their valley margins—progressively decreases from the gateways in the mountain to the sea. The lower terraces composed of soft material far out on the plains have melted down and been removed to a great extent, under the action of the atmosphere, while the higher terraces in firmer material have retained their characteristic topographic forms.

In the terraces of the Rocky Mountains and adjacent portions of the Great Plains, the wide-reaching influence of the Glacial epoch is again recorded. The Rocky Mountains had their local glaciers at that time, and the streams were

12

flooded especially during the final melting of the ice, when, it is inferred, the rain-fall was also abundant, but the swollen streams were overloaded and their channels became deeply filled. The effects of more or less periodic changes in the elevation of broad areas above the sea may perhaps be made out in this region from the terrace records, but as' yet too little attention has been given to this subject, and in fact to the general surface features of the Rocky Mountain region, to warrant one in offering anything more than provisional answers to the questions here suggested.

In the Great Basin region variations of climate are again recorded by the work of the streams. Changes in the rate at which streams deposit, it will be remembered, depend on changes in velocity and in load. Velocity depends in part on volume. A change in climatic conditions from arid to humid means an increase in the volume of the draining streams. Whether this increment in velocity will be accompanied by deeper corrasion or by aggrading, is determined by the accompanying change in the rate at which the streams are loaded. An increased rain-fall would be accompanied by a greater removal of loose material from the highlands, and consequently a greater contribution of debris to the stream. There would, therefore, be a balancing of conditions in any one part of a stream's course. If the supply of debris was not in excess of the transporting power of the draining streams, they would corrade, but if the loads delivered to them were too great, deposition would result. When the whole extent of a river is considered, a change from arid to humid conditions must increase both corrasion and deposition. More active corrasion in the upper portion of a drainage system usually necessitates a greater rate of deposition lower down.

The streams of the Great Basin felt the effects of the change of climate which caused, or accompanied, the Glacial epoch, and, as the results indicate, were overloaded. Many of them are bordered by terraces in such a manner as to show that they were formerly of greater volume than at present, and subsequently decreased in volume, but were able for a time to cut channels and broaden their valleys in previously formed flood-plains. In many instances the streams have diminished to such an extent, however, that they are now aggrading. In their enfeebled condition they are unable to carry even the small burdens that are imposed upon them.

In the region of the high plateaus drained by the Colorado and its branches, there are many terraces. The majority of those which attract the eye, however, are due to the weathering of the outcrop of alternating hard and soft strata, but stream terraces also occur. Many broad valleys are deeply filled and without terraces, as is illustrated by Fig. A, Plate XVI., owing to the fact that aggrading has been in progress throughout a large portion of the present arid period.

The Colorado River, as is well known, flows through a canyon within a canyon. The outer canyon is in places some fifteen miles broad and comparatively level-floored. Sunken in this floor is the deeper, inner canyon, which in places is from one to two miles broad. The floor of the outer canyon is thus a great terrace, as may be seen on inspecting Plate XVII. The general history to be read in these features is that the region was at one time lower than now by an amount about equal to the depth of the inner canyon. The Colorado cut down its channel to baselevel and then broadened it into a wide valley. Subsequent elevation renewed the energy of the stream and enabled it to cut down nearly to baselevel once more, leaving large portions of the bottom of its older valley as a terrace on each side of its later gorge. The terrace thus formed extends into many of the tributaries of the main river, and in fact the change to which it was due affected a large part if not the entire drainage system.

Our knowledge of the terraces in the valleys of North America is too immature to permit us to state with confidence their distribution throughout the continent, and one more illustration must suffice for this brief review.

Columbia River, in the portion of its course known as the Big Bend, flows through a narrow, canyon-like valley on the side of which there are numerous terraces. A short account of these taken from a report by the present writer,[1] will indicate not only the nature of the stream records so abundant on the sides of many of the canyons and valleys of the far Northwest, but also show how stream terraces are frequently associated with similar topographic forms originating in other ways:

" On descending the side of the canyon [of the Columbia, opposite the entrance of Chelan valley] by means of a road following a deep, high-grade gorge, we notice that there are many terraces on each side of the river. The most remarkable of these, and

[1] I. C. Russell, "A Geological Reconnoissance in Central Washington," *U. S. Geological Survey, Bulletin* No. 108, pp. 78, 79, 1893.

one of the finest examples of terrace structure that can be found anywhere, is a level-topped shelf formed of gravel and water-worn boulders, the surface of which is seven hundred feet above the Columbia. This truly remarkable terrace is best developed about two miles below where we descended into the canyon. It is there several hundred feet broad and runs back into lateral gorges, showing that the sides of the main canyon were deeply scored by lateral drainage before the gravel forming the terrace was deposited. On the west side of the valley there are other fragments of the same deposits, forming a less conspicuous shelf, which has been built against the steep slope, and has the same level as the great terrace on the east side of the river. The valley was excavated lower than the bottom over which the Columbia now flows, and then filled in from side to side with stream-borne stones, gravel, and sand before the present channel was excavated. In the re-excavation, fragments of the deposits filling the canyon have been left clinging to its slopes. Streams flowing down lateral gorges have cut channels across the terrace, thus revealing the structure even more plainly than the steep slope leading to the river.

" Above the valley opening in the west wall of the canyon and leading to Lake Chelan, there are other large remnants of the same great terrace, this time on the west side of the river. In the broad plain formed by the surface of the terrace, there stands a lofty pyramid of solid rock completely surrounded by the gravel deposit and rising like an island from its level surface.

" The terrace gravels extend into the valley of Lake Chelan and form conspicuous terraces about its lower end. For many miles both up and down the Columbia, other fragments of the same level-topped deposit occur, always forming striking features in the landscape, owing to the marked contrast of their smooth horizontal lines with the vertical line due to the erosion of rills and creeks.

" Beside the great terrace described above there are many other but less conspicuous horizontal lines on the sides of the Columbia canyon. Some of these below the horizon of the main

terrace are stream terraces, made by the river in lowering its bed.
A more numerous but much less regular class are due to landslides, of which there have been many. Other horizontal lines
are due to the unequal weathering of the strata of basalt and of
interstratified sedimentary beds.

" Still another class of terraces, both numerous and conspicuous, has been formed as moraines on the sides of the glacier
that once filled the canyon up to an elevation of 1200 feet above
the river as it flows to-day. The moraine terraces are of older
date than the great terrace described above, and about the entrance of Chelan valley have been partially buried by it.

" In the canyon of the Columbia for several miles above Lake
Chelan its rugged sides are strewn with thousands of perched
boulders, left by the retreat of the ice. These have a definite
upper limit, but mingled with them are masses of basalt that have
fallen quite recently from the cliffs above.

" In embayments along the sides of the main canyon and back
of the ridges of stone and boulders left by the ancient glaciers,
there are flat areas which have been filled in with fine material,
washed from higher levels. These plains have in some instances
been cut by small streams flowing across them, thus adding other
horizontal lines to the complex topography of the canyon
walls.

" It is not practicable to describe these terraces in detail, but
those who visit Lake Chelan will have an opportunity to read for
themselves the remarkable history which they record. In studying them, however, the traveller must bear in mind that the
canyon, after being cut through various rocks to a depth greater
than it now has, was occupied by a large glacier, and then by an
arm of a large lake, and that river, glacial, and lacustral records
are inscribed on the same slope. In addition, there have been
many landslides, producing deceptive, terrace-like forms, and
terraces due to the unequal weathering of hard and soft
beds."

A continuation of this review of the distribution of terraces would lead us northward to the Mackenzie and

Yukon,[1] where many records similar to those just considered are known to exist, but our present knowledge of the changes these streams have experienced is even more scanty than for the central and southern portions of the continent.

The most important result of this hasty excursion through terraced river-valleys is perhaps the recognition of the fact that terraces exist along the sides of stream-cut valleys throughout the length and breadth of North America. Volumes of history are recorded in those graceful curves which give beauty to the varied scenery of valley borders from the tropical forests of Central America and Mexico to beyond the Arctic circle. The interpretation of these records has only recently been undertaken, and much that is new unquestionably awaits the patient explorer. The general principles to be used in this study have been presented in the present chapter, but as investigation progresses, much that is novel in details, and probably also the discovery of as yet unknown laws or modifications of those now recognised, will reward the student.

[1] I. C. Russell, " Notes on the Surface Geology of Alaska," in *Bulletin of the Geological Society of America*, vol. i., pp. 144-146, 1890.

CHAPTER VII

STREAM DEVELOPMENT

Consequent Streams.—In case a portion of the sea floor should be upraised so as to make what geographers term a new land-area, the streams flowing from it would take the easiest courses, as determined by the slope of the surface, regardless of the structure of the rocks beneath. If a dome-shaped uplift should occur in a broad plain underlain by previously horizontal layers of rock, the rain falling on its surface would form rills, and these uniting would give origin to creeks and perhaps to rivers, which would flow away in all directions from the summit portion of the uplift. In each of these hypothetical cases the streams would evidently have their directions determined by the pre-existing topography, and hence may be termed *consequent streams.*

Subsequent Streams.—As consequent streams deepened their channels they might discover differences in the rate at which they can remove the rocks, and hence have their directions variously modified by differences in hardness or by the greater or less solubility of the various beds that they encountered. New branches or tributaries to the main streams would be developed, the positions of which would be determined by the down-cutting of the channels of the

184

master streams, and by the relative ease with which the various rocks coming to the surface could be removed. That is, as a drainage system develops, streams originate, the directions of which are regulated by the hardness and solubility of the rocks. Such streams appear subsequently to the main topographic features in their environment, and are termed *subsequent streams.*

Ideal Illustration of Stream Adjustment and Development. —Perhaps the best way in which to obtain a graphic idea of the changes passed through by a river system in the course of its development and adjustment to the geological conditions it discovers, when unaffected by marked climatic changes and not seriously disturbed by movements in the earth's crust, is to form a mental picture of a gently sloping plateau with an essentially even surface on which rain falls and gives origin to rills and brooks which unite to form larger consequent streams, and picture to ourselves the changes that would result under the influence of a moderately humid climate. Imagine such a plateau, we will say, one hundred miles long from right to left and fifty miles broad, sloping gently toward an assumed point of view, and follow in fancy the changes in the streams, and the resulting modifications in the relief of the surface as normal stream development progresses. To complete our conception, we may assume that, beyond the sky-line bounding the far side of the landscape, the surface gently declines in the opposite direction. That is, the plateau before us is the side of a long ridge, the central axis of which is raised, we will say, one thousand feet above sea-level.

The rocks beneath the surface of the tilted plane, we will

assume, are in inclined layers, which slope toward our point
of view, at a greater angle than the surface of the plane, and
besides are composed of hard and soft beds. A section
through the tilted plane at right angles to the axis of the
uplift has the structure indicated in the following diagram.

The harder rocks are shaded. The lines in which the inclined
beds join the surface of the plane run in the direction of its
length. The conditions here assumed are such as might
result if a region underlain by inclined stratified rocks had
been planed away nearly to baselevel and then upraised so
as to produce a gently sloping peneplain.

The rain-water, falling on the surface of the plane before
us, gathers in part in depressions on its surface and forms
ponds and lakes. These are but temporary, however, as
the shallow basins are soon filled with sediment, or have
their outlets cut down by the overflowing water, and are
drained. The rills supplied directly from the rain and those
starting from the lakelets unite to form larger streams, which
flow down the inclined plane to the sea in obedience to
gravity. The directions of these initial streams are determined by the slope of the surface. They are, therefore,
consequent streams. Their number will be determined by
the inequalities of the surface which cause the rills and
rivulets to unite. Some will be longer than others. Some
will have a greater volume than others. A common feature,
shared at first by all, is that they have but few tributaries.

A diagram showing these initial consequent streams, in their infancy, is presented in the following ideal map.[1]

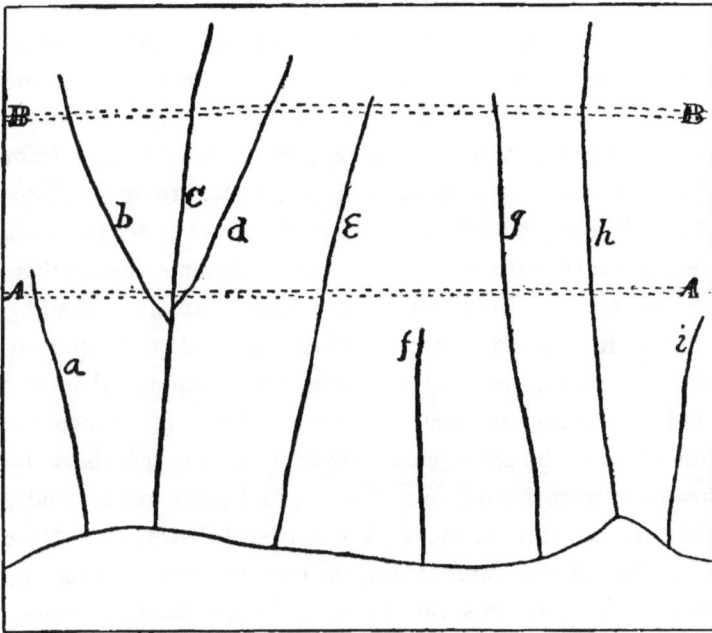

FIG. 16. Ideal Sketch-Map Showing Young Consequent Streams.

The consequent streams, *a* to *i*, follow courses determined by the slope of the surface and approximately straight. The hardness or softness of the underlying rock does not affect them at first, for the reason that they are surface streams. They differ in volume, as is indicated to some extent by the length of the lines representing them in the diagram. All

[1] Figures 16, 17, and 18, together with almost all of the account of the development of streams here presented, have been taken from a highly instructive article by W. M. Davis, on " The Development of Certain English Rivers," in *The Geographical Journal* (of the Royal Geographical Society), vol. v., pp. 127–146. London, 1895.

of them begin at once the task of deepening their channels
to a certain grade determined by their volumes and their
loads.   This work would not progress at the same rate in
all the streams because they are of unequal length, of different volumes, and are variously loaded.   The longer streams
would, under most conditions, be the larger, and would
corrade their channels most rapidly.   The drainage from
the inter-stream spaces flows to the master streams and develops feeding branches.   The gradients of these branches
depend on the rate at which the master streams deepen their
channels.   The branches of the more rapidly corrading
master streams have their velocities, and consequently
their corrading power, increased more rapidly than the
similar branches of their weaker neighbours.   Hence the
branches of the stronger consequent streams cut back by
head-water corrasion and increase in length more rapidly
than the branches of the weaker consequent streams.   More
and more of the water falling on the territory between the
main streams is thus carried to the more favoured consequent streams, and increases still more their advantage
over their weaker neighbours.

The initial streams, it will be remembered, flowed down
the original slope, as shown in Fig. 15, at right angles to
the strike, that is, across the edges of the strata composing
the tilted block of the earth crust we have in mind; the
branches of the streams, however, flow parallel with the edges
of the strata where they come to the surface, and hence
find hard and soft bands parallel with their courses.   As
erosion progresses, the edges of the resistant beds are left
in relief, forming ridges, while the less resistant beds are

more rapidly removed and determine the courses of the
subsequent branches. As this process goes on, our sloping
plane loses its smoothness, channels are cut by the consequent streams, and depressions are made by their branches
trending in general at right angles to their courses. Between the lateral valleys ridges appear, marking the posi-

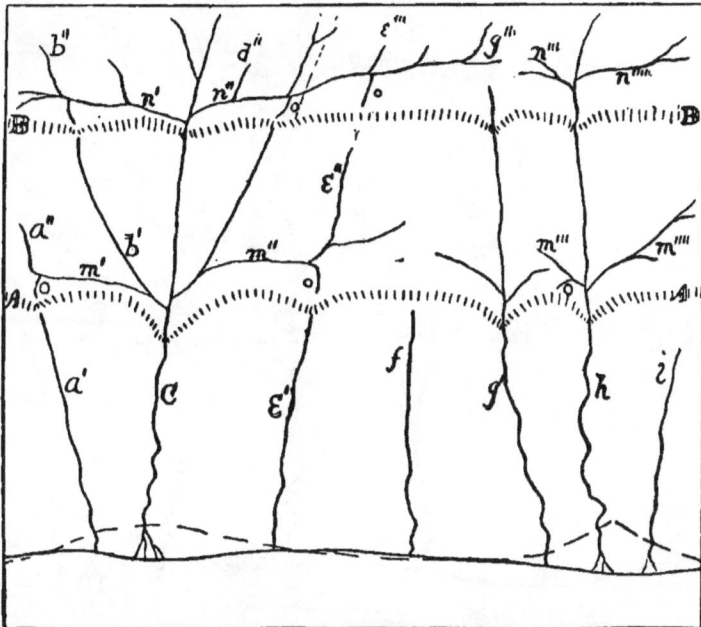

FIG. 17. Ideal Sketch-Map Illustrating Stream Development.

tions of the edges of the resistant beds. These ridges are
at first straight, and mark the intersection of the hard beds
with the original, gently sloping surface. As the strata are
inclined, however, one side of a ridge formed by the outcropping edge of a hard bed will have a more gentle slope
than the opposite side. The sides of the ridges slope gently

toward our assumed point of view and present steep escarpments in the opposite direction. The condition of the
sloping surface before us at this stage is shown in Fig. 17.
The hard layers, indicated by broken bands, stand up as
ridges, and the branches of the original consequent stream
have begun to develop valleys in the soft rocks.

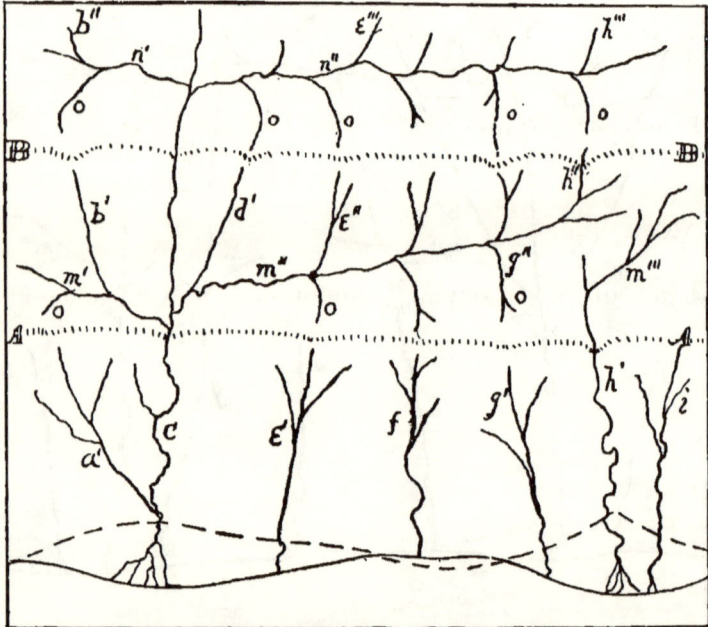

FIG. 18.   Ideal Sketch-Map Showing an Advanced Stage in Stream Development.   Former Shore Shown by Broken Line.

The consequent stream *c*, being stronger and corrading
more rapidly than *a*, deepens its channel through the hard
ridge A A more rapidly than its weaker neighbour. The
branch *m'* of the strong consequent stream *c*, having its
place of discharge lowered by the corrasion of the stream

to which it is tributary, is able to remove the soft rocks forming its bed and to grow in length by head-water corra-sion more rapidly than the corresponding subsequent branch of *a*. As *m'* increases in length, it captures more and more of the drainage of *a*, thus weakening that stream, and at length draws off all of its water above *o*. The original stream *a* is thus broken in two, or is *beheaded*, to use a term proposed by Davis. The notch that *a* has cut in the ridge of hard rock A A is left as a wind-gap. The bottom of this gap is a divide from which the waters flow each way. The beheaded stream *a'* holds its former course below the divide, but is weakened by the loss of its head-waters; the portion of the stream *a*, from the divide on the hard bed to where the subsequent stream *m'* intersected it, is *reversed*. For such reversed streams Davis has proposed the name *obsequent*. As time goes on, changes similar to those accompanying the backward cutting of *m'* take place also in the other streams, as may be seen from Fig. 18, in which a more advanced stage in stream development is indicated.

Another feature of the changes in progress is shown by the fact that the ridges of hard rock, indicated by the bands A A and B B, are no longer straight. When the stronger streams cut through them, forming water-gaps, the cliffs recede by weathering and by the sapping of their bases by the streams. This wasting of the hard ridges goes on most rapidly on the side toward which they slope most steeply; that is, on the farther side from our assumed point of view. The cliffs, formed by the steeper slope of the ridges of hard rock, thus gradually migrate in the direction of the dip of the hard beds, that is, toward our point of view, under the influence of general erosion and sapping throughout their entire length. But this recession is most rapid where the stronger consequent streams cross them, and they become lobed or scalloped, as shown in Fig. 17. With the process of stream development, the alignment of the cliffs becomes more and more modified, until the recession in the neighbourhood of the master stream is checked by the streams having cut down nearly to baselevel. At this stage, the cliffs at the ends of the V-shaped gorges, at the apex of which the master streams cross the hard beds, will remain stationary and crumble away, while those portions of the cliffs between the master streams, which before receded more slowly than the portions near the stream, will retreat more rapidly than the portions of the escarpment near where the master streams have cut to baselevel. In an advanced stage of stream adjustment and of topographic development, the lines of cliffs, at first straight and then deeply lobed, will again approach an even alignment, but the position of the ridges will change with this development, and move in the direction of the dip of the hard beds. The cliffs in an early stage of development were of faint relief; when cut into deep lobes, they stand up prominently, but as their alignment is again established, they become subdued, and when the process is far advanced nearly or quite disappear.

To return to the development of drainage. The manner in which the subsequent stream m', Fig. 17, captured and diverted the head-water of a and divided that stream into a *beheaded* portion, a', a *reversed* portion, o, and a *diverted* portion, a'', will serve to illustrate the similar process followed by other streams. In each instance, the subsequent branches of the stronger primary stream cut back until they divert a portion of the drainage of their weaker neighbours. The result of this process can be easily predicted from a study of the map. At a certain stage in the process, the stronger streams c and h, will have captured the head-water of all of their rivals above the ridge A A, and a competition between the two conquering streams will ensue. An advanced stage in this struggle is indicated in Fig. 18, where the subsequent branches m'' and n'' of the stronger master stream c have captured and diverted the head-waters of h'.

In the map forming Fig. 18, it will be noted that the ridges of hard rock are again nearly straight, and also that the lower courses of c and h have become tortuous. The reason for the curves in the lower courses of the stronger stream is that after cutting down their channels nearly to baselevel and becoming sluggish, they continue to corrade laterally and form flood-plains on which they meander from side to side, at the same time broadening their valleys. As has been shown on a previous page, a sluggish stream, having little power to overcome obstacles, is more easily deflected than a swifter stream, and besides, the lower portions of the valley and plains tracts of a stream during advanced stages in development are regions of deposition. The migrations of the streams a and c have brought them together, as shown in Fig. 18, thus illustrating another process of capture.

The examples of stream development we have been following are ideal, but, I believe, true to nature. The reason for sketching an ideal illustration is that in nature various disturbing conditions usually modify the process and increase the difficulty of separating what is normal from that which may be termed accidental. Stream development is a slow process even when not disturbed by marked climatic changes or by movements in the earth's crust. The life of a man, or even of a nation, is too short to embrace the time necessary for the development of a river system. It is only by studying many streams in various stages of their development that geographers are able to sketch generalised pictures of the normal changes a great river passes through in its lifespan of millions of years.

When one attempts to apply the elementary conceptions of stream development outlined above to actual streams, it is found that many modifying conditions have to be taken into account. Broad surfaces with even initial slopes are rare; the rocks forming the earth's crust are frequently folded and faulted, especially in uplifted regions, and consequently the development of subsequent streams is frequently greatly modified; more puzzling complications arise, however, from the fact that the land is not stable, but is subject to up-and-down movements, which disturb or entirely arrest the slow process of stream development before it can run its normal course. These and still other modifying conditions have to be considered in studying the history of the streams which drain the land and throughout their history are continually modifying the relief of the surface.

With the introduction to the principle of stream development in mind, let us turn to a portion of our own land where the processes just outlined have been long in action and see if we can read a portion of the history recorded by the valley and intervening hills.

EXAMPLES OF STREAM DEVELOPMENT AND ADJUSTMENT IN THE APPALACHIAN MOUNTAINS

The leading geographical feature of the Appalachian Mountains, more especially of their northern half, is the large number of curving but generally parallel, level-topped ridges with valleys between, which compose the uplifted region. Crossing the ridges and valleys approximately at right angles is a series of rivers, such as the Delaware, Susquehanna, Potomac, and James, which have their sources to the west of the mountains, and flow eastward to the sea. These master streams receive many branches from the valleys crossed by them. The general features referred to are shown on the map forming Plate IX.

The ridges in the northern Appalachians are known to be due to folds in the rocks, which have been truncated or planed off to a certain general level, and the surface thus formed upraised and eroded so as to leave the edges of hard beds in bold relief. The first question suggested by an inspection of the accompanying map is: How has it come about that the main rivers flow through the ridges of hard rock by means of gaps cut in them, instead of being turned aside and pursuing what would seem to be much easier courses to the sea? The ideal case of river development we now have in mind will assist in solving this problem.

The study of the northern Appalachians, conducted by a large number of geologists, and especially by Davis and

Willis, has shown that after the rocks were folded the region existed as a land area, probably more elevated than now, and was worn down nearly to sea-level, or, in other words, was reduced to the condition of a peneplain. This peneplain was subsequently elevated and tilted so as to slope toward the south-east. The conditions were then essentially the same as in the ideal case already discussed, except that the rocks beneath the tilted plane had a complex structure. The rocks were also of many degrees of hardness and solubility. The south-eastern margin of this tilted peneplain was at sea-level, while its north-western border, in the region now embraced in the central and western portion of New York, Western Pennsylvania, and West Virginia, was elevated, not all at once, but slowly, to a height of probably two or three thousand feet.

We have designated the sloping surface referred to as a tilted plane, more accurately it should be considered as the side of an elongated dome-like uplift.

The pre-existing streams flowing with slack currents in their old age, and young consequent streams originating on the tilted peneplain, took the direction of easiest descent, and flowed south-eastward to the sea. The courses of these streams were determined by the slope of the surface irrespective of the position or character of the rocks beneath, and hence are consequent streams. As they deepened their channels, the edges of hard and soft beds were cut through. With this process of deepening the channels of the consequent streams, many subsequent branches originated which also entrenched themselves, but their directions were controlled by the hardness or solubility of the rocks. Those

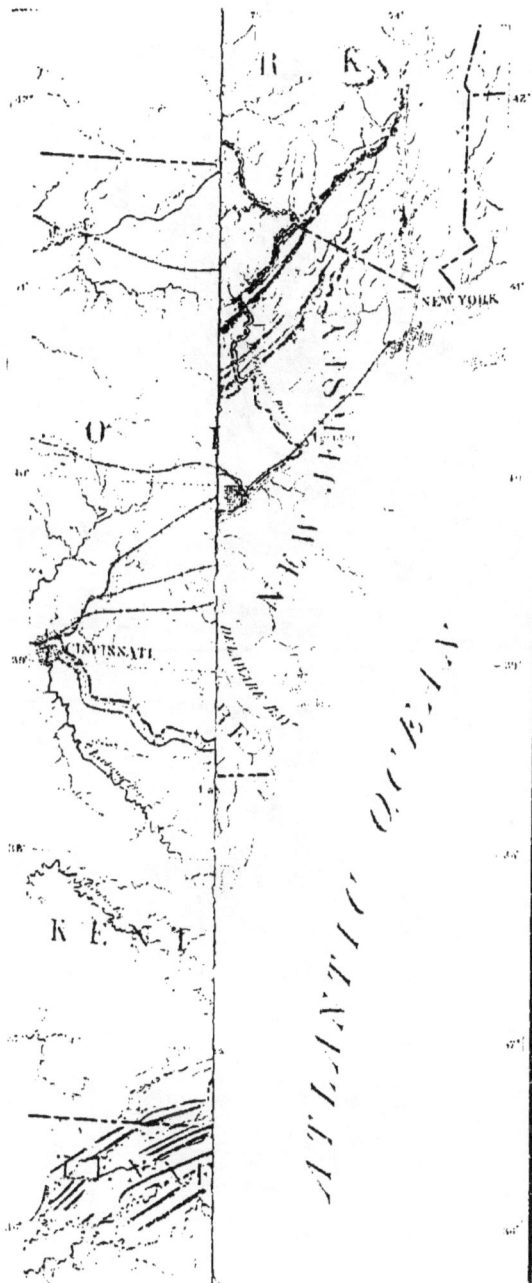

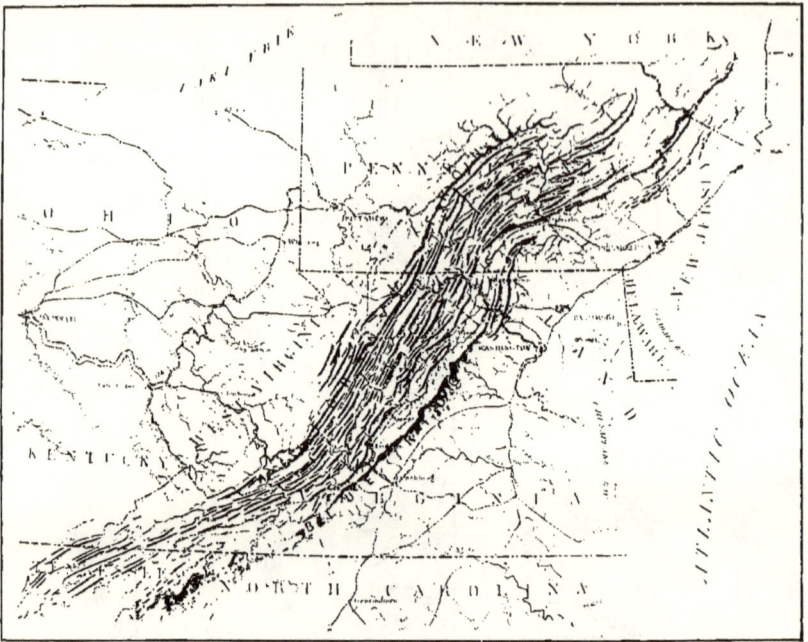

The Northern Appalachians. (After Bailey Willis.)
Approximate scale: one inch = seventy-seven miles.

originating on soft beds maintained their positions, while those which flowed at first along the outcrops of hard beds were soon shifted to the softer beds adjacent. The hard beds were thus left as ridges between the valleys excavated by the subsequent streams along the outcrops of soft beds. As the master streams flowing south-eastward lowered their channels their subsequent branches were given greater velocity and deepened their channels also. This sinking of the rivers and of all their branches produced a roughening of the topography and the once nearly smooth plain became a rugged mountainous region. In this general down-cutting the large consequent streams first reached baselevel at their mouths, and then a low gradient, or an approximation to baselevel, was produced progressively up stream. The tendency of all the streams, or their chief aim, as we may say, was to reduce the land to a second baselevel. This would be accomplished by the downward corrasion of the streams in their upper courses, and a broadening of their valleys in their lower courses; the broadening process progressing up stream as fast as the valleys were deepened at a certain progressively decreasing rate.

During the process outlined above, each of the subsequent branches of the main streams entered into competition with its neighbours for the possession of the territory between them, as in the ideal illustration of stream development previously considered. The branches of the larger master-streams, by having their places of discharge lowered more rapidly than adjacent subsequent streams flowing to weaker consequent streams, were able to extend their head branches and capture new territory in the manner already discussed.

This process was modified in many ways, however, owing to complex folding in the rocks exposed by erosion.

Influence of Folds in the Rocks on Stream Adjustment.—A fold in stratified rocks of various degrees of resistance, when the axis is horizontal, will produce parallel ridges and valleys with tapering ends.   If the axis of the fold is not horizontal but inclined so as to pass below a horizontal plane in one direction and rise above it in the opposite direction, it is evident that if the region where the fold occurs is carved away to a horizontal plane, and then etched so as to leave the edges of the hard layers in relief, the resulting ridge will not be parallel throughout, but form more or less elliptical curves.[1]

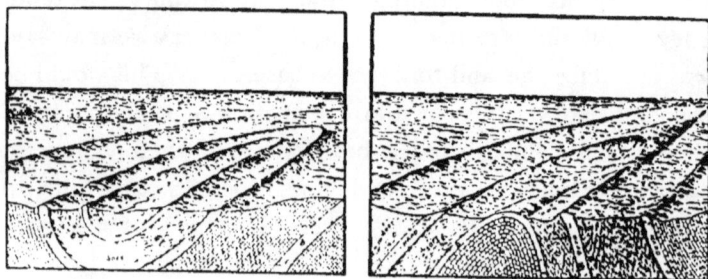

Synclinal Fold, with Central
Canoe-Shaped Valley.

Anticlinal Fold, with Hemi-
Cigar-Shaped Mountain.

FIG. 19.   Topographic Forms Resulting from the Erosion of Folded
Rocks.   (After Bailey Willis).

The topographic changes resulting from the weathering and erosion of rocks of various degrees of resistance, when

---

[1] Folds in the rocks, if traced to where they die out, will be found either to flatten and spread so as to merge with undisturbed areas or become narrow and more or less sharp-pointed.   Individual folds are more or less conical and when cut by planes of erosion give figures which are conic sections.

folded, are shown in Fig. 19. In one instance the fold is downward, so that the strata on the borders dip toward the longer axis, and is termed a *synclinal;* and in the other instances the strata forming the arch dip away from the longer axis, making an *anticlinal.*

Water-Gaps and Wind-Gaps.—The Appalachian Mountains are due to the upraising of a great belt of country in which the rocks have been folded into anticlinal and synclinal, as in the illustration just given. The longer axes of the folds trend N. E. and S. W., and are either horizontal or pitch at various angles. The western side of each fold is usually steeper than the eastern side. The ends of the folds frequently overlap, one dying out and another begin- ning and continuing sometimes for scores of miles, before it in turn disappears and is replaced by another similar fold. It is the ridges in these variously truncated folds, due to the weathering out of resistant layers, that give to the Appalachians their highly characteristic topography. The softer beds have been eroded away by the subsequent streams. The ridges of resistant rock form the divides be- tween the branches of the large rivers. The crests of the ridges are nearly level for the reason that the region was worn down to a peneplain before the etching process which gave them prominence was initiated. These level crest- lines are broken, however, by deep notches where the master streams pass through them, and are also indented by less deep notches where streams which have been beheaded formerly crossed them.

The process of river conquest, as it has been termed, by which notches have been left in the crest-lines of the ridges, is illustrated by the following typical example in Virginia, borrowed from an admirable essay on the northern Appalachians, by Willis.[1]

The Potomac near Harper's Ferry flows through two deep

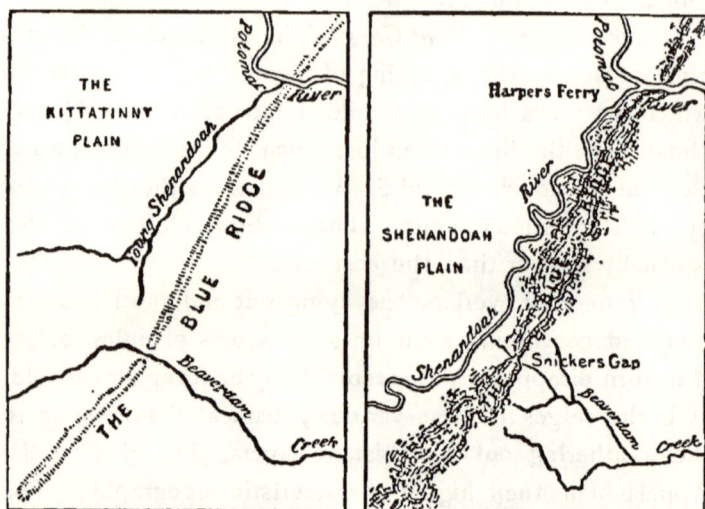

Arrangement of Streams on the	Adjusted Streams on the
Kittatinny Peneplain.	Shenandoah Peneplain.

FIG. 20.   Methods and Results of River Piracy.   (After Bailey Willis.)

picturesque notches in ridges of hard rock, as may be seen from the photograph forming Fig. B, Plate XVI. Such a notch in a mountain crossing the course of a stream, and still occupied by the stream which excavated it, is known in the language of geography as a *water-gap*. In the Blue Ridge, a few miles south of Harper's Ferry, there is a similar notch, but not so deep, the bottom of which, like the crest

[1] Bailey Willis, "The Northern Appalachians," in *National Geographic Monographs*, vol. i., pp. 169–202, published by the American Book Co. under the auspices of the National Geographic Society.

of the ridge to the north and south, is a divide between the streams flowing east and those flowing west. The air-currents flow through such notches, and this has gained for them the name of *wind-gap* among the inhabitants of the Appalachian region. This familiar name has been adopted by geographers as a generic term by which to designate a class of notches in the crest-lines of ridges and mountains having a certain origin. The particular notch in the Blue Ridge here referred to is known as " Snickers Gap," and is a typical illustration of a wind-gap. Its history is shown graphically on the two accompanying sketch-maps by Willis.

It will be remembered that the country about Harper's Ferry was at one time in the condition of a tilted peneplain, and that a strong consequent stream, the Potomac, flowed across it toward the east; and that this river and its tributaries deepened their channels and entrenched themselves in the plain. As a result of this process and of general erosion, the edges of the layers of hard rocks beneath the surface of the plain were left in relief. The Blue Ridge, composed of hard, resistant quartzite, is a typical illustration of a ridge originating in this manner.

The conditions after the Potomac had begun to deepen its channel, and the Blue Ridge was a line of faint relief, are shown in the ideal sketch-map to the left of Fig. 20. The infant Shenandoah River entered the Potomac above the water-gap at Harper's Ferry, flowing northward along the west base of the Blue Ridge in a valley excavated in limestone. At the stage in the history shown in the map just referred to, the Shenandoah was a young subsequent stream. To the south of the Potomac, as indicated on the map, there was another but weaker consequent stream, Beaverdam Creek, which also crossed the Blue Ridge in a water-gap. It will be remembered that all of these streams were flowing at a higher level than the Shenandoah occupies to-day, and that the Blue Ridge was a much less prominent topographic feature than at present. The Potomac, being a larger stream than Beaverdam Creek, deepened its channel more rapidly, and thus lowered the mouth of the Shenandoah and caused it to flow more swiftly. The Shenandoah was thus enabled to deepen its channel and to extend its head branches more rapidly than its neighbour and rival. As a result, the Shenandoah captured the drainage of Beaverdam Creek to the west of the Blue Ridge, thus beheading that stream. The ability of Beaverdam Creek to deepen its channel in the hard rocks forming the Blue Ridge was thus lessened, and as the Shenandoah continued to lower its chan-nel, the portion of Beaverdam Creek situated between the places of capture and the bottom of the notch it had cut in the Blue Ridge was reversed, and also contributed its waters to the capturing stream. Beaverdam Creek was thus broken in two at the place where it formerly crossed the hard layer forming the Blue Ridge, and stream corrasion there ceased. The notch previously made was thus changed from a water-gap to a wind-gap. Subsequently the Blue Ridge became more and more prominent owing to the removal of the softer rocks on each side of it, but the notch in its crest-line re-mained. The conditions as they exist at the present day, when the bottom of the notch is a water-parting or divide, between streams flowing in opposite directions, is shown on the right-hand map of Fig. 20. Another illustration of the robbing of one stream by a more favourably circumstanced rival is illustrated in Plate XIII, and described in advance in connection with a discussion of the migration of divides.

Stream Conquest.—The process of capture by the subsequent branches of strong consequent streams, just illustrated, has gone on, with various modifications in detail, throughout the Appalachians, and great variety both in the direction of the streams and in the relief of the land has resulted. The principal conditions which give one stream an advantage over its neighbour on the opposite side of a common divide, are a shorter course to the sea, greater volume, and softer rocks in which to sink its channel.

If one of two streams heading against a common divide has a shorter course to the sea than its rival, other conditions being the same, its gradient will be greater, and hence it will have greater velocity and be able to corrade more rapidly, and, also, the amount of rock to be removed in order to reach baselevel is less. If the rain-fall on one side of a mountain range is greater than on the opposite side, other conditions being the same, the streams on the side having the greater rain-fall will be larger, and hence able to deepen their channels and extend their head branches more rapidly than the streams on the opposite side of the divide.

In a similar way, it will readily be seen that of two competing streams, one flowing over hard and the other over soft rocks, the one with the easier task will deepen its channel more rapidly than the one flowing over hard rock, and lead to the capture of some of the territory previously draining to its rival.

In the sculpturing of the Appalachian Mountains all of

these variations in conditions, and possibly still others, have been in progress at the same time. Many of the features of the northern Appalachians resulting from this process of the adjustment of streams to the structure of the rocks into which they sink their channels may be read on the map forming Plate X.

This map illustrates in an admirable manner the way in which the Susquehanna, a strong consequent stream, flows across the edges of both hard and soft strata, independently of the topography, while the secondary streams follow the outcrops of the soft rocks, although occasionally flowing directly through a ridge of hard rock, and continuing their general course in the next valley. Evidently the secondary streams, flowing through ridges of hard rock, had their right of way established on the original peneplain, or, by a process of adjustment, described below, have made for themselves a way out of synclinal valleys and into depressions excavated in the tops of anticlinal ridges.

The student should study also the well-developed dendritic drainage in Lebanon valley at the bottom of the map, where the rocks are soft limestone which yield readily to solution; in comparison with the remarkably straight course of Stony Creek, confined between two ridges of hard sandstone. The crooked courses of the streams, particularly where they have cut down their channel nearly to the level of the master rivers, indicate the tendency of streams well advanced in their task of valley-making, to become sluggish and meander. Especially does this excellent map illustrate the fact that the relief of the land is due to the action of the stream in removing soft rocks and allowing the hard rocks

PLATE X.

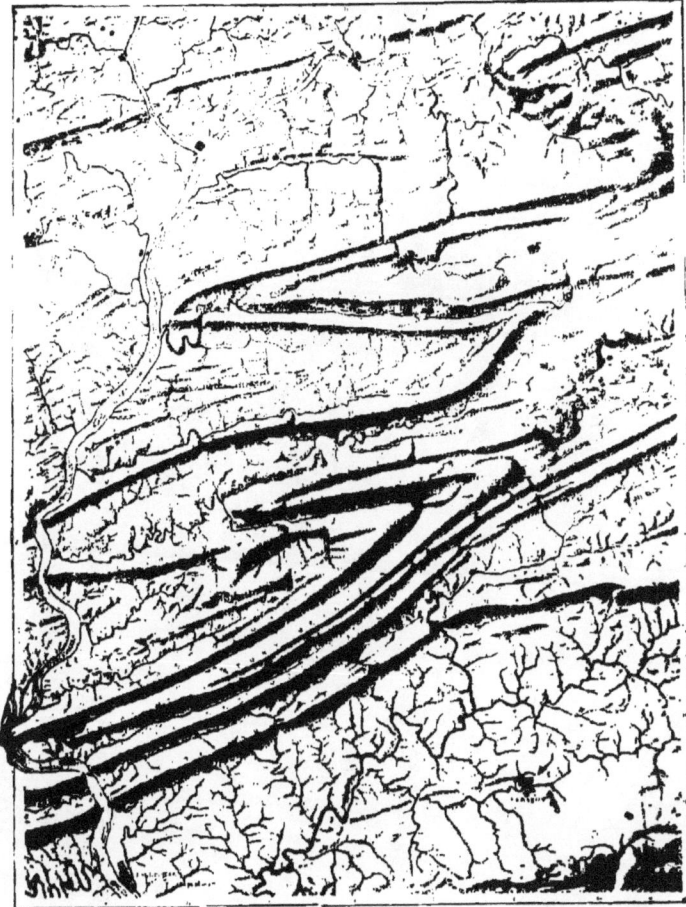

Western Portion of the Anthracite Basin, Pennsylvania, Showing Canoe-Valleys and Mountains and the Course of the Susquehanna across them. (After Bailey Willis.)

Approximate scale: one inch = twelve miles.

to stand in relief. Instead of the topography controlling the stream, the stream gives origin to the topography. As long since explained by Hutton, each stream flows in a valley of its own making.

Ancient Peneplains.—Only a part of the history of the northern Appalachians has been read when the adjustment of the streams to geological structure and the growth of certain drainage areas at the expense of others has been worked out. The land has not remained stationary during the millions of years required for this process, but have been upheaved and depressed. One immensely long period of rest is recorded by the broad, featureless peneplain which was tilted, as already explained, so as to cause the master stream to flow across the future site of the mountains to the sea. A portion of this peneplain not yet consumed forms the Kittatinny Mountains in Eastern Pennsylvania. The plain referred to is hence named the Kittatinny peneplain.[1] After this plain had been deeply dissected and the streams had broadened their valleys so that only isolated remnants of the rocks remained above sea-level, the region was again elevated, but the second upward movement was not so great as the one just considered, and another attempt to reduce the region to baselevel was begun. A second peneplain was formed, but not carried to completion before the region was again raised. As stated by Willis, the upheaval leading to the dissection of the Kittatinny peneplain, caused an elevation of two hundred feet in New Jersey, six hundred feet in Pennsyl-

---

[1] Also known as the "Schooley peneplain" in New Jersey. See "Physical Geography of New Jersey," in vol. iv., of the *Final Report of the State Geologist of New Jersey*, p. 85, 1898.

vania, one thousand seven hundred feet in Southern Virginia, and thence southward decreased to the Gulf of Mexico. A typical illustration of this second peneplain is found in the broad bottom of the Shenandoah valley, and for this reason it has been named the Shenandoah peneplain. In the illustration forming Fig. B, Plate XVI, the Shenandoah peneplain is on a level with the point of view, while the hills rise to the level of the Kittatinny peneplain.

In consequence of renewed elevation after the broadening of the Shenandoah peneplain was well under way, the energy of the streams was again revived. Once more falling swiftly, they have sawed and are sawing their channels down, and are preparing for the development of a future baselevel.

In the southern Appalachians, the Kittatinny peneplain was not so completely developed as farther north, and a group of mountains representing the previous uplands from which the plain was carved was left. These mountains have maintained their existence to the present day, and still furnish the highest and most picturesque peaks in the system. This great group of peaks, of which Mount Mitchell, Rhone Mountain, and other prominent summits in Eastern Tennessee and Western North Carolina are examples, it will be seen, are of the nature of remnants rising above a broad and nearly completed peneplain, or, to use a technical name previously explained, they are monadnocks.

At the south, the great Kittatinny peneplain was not tilted south-eastward as in Eastern Pennsylvania and adjacent States, but toward the south-west. Hence the streams flowing down its inclined surface had their sources to the east of the ridges and mountains subsequently developed by the erosion of its surface and flowed westward to the Mississippi and south-westward to the Gulf of Mexico. The principal consequent streams in this region are New River and the Tennessee. The Coosa at present belongs also in this category, but, as has been shown by Hayes,[1] was formerly a continuation of the Tennessee.

Synclinal Mountains and Anticlinal Valleys.—The process of stream adjustment to geological conditions, discovered as erosion progressed, was much the same in the southern as in the northern Appalachians, but the details were in some respects different. One of the characteristic features in the structure of the southern Appalachians, but more especially of their western half, which departs somewhat widely from the typical structure at the north, is the presence of broad downward curves in the rocks, or synclinals, separated by comparatively narrow upward folds, or anticlinals. If the land had been elevated without being eroded, we should find to-day a series of prominent but narrow ridges running north-east and southward, intervening between much broader, trough-shaped valleys. If streams should come into existence on such a surface where it was inclined 'in the direction of the longer axis of the ridges and troughs, they would evidently follow the depressions as consequent streams.

In marked contrast to what would have been the topography of much of Eastern Tennessee and the northern portions of Alabama and Georgia had there been no ero-

---

[1] C. Willard Hayes, "Geomorphology of the Southern Appalachians," in *The National Geographic Magazine*, vol. vi., pp. 109–119, 1894.

sion, we find that where the ridges would have been, there are now valleys occupied by well-developed drainage systems, while the synclinals, which would have been valleys under the conditions just assumed, in reality stand in relief and form broad ridges or mountains, with shallow depressions in their surfaces. This reversion of what would have been the topographic relations of the anticlinals and synclinals had there been no erosion, is one of the most interesting chapters in Appalachian history. Let us see how this topographic revolution has come about.

A good example of a synclinal plateau is furnished by Lookout Mountain, which terminates at the north in a bold escapement over one thousand five hundred feet high at Chattanooga, Tennessee, and extends south-west about seventy miles to Atalla and Gadsden in Alabama. It was at the extreme northern end of this synclinal, the axis of which declines gently southward, left in bold relief by the erosion of the bordering valleys, that the battle of Lookout Mountain was fought. To the west of Lookout Mountain is a deep anticlinal valley from four to five miles wide, and to the west of this, again, another broad synclinal plateau known as Sand Mountain. The present relief and drainage of this region are shown on the sketch-map forming Fig. 4, Plate XI.

The origin of the present strongly pronounced and characteristic topography of the region just referred to, has been studied by Hayes, and I cannot serve the reader better than by presenting an extract from his report.[1]

[1] *Geological Survey of Alabama, Bulletin*, No. 4, pp. 23-29, and Plate I 1892.

The four maps presented on Plate XI. illustrate four successive stages in the history of the streams in the Lookout-Sand mountain region. An early stage in the topographic development is shown in Fig. 1, where a stream flowed southward in each of the synclinal troughs and received tributaries from the adjacent anticlinal ridges.

" At first these streams were all flowing upon the same kind of rock, probably coarse sandstone, so that they were able to erode their channels most rapidly where the fall and consequently the transporting power of the stream was the greatest. But the slope of the synclinal troughs was very slight, so that the main streams had little power to deepen their channels, while the side streams flowing into them from the intervening ridge, although they were much smaller, still by reason of their greater fall eroded their beds more rapidly.

" If the rocks of this region had been uniform in character for a long distance down from the surface, the effect of the more rapid cutting of the side streams would have been simply to reduce the height of the intervening ridge, leaving the main streams in their original position in the synclinal troughs. But the rocks are not homogeneous. They consist of alternating hard and soft beds, and after the side streams had cut down a few hundred feet they came to layers of shale and then limestone which they could remove much more rapidly than the overlying sandstone. As soon as a side stream reached these soft rocks at any point, it tended to widen its valley at that point by removing the soft rocks so as to undermine and thus break down the overlying harder beds. By a continuation of this process lateral valleys were formed, Fig. 2 [Plate XI], extending in the direction of the ridge and at right angles to the side streams.

" The two streams w and w' cut away at the divide d and the stream w having the lowest outlet was able to erode more rapidly than w' and so pushed the divide farther and farther toward the side stream l' till finally it tapped the latter and led

14

EXPLANATION OF PLATE XI.

Sketch map of a portion of Lookout Mountain, Wills Valley, and Sand Mountain ; showing various stages in the development of the present drainage system and topography.

Fig. 1. Showing the undulating surface which determined the initial position of the streams. B, B and T, T flow in synclinal troughs and receive side streams l, l, l and s, s, s from the intervening anticlinal ridge.

Fig. 2. Showing a stage in the development when the side streams l, l, l and s, s, s have cut through the hard surface rocks to soft beds beneath and lateral valleys, w, w', etc., are being formed parallel with the anticlinal axis.

Fig. 3. Showing a further stage in the development when the lateral stream w has cut through the intervening divides and diverted the drainage of l' and l". A second series of lateral streams, W, etc., is being developed along the anticlinal parallel with the first series, W, W, etc. The upper portion of the synclinal stream, B, B has been diverted by a side stream, R, R.

Fig. 4. Showing the present drainage system and topography. Both lateral streams, w and W, have continued to encroach upon the basins of those adjacent, w resulting in the present Little Wills Creek and W in Big Wills Creek. The latter now occupies the axis of the anticlinal throughout its whole length and has become the dominant stream of the system under consideration. The stream B, B has been further robbed of portions of its drainage basin by streams flowing eastward to the Coosa. The synclinal stream T, T has been tapped at various points by streams flowing westward into the Tennessee and the drainage thus diverted from its original course toward the south.—C. W. HAYES.

PLATE XI.

Fig. 1

Fig. 2

Fig. 3

Fig. 4

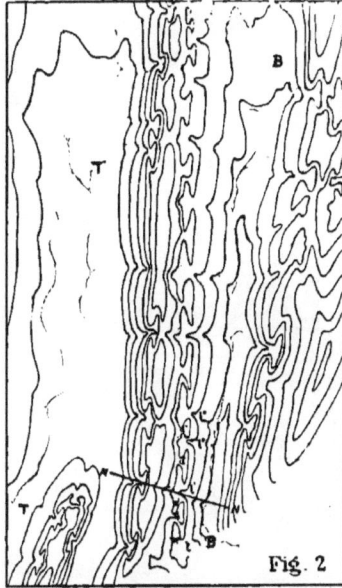

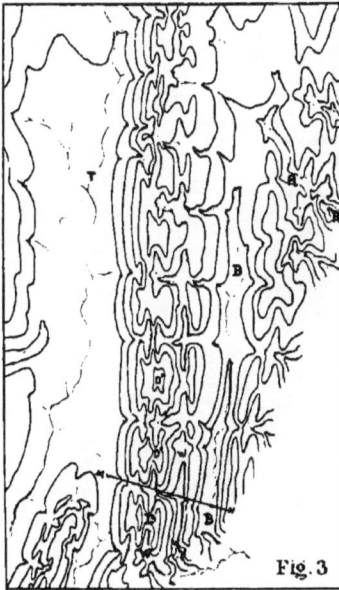

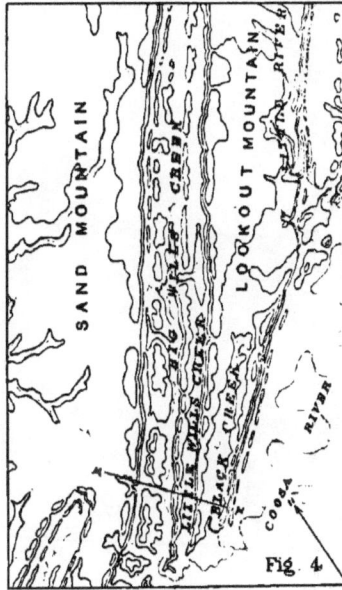

Lookout Mountain Region, Alabama, illustrating stream adjustment.
(After E. W. Hayes).

Approximate scale: 1 inch = 15 miles.

its waters off by way of *l*. The lateral stream thus formed (*w w*, Fig. 3) was the beginning of the present Little Wills Creek. The same process would have continued till this stream had tapped successively all the drainage basins above if it had not encountered a second hard bed through which erosion was very slow. After the soft rocks were removed which lay above this hard bed, then the same process was repeated which had taken place on the original anticlinal ridge; that is, side streams with greater fall were able to cut through the hard bed more quickly than the main stream and reaching soft rocks below began to widen their valleys and then form lateral valleys at these points. The same process was repeated with this second set of lateral streams. By erosion at the divides D D' D", etc., Fig. 3, that one having the lowest outlet tapped the drainage basin of the one adjacent and led its waters off along the axis of the anticlinal. The side stream W, Fig. 3, possessed a great advantage over any of the others in having a much lower outlet and hence it was able to encroach upon them and divert their head-waters to its own channel. But with each conquest of new territory, by the additional volume of water thus gained, it became more efficient in eroding its valley while the streams whose drainage basins had been thus diminished were even less able to hold their own. Thus the process was cumulative in its effects, and finally the stream last formed became the dominant one of the drainage system.

" This process by which the ridge was removed and the streams shifted from their original position in the synclinal trough to the axis of the anticlinal may be further illustrated by the diagram [Fig. 21], representing a section through the ridge and adjacent troughs. The heavy line represents the present surface and the unbroken lines the beds of rock as they exist at present, below the surface. The curved, dotted lines represent the position of the beds as they originally existed before their removal. Two of these beds, Cl and Sr, which are sandstone, offer much greater resistance to erosion than the limestones, Cb, Sc, and Sk. The upper curved line represents the profile of the land surface on which drainage originated, corresponding in position to the line M N in Fig. 1

[Plate XI.]. B and T indicate the position of the main streams in the synclinal troughs into which the side streams flowed from the intervening anticlinal ridge. As already explained, the first point at which the upper hard bed C 1 was cut through was on the steep slopes of this ridge, as at w and v, where the lateral valleys were subsequently formed in a direction parallel with the ridge. The upper broken line, then, will represent the surface at the second stage of its development, represented in Fig. 2. Continuing to erode their channels downward through the soft rocks Cb, the streams encountered the second hard bed Sr, and

FIG. 21. Section through Lookout Mountain, Wills Valley, and Sand Mountain ;. Showing Profile of the Land Surface at Four Stages in the Development of the Present Drainage System. (After C. W. Hayes.)

the process above described was repeated, producing the surface represented by the lower broken line. This is the third stage in the development of the drainage system in which the streams had the positions indicated in Fig. 3. Finally, the lateral stream which started at W, being already through the two hard beds, easily distanced its competitors and robbed them of successive portions of their drainage area until it became the dominant stream of the system, Big Wills Creek.

" The stream B B Fig. 1, which originally flowed the whole length of the Lookout synclinal trough, was not permitted to retain that position. Robbed of all its western tributaries by the process above described, it was unable with its diminished volume to lower its channel sufficiently fast for its own protection. At a point on the eastern side of the synclinal a stream, R R, Fig. 3, has cut back from the valley of the Coosa and diverted the upper portion from its original channel. Hence the present course of Little River, Fig. 4, follows the synclinal to this point and then turns sharply to the south-east by a deep rocky gorge. Other portions have been more recently diverted by Wolf and Yellow Creeks. Thus the stream which originally drained the whole of the synclinal trough and the slopes of the adjacent anticlinal ridges has been robbed of the greater part of its drainage basin, and Black Creek alone, a mere remnant of the original stream, retains the course which it has followed from the beginning. For a short time during the stage represented by Fig. 3, Little Wills Creek, w w, was the encroaching stream, but reaching a hard stratum, its career of conquest was checked, and the stream W, more favourably situated, although last born, became the dominant stream of the system. In the meantime the anticlinal ridge had been entirely removed, and in its place a deep valley excavated, while the original stream channels were left high up in the synclinals now forming the tops of the mountains.

" This is but one of numerous examples in this region which might be followed out in detail to show how the drainage system has adjusted itself to the structural surface and how the present position of the streams is dependent on the dip of the strata and the alternation of hard and soft rocks.

" It must be borne in mind, however, that only the latest stages in the development of the present topography can be followed with certainty. The condition which immediately preceded the present is easily inferred, but as the processes are followed backward they become more obscure, and finally are only to be conjectured. Hence in the development of Wills Valley, as it has been sketched above, the explanation becomes more largely pure hypothesis as the more remote stages are reached. The explanation offered for the earliest stages is not the only one possible, but is perhaps the most probable of a number which might be given.

" Also in the above sketch several complicating factors have been purposely omitted for the sake of greater simplicity in presenting the essential points of the theory. Thus the anticlinal arch probably continued to rise during the process of erosion, and the effect which this may have had on the resulting topography has not been taken into consideration."

The explanation accompanying Plate XI, also borrowed from Hayes's report, will assist the reader in understanding the bit of ancient history just outlined.

An analysis of stream adjustment, in a region of folded rocks similar to that just presented, was published in 1889, by Davis[1] in discussing the origin of the peculiar topography of Pennsylvania. The paper just referred to, the first ever published that offered a rational explanation of the development of the intricate Appalachian drainage, should be read by all students of the events in the earth history here discussed.

EFFECTS OF ELEVATION AND SUBSIDENCE ON STREAM DEVELOPMENT

The effect of a general rise of the land throughout a broad region is to increase the gradients of the streams, and hence to give them greater velocity and greater corrading power. If subterranean forces affect the surface in such a manner as to tilt a broad area, the streams flowing in the direction of downward tilting, other conditions remaining unchanged, will have their energy increased, and will therefore deepen their channels. This will give their lateral tributaries, coming to them more or less nearly at right angles, increased energy by lowering their mouths, and still other results will follow.

The reader, no doubt, has already reached the conclusion that a river system is similar to a delicately adjusted machine. A change in the adjustment in any one

[1] W. M. Davis, " The Rivers and Valleys of Pennsylvania," in the *National Geographic Magazine*, vol. i., pp. 183-253.

part, or in the complex and far-reaching conditions on which stream life depends, necessitates changes throughout large portions and perhaps the whole of the system. Of the changes which interfere with the regular and systematic development of streams, none are more common or have produced more conspicuous results than movements in the rocks resulting in upheavals or depressions of the surface.

Some of the effects of uplift and subsidence of portions of the earth's crust have already been considered in connection with the discussion of the origin of stream terraces, and of the adjustment of stream to geological conditions. There are many other results of such changes, however, which are of interest to the geographer and geologist.

Some of the Effects of Elevation.—A rise of a region adjacent to a shallow sea would bring a portion of the sea-floor above water, and thus increase the area of dry land. The length of the streams entering the sea in the area thus affected would be increased, and necessitate a readjustment of grade for a long distance up their courses. The lengthening of a river by the addition of a broad strip of new land to the border of a continent might necessitate such a readjustment of grade by deposition, in order to enable the stream to carry its burden to the sea, that much of the increase in energy due to the upheaval would be counteracted so as to cause the stream to aggrade its channel at localities where corrasion was previously in progress. Elevation, it may thus be shown, is not always immediately followed by deeper cutting, as might at first be inferred.

An elevation of the land of the nature just considered, tends in general to straighten coast-lines, for the sea bottom, as a rule, is more even than land areas, and to trans-form previous bays and estuaries into river valleys.

Increased complexity in the influence that elevation has on stream development occurs when, instead of a tilting of broad areas along a single axis, the rocks are folded, as in the early history of the Appalachian Mountains, so as to produce many lines of elevation. In certain regions, especially in the central portions of continental areas, the rocks have been elevated into vast domes by forces acting from below upward. Examples of such domes, and of their influence on drainage, are furnished by the Black Hills of Dakota and other similar uplifts in the eastern part of the Rocky Mountain region.

Again, throughout broad belts of the earth's crust the rocks have been broken by lines of fracture, and the blocks thus formed variously tilted and displaced. The displace-ment of the broken edges of the same bed, on the opposite sides of such a break, is in many instances thousands and even tens of thousands of feet. The Great Basin region illustrates, more clearly than any other portion of North America, the influence of such faults, as they are termed, on the relief of the surface.

The changes in topography produced by faulting probably progress slowly with many intermittent movements. If the growth of the faults is so slow that streams flowing across the affected region can deepen, or aggrade, their channels as rapidly as the changes occur, the streams may hold their right of way and deepen or fill their channels as rapidly as the land is elevated or depressed. When, for example, a fault or fold rises athwart the course of a river, it may corrade its channel as rapidly as the land rises and excavate a trench through the growing mountain. Illustrations of such a history are furnished by the Columbia and many of its branches, which cut through the upturned edges of fault blocks and produce water-gaps.

Should the growth of a mountain formed either by a folding of the earth's crust, by the elevation of a dome, or the growth of an escarpment due to faulting athwart the course of a river, be more rapid than it can deepen its channel, evidently it will be broken in two. Its lower course will be beheaded, its upper course reversed, or its waters ponded so as to form a lake.

When the normal development of a drainage system is interrupted by such changes as have just been instanced, a new adjustment is made, and the process of development continued under the changed condition.

The broad conclusion reached in reference to the effects of upheaval on drainage is, that land is raised above the sea by movements in the earth's crust, due principally to the cooling and consequent shrinking of the earth's hot interior, and the adjustment of the cooler and more rigid crust to keep in contact with the continually shrinking central mass on which it rests; and streams and other denuding agencies cut away the areas thus raised. There is a continued warfare between these two contending series of agencies.

Some of the Effects of Subsidence.—One of the most conspicuous effects of a downward movement of the land on the streams draining it and on the valleys that the streams have made, is to be seen when coastal plains crossed by

large rivers are submerged.   In such instances the sea enters
the river valleys and converts them into bays and estuaries.
Ridges between adjacent valleys then become capes or pro-
montories, and the more isolated peaks are perhaps converted into islands.   Examples of conspicuous changes due
to subsidence are furnished by the Atlantic and St. Lawrence drainage slopes.   The mouth of the Hudson, as is
well known, was formerly some seventy miles eastward of
Long Island, but now, owing to a depression of the land,
the tide rises and falls at Troy.   The St. Lawrence formerly
discharged to the eastward of what is now Nova Scotia,
but at present the trunk of the river is shorter by a thousand miles, and tide-water reaches nearly to Montreal.

The St. Lawrence below Montreal and the Hudson (Plate
XV.) below Troy illustrate what is termed a drowned river.
The former rivers have been betrunked by subsidence.
Other illustrations of the same occurrence are furnished by
Delaware and Chesapeake Bays, which are estuaries formed
by the drowning of river valleys.   Chesapeake Bay is also a
typical example of the way in which a river system may be
dissected by subsidence.   The trunk of the stream has been
lost by drowning, and several of the former branches enter
independent estuaries.

Many other illustrations of similar geographical changes
are furnished by the coast-lines of North America.   The
ragged coast of Maine, with its multitudes of capes and
bays and its fringe of islands, owes much of its picturesque-
ness to the fact that a rough land-surface has been depressed
so as to allow the sea to encroach upon it.   In this instance, however, the land was formerly covered by glacial

ice, and in part the roughness of its surface is due to hills and ridges produced by glacial deposition.

On the Pacific coast a partially drowned river-valley furnishes the magnificent bay opening to the sea through the Golden Gate. Puget Sound and the fringe of islands adjacent to an extremely irregular coast, northward to Lynn Canal and Glacier Bay, Alaska, also show the effect of the sea entering the depressions on the border of a continent and leaving the hills and mountains rising above a certain level exposed to the air. Here again, as on the Maine coast, the roughness of the land is due in part to glacial action.

FIG. 22.—Map of Chesapeake Bay, Showing by Heavy Lines the Way in which Various Streams would Unite to Form a Single Trunk-Stream if the Land were Elevated. (After R. S. Tarr.)

Puget Sound and the similar depression northward for a thousand miles were formerly occupied by glacial ice, which lingered in the depressions, and allowed deep accumulations of stream and glacial-born debris to be deposited around it. When the ice finally melted, the present tide-ways were left unfilled.

In general, land exposed to the atmosphere is rendered rough and uneven by stream corrasion up to a certain stage in its topographical development, and then the prominences are removed, the relief becomes subdued, and a plain is the ultimate result. If partial submergence occurs during the earlier stages of topographical development, a ragged coast-line results. Beneath the sea-level the detritus washed from the land, together with shells and other material of organic origin, is deposited, and inequalities in the bottom filled. A rise of the sea bottom, therefore, as previously stated, tends to produce even coast-lines.

The action of the waves and currents of the ocean on its shores is analogous in many ways to the action of rivers on the bottom and sides of the valleys through which they flow, and analogous topographic changes result, which are of great scenic as well as geographic importance. Another branch of geographic study full of interest and novelty, is here open to the student, but at present we must deny ourselves the pleasure of a stroll on the salt-sea strands and return to the consideration of river development.

The topographic changes resulting from the drowning of a river valley, owing to a subsidence of the land adjacent to the ocean, find a counterpart along the shores of lakes when their waters rise. In the case of lakes without outlets, as Great Salt Lake, Utah; Pyramid, Winnemucca, and Walker Lakes, Nevada, etc., a climatic change, resulting in an increased rain-fall or a decrease in evaporation, would cause the lakes to rise and flood the lower portions of low-grade tributary stream-valleys. The extension of the waters of Great Salt Lake into the channel of Bear River at the present time is an illustration of the drowning of a river by this process. The many changes of level experienced by the Laurentian lakes, owing to a tilting of their basins, has in some instances led to the submergence of river valleys. For example, at a time when the waters in the western part of Lake Ontario were lower than now, Niagara River excavated a channel leading past Lewiston, which, owing to a tilting of the lake basin, was subsequently flooded. Other geographical changes, produced by fluctuation of water-level in the lakes referred to, illustrate on a comparatively small scale the modifications in coast-lines which result from movement in the land.

SOME OF THE INFLUENCES OF VOLCANIC AGENCIES ON STREAM DEVELOPMENT

Important modifications in stream development have resulted in numerous instances from interruptions due to volcanic agencies. The influences of volcanoes on the histories of streams are diverse, but only a few of the more pronounced changes of this nature need be noted at this time to enable the reader to recognise others without the aid of suggestions.

Volcanoes frequently emit streams of lava which flow over the surface of the land in obedience to gravity, and take the most favourable courses available. A lava stream sometimes flows down a previously eroded valley, and on cooling and hardening leaves it partially or wholly filled with resistant rock. The adjustment of the stream is thus greatly disturbed, or perhaps an entirely new start in channel-making initiated. Lava streams sometimes cross river valleys and dam them so as to form lakes. Instances of such a nature are described in the author's book entitled *Volcanoes of North America*.

Vast lava inundations have occurred in the history of North America, as when the Columbia lava of Washington, Oregon, Idaho, and California was spread out in successive sheets over an area of between two hundred thousand and two hundred and fifty thousand square miles and attained a thickness in certain regions of over four thousand feet. In such an instance, the topography of the inundated region is entirely obliterated, the lives of its streams are terminated, and a new start in stream development has to be made on the surface of the lava covering. The streams from neighbouring mountains are dammed, lakes are formed which discharge perhaps across the lava plain, as in the instance of Snake River, and a canyon is carved. In the case of the river just mentioned, the outspreading of a vast lava plain over the region across which it previously flowed, was in a measure equivalent to an elevation of the land in its lower course.

Volcanoes also discharge projectiles in the form of scoria, bombs, small rock fragments (*lapilli*), and dust, which accumulate about the vents from which they came and build up elevations, usually conical in form, or are carried away by the wind, as in the case of volcanic dust, and widely distributed. Deposits of this nature also modify the normal development of streams, and may even terminate their existence.

Volcanic eruptions are frequently accompanied by earthquakes, which cause fissures to open in the soil and rocks, and in this manner other accidents, as they may be termed, to river development come about. Earthquakes are also accompanied by changes of the level of the land, perhaps as a cause or as an effect of the changes to which the shocks are due, but the influence of such movements in stream development is not essentially different from that produced by the changes in elevation already considered.

Another method by which volcanoes influence the lives of streams is through the action of the acids they emit. This chemical phase of the subject has received but slight attention, but it is evident, from the vast quantities of various acid gases poured out during eruptions and even for centuries after a volcano has passed to the condition of a fumarole or a solfatara, that the chemical action of surface waters must thereby be enhanced.

Volcanoes also exert an influence on climate both on account of the heat emitted and the vapours poured into the air, and again, by reason of their influence on air currents, etc., when prominent mountains are built. All of these changes in what may be termed the geography of the air, as well as of the relief of the land, exert an influence on the history of streams.

SOME OF THE MODIFICATIONS IN STREAM DEVELOPMENT DUE TO CLIMATIC CHANGES

To appreciate the effects of climatic changes on normal stream development, perhaps the best method is to have in

mind an example of a river with numerous branches which
has become well adjusted to the structure of the rocks
underlying its hydrographic basin, and then postulate
atmospheric changes and see what variations in the behaviour of the stream would necessarily result. The conclusions reached by this process of mental analysis may
be checked by making comparisons between the changes
thought to logically follow certain climatic variations and
the condition of the streams in regions where similar
changes have actually occurred.

Of the elements in the highly complex atmospheric conditions embraced in the term climate, those having the
most direct and tangible influence on the behaviour of
streams are precipitation and temperature.

Variations in Precipitation.—An increase in precipitation
in a region where the mean annual temperature is such that
all of the water coming to the earth is in the form of rain,
or if snow falls during a part of the year it is all melted before the next succeeding winter, is to increase the volumes
of the streams and enable them to carry on their work more
rapidly.

An increase in rain-fall, other conditions remaining the
same, means, then, that more debris is transported, and
when the relation of load to velocity is such as to favour
corrasion, the stream channels are deepened more rapidly
than previous to the postulated change. Increased corrasion in the branches of a drainage system, however, means
usually more rapid deposition, or aggrading, in those portions of the main stream, or in its branches, where the swift
up-stream reaches deliver their loads to less rapidly flowing

waters. On the whole, streams carry on this work more rapidly, and lower their drainage basin to baselevel more quickly, under humid than under rainless skies. That is, increased volume favours corrasion and hastens the coming of the final stage in the history of streams, when they have reduced their basins to baselevel. There may be a check in this increased activity, however, due to greater rain-fall, through the influence of more luxuriant vegetation.

The effects of a long-continued or secular decrease in precipitation on stream development and erosion are illustrated on a small scale each summer in the eastern portion of the United States and Canada. After the spring rain, as is well known, the monthly precipitation greatly decreases, the streams become less and less in volume; many of the weaker ones disappear, their supplies diminish, their waters are evaporated, or absorbed by the material over which they flow. When one follows up a dry stream-channel in late summer he comes at length in many instances to where it is still occupied by water. The trunk of the drainage system has disappeared and the branches fail to unite. The streams have been betrunked by a decrease in water supply and an increase in loss by evaporation. The weakened streams fail to abrade their channels where active corrasion was in progress a few months previously, and all the debris carried by them is deposited within their channels.

On account of decrease in load, however, many streams are enabled to corrade their channels in certain tracts during the dry season, where previously overloading led to deposition.

The changes experienced by streams in a region where
15

seasonal changes occur, as just referred to, illustrate the more marked results of secular climatic changes. If precipitation slowly decreases century after century, even the larger rivers may fail to reach the sea, but annual pulsations in their branches and even in the main channels may still continue. The channels of the main streams and of many of their tributaries will then become deeply filled. Some of the branches will fail to reach the main stream-channel, and the drainage tree, as it appears on a map, is betrunked.

Many streams illustrating an advanced stage in the shrinking and betrunking of once vigorous lines of drainage, owing to increased dryness of climate, occur in the arid portions of the United States, between the Rocky Mountains and the Sierra Nevada, and also in Texas and New Mexico. An examination of a fairly good map of these regions will show many branches of previously extensive rivers, which end without uniting so as to form trunk streams. These *lost rivers* furnish illustrations of the dissection of streams by a secular decrease in rain-fall and general desiccation.

In other instances, as in the case of Humboldt River, Nevada, a trunk stream is formed from year to year during the rainy season, which discharges its waters on to a broad desert valley where they spread out in a saline lake and are evaporated. During the next succeeding summer, the trunk stream fails to reach the lake into which it previously discharged and shrinks in volume throughout, leaving isolated ponds in the deeper portions of its channel; its branches then correspond to the branches of a fallen tree from which the trunk has been removed.

An instructive phase of the drainage of an arid country is

furnished when a stream rising in more humid and usually mountainous regions, flows across it, and has sufficient volume to sustain the losses due to evaporation, and maintains its course to the sea. Under such conditions a river may continue to deepen its channel through an arid country without developing branches in its middle and lower courses. Such a stream, returning to the analogy between the outline of a drainage system and a tree, resembles one of the monarchs of a forest having a tall trunk without branches until the spreading crown of foliage is reached. An example of such a river, with an immensely long trunk from which lateral branches have fallen away, is furnished by the Colorado. The trunk of the Nile measures about eleven hundred miles to the first branch.

The character of the trunk of a river flowing through an arid country will depend largely on the altitude of the land through which it flows. If the region is an elevated tableland, as in the case of the Colorado, it will corrade its channel down to baselevel and form a deep canyon, for the reason that general degradation in an arid climate is greatly retarded. The walls of the canyon will be precipitous because the stream deepens its channel more rapidly than its broadening cliffs are eroded. If, however, the arid region through which the river flows is low, aggrading will take place.

Between the two extremes just cited, many intermediate phases may be discovered, dependent mainly on the height of the land above the sea. When the topography of the region through which flow such tall drainage trees, as we may venture to call them, is more carefully studied, the influence of many secondary conditions such as rock texture, character of the infrequent storms, nature of the vegetation, etc., will furnish interesting subjects for investigation.

Variation in Temperature.—If we dissect out, as it were, the effects of secular variations of temperature on the development of streams, from other climatic conditions, we find that an increase of temperature promotes evaporation and thus decreases the volume of streams; a gradual lowering of the mean annual temperature for a series of decades, or centuries, will favour an increase in the volume of streams. But secular variations in temperature mean a profound change in other climatic conditions, and start a wave which is felt also throughout the organic kingdom in the region affected. The resultant changes in fauna and flora react on the inorganic kingdom, and notably on the volume, variations, and development of streams. An increase in mean annual temperature in many regions is followed by a greater luxuriance of the flora; while over other extensive areas, as, for example, in arid and desert countries, it means a decrease in the previously scanty vegetation. A reverse wave of solar energy means in general a decrease in the luxuriance in the flora of previously warm and humid regions and an increase in the vegetation of previously hot and arid regions; while cold, humid regions will become still more arctic and arboreal vegetation decline. Some of the influences of plant-life on the behaviour and growth of streams have already been noted and others will be considered.

The variation in temperature which most directly affects the streams is a change from temperate to arctic conditions. A lowering of the mean annual temperature in regions which previous to the change had a temperate or sub-arctic climate, means an increase in the length of the winters and a shortening of the summers. A progressive and cumulative change in this direction would be accompanied ordinarily by an increase in the winter's snow-fall and the preservation of the snow until late in the spring or even far into the summer, and when the accumulated snows finally yielded to the increasing temperature of the warm season, floods would result. While the ground was frozen and snow-covered, erosion would be nil, the streams clear and ice-bound, and all the varied processes of corrasion and deposition greatly retarded. With the breaking of the river ice when warm rains melted the snow, the increased volume of the streams, a generous supply of debris loosened by the winter's frost, and yet other conditions would favour stream work. In many ways, therefore, a moderate or at least not excessive lowering of the mean annual temperature, especially in previously temperate and sub-arctic regions, would be accompanied by increased activity in stream development. A more excessive refrigeration would lead to the accumulation of perennial snow and the formation of glaciers.

Fluctuations of Streams.—The amount of water flowing through most stream channels is subject to many fluctuations. The most constant streams are such as are fed by large springs or by the overflow of broad lakes, for the reason that, in instances of this nature, the water comes from reservoirs of such size as not to be materially influenced by sudden rains or by ordinary droughts. The subterranean reservoirs referred to as supplying springs are not usually definite water-bodies like the lakes in caverns, but masses of porous soil and rock which became saturated by percolation.

It is to be noted, however, that streams flowing from large lakes do experience some variation in volume, as when a strong wind blowing over a lake causes its waters to rise on the side towards which the wind blows; when this side is the one from which the water escapes, a sudden rise is experienced in the draining stream. A reverse direction of the wind would cause a diminution in the volume of the outflowing water. There are also other atmospheric changes, such as those producing sudden variations in the level of lake water, known as *seiches*, which at times have a temporary influence on the volume of streams flowing from lakes.

The principal influences which cause streams to vary in volume, although diverse and frequently complex, may be provisionally classified in three groups, namely, seasonal changes of climate, weather changes, and the breaking of dams. There are, besides, and perhaps most important of all, secular climatic changes, like those that accompanied the Glacial epoch, to which the greatest variations in the histories of streams are due, but these are beyond our immediate dreams.

Of the changes in climatic conditions accompanying the orderly march of the season, those producing alternate wet and dry periods have the most direct and conspicuous influence on the volume of the streams. This, however, is a matter of every-day knowledge, and need claim but little space at this time.

Throughout nearly the whole of North America, the rainy season is also the cold season; the ground is frequently frozen, thus checking percolation, and the country over large areas is snow-covered. When a thaw occurs, the water formed by the melting of the snow, increased perhaps by a copious rain-fall, flows quickly over the frozen soil and causes floods in the valleys.

At times when the ground is not frozen, a portion of the surface water flows directly to the stream, while another, and frequently the larger portion, sinks below the surface and percolates slowly away. Under these conditions, there are commonly two well-marked periods of rise in the adjacent streams ; the first and quickest rise following the inrush of surface run-off, and the second usually involving a greater volume of water, caused by the sub-surface water percolating out from the sides of valleys and flowing from springs. There is marked difference between these two floods referred to in various regions, dependent on the permeability of the soil and of the rock immediately beneath. When the material composing the hills and valley sides is deep and porous, the first rise is small, unless the rain-fall is remarkably heavy, and quickly subsides, while the slower rise which follows is of longer duration and of much greater volume. In regions with an impervious covering, such as clay, the first rise of the stream, after a heavy rain-fall, is marked both by its suddenness and by the large volume of the run-off. The second rise may then be slight, or even not recognisable.

Each of the two conditions of soil referred to is accompanied by characteristic topographic forms. In regions covered by impervious soil, as in the case of very large areas in the South Atlantic States where residual clays predominate, the land is everywhere trenched by stream channels, which ensure a quick escape for surface water. On the other hand, where deep, porous soils occur, as in much of the formerly glaciated region of the United States, the surface waters are quickly absorbed, and percolate slowly away, leaving broad areas between the large stream-cut valleys without rill marks.

Floods in streams are caused by seasonal changes in rainfall and also by the melting of the snow on high mountains. In early summer, for example, when the snow is melting on the Rocky Mountains, the Missouri and the lower Mississippi undergo what is known as the June rise. Rain-fall floods follow excessive rains and may occur in a part or the whole of a river system. When the swollen tributaries of a trunk stream deliver their waters to the main channel at the same time, great floods occur below where the branches unite. This class of floods can be readily predicted when a sufficient number of weather records and of gauge readings in the principal tributaries are available. Valuable work in this connection is being done by the United States Weather Bureau. The floods of the Ohio are of this character, but the highest rises are augmented by the melting of winter snow. The highest waters occur usually in February, when a height of over fifty feet above the summer stage frequently occurs.

The waters of streams are in many cases held in check by glacial dams, ice-gorges, accumulations of drift-wood, land-slides, avalanches, etc., until the breaking of the obstruction permits of the emptying of the reservoirs above them, and floods sometimes accompanied by great loss of life and destruction of property occur in the valleys below. Floods of

this character can seldom be predicted for any considerable time in advance, and to this fact is due much of the
destruction wrought by them.

Inundations of portions of valleys and flood-plains, not
usually in danger during annual high-water stages of the
streams flowing through them, occur when the necks of
land left by the migration of streams are cut through and a
new channel is rendered available. The aggrading of stream
channels on alluvial cones and deltas leads to similar results.
The clogging of stream channels, owing to abundant deposition, also causes them to overflow their banks, especially
during the annual high-water stages.

River floods are now being systematically studied in the
regions occupied by the more civilised nations, and most
valuable results may be expected from these scientific in-
vestigations, particularly in the direction of predicting when
floods are to be expected, thus allowing opportunities
to counteract their destructive effects, and to utilise the
inundation of farm lands so as to enrich them by the
silt thrown down. Much of the richest land in the world
is situated on the flood-plains of great rivers. These
plains owe their origin, as has been already explained,
to the deposits made during high-water stages of the
streams. In general, it seems better for man to adapt
his industries to these natural conditions and endeavour to
utilise the floods to enrich his land, rather than to build
levees for the purpose of preventing inundations. This
branch of river study falls properly in the field of the engineer, and is too technical to be treated at length at this
time.

SOME OF THE INFLUENCES OF GLACIERS ON STREAM
DEVELOPMENT

The origin, growth, and retreat of glaciers in a region previously occupied by streams have a varied influence on their
lives. In the case of alpine glaciers originating about
isolated peaks or on the summits of mountain ranges, the
previously excavated stream-valleys become avenues of ice-
drainage, and in the more elevated portions of such valleys
all stream work is stopped. Subglacial streams originate
which are heavily charged with silt, and, judging from
existing examples, would be in a condition to abrade the
rocks over which they flowed. The streams below the ends
of the glaciers, and supplied by their melting, would be
swollen in summer and greatly diminished in volume in
winter. Their efficiency as transporting and corrading
agencies would thus be increased beyond the power they
would have if the water supplied to them was delivered with
more uniformity. But the chief effect of such a change as
has just been postulated, as is shown by the study of existing glaciers, would, in general, be the overloading of the
streams below where the drainage changed from a solid to a
liquid form. Alpine glaciers normally deliver to their drainage streams more debris than the latter are able to transport,
and aggrading begins at their very sources unless the stream
channels are remarkably precipitous. Many valleys at the
present day, which are occupied by glaciers of the alpine
type in their upper courses, are deeply filled with debris all
the way from the lower extremities of the glaciers to the
lake or sea into which they discharge. Broad flood-plains,

bifurcating streams, and valley sides without terraces are •
some of the more striking features of valleys which have
experienced such changes.

The modifications in the behaviour of streams flowing
from an isolated peak or mountain range on which glaciers
have been developed at the heads of previously excavated
stream-valleys, are similar to the changes in the lives of
streams draining a region where a continental glacier
originates and expands.

As a continental glacier advances and occupies a previously well-drained region, the streams are obliterated over
most of the area that becomes occupied by the ice. Near
the outer border of the ice-sheet, however, and perhaps for
scores of miles back from the margin and beneath the ice,
preglacial streams may continue to flow or new subglacial
streams originate. The gradients of these streams will not
be high, and, judging from the subglacial stream recorders
in regions occupied by Pleistocene glaciers, will be overloaded and consequently forced to drop debris and raise the
beds of their channels. When the streams leave the ice and
expand and bifurcate, as usually happens, their velocities
will be still further decreased and still more of their loads
deposited. Flood-plains and alluvial cones merging into
sand and gravel plains will be the more striking results of
such conditions When the streams leave their tunnels in
the ice, aggrading may be so active that their beds will be
raised and a check imposed upon the flow of their waters
through the tunnels from which they bring their loads of
debris, thus necessitating the raising of the bottoms of the
tunnels and their enlargement above by melting the ice.

*   This process, by which ridges of gravel and sand, or *osars*, are formed beneath ice-sheets both of the continental and piedmont types, has been considered, to some extent, in a former chapter, and at greater length in a previously published volume by the present writer.[1]

When a continental glacier wastes away and its outer border retreats, the zone of marginal deposition recedes also, and will be followed in turn by conditions which favour corrasion, and the previously formed flood-plains, etc., will have channels and valleys cut through them.

The considerations just presented are necessarily of the nature of an outline sketch, but I trust furnish sufficient suggestions to enable the reader to fill in the details in the case of any special field that may come under his notice.

SOME OF THE INFLUENCES OF VEGETATION ON STREAM
DEVELOPMENT

In a region bare of all vegetation and where the surface is inclined, the rain-water gathers quickly into rills and rivulets which at once begin to excavate channels. When the ground is grass-covered, it is protected from the impact of the falling drops, and the plant roots bind the soil together so as to greatly retard its removal. If shrubs and trees rise above a grass-covered surface, still greater protection is afforded. The tendency of vegetation is thus to shield the land and allow surface water to be absorbed by the soil and percolate quietly away, thus robbing it of the power to cor-

---

[1] I. C. Russell, *Glaciers of North America*, pp. 28, 29, 123-125. Ginn & Co., 1897. The name *osar* was adopted in this volume in place of *eskar*, *kame*, or *ôsar*, in conformity with American usage.

rade. This is illustrated especially in humid regions where ploughed fields are adjacent to meadows, pastures, and woodlands. Ploughed fields, if neglected for a few years, will become channelled by stream courses, and immature drainage systems developed where the slopes are favourable, while adjacent fields covered with grass and other plants are not visibly affected. The abandoned fields of Virginia and the more southern Atlantic States, cut by thousands of gullies, furnish sad testimony of the disasters which follow the breaking of the soil in regions where the waters are retained at the surface and gather into rills instead of percolating slowly away. If the soil and subsoil are deep and porous, however, the fields may not be seriously affected by the breaking of the soil.

While vegetation retards mechanical corrasion, it favours the chemical action of percolating waters by supplying them with organic acids, as has already been explained, and hastens chemical corrasion.

Vegetation has an effect on streams also, from the fact that it promotes evaporation and retards the gathering of surface waters in channels. Evaporation is favoured by the retention of the water, and yet still more efficiently through the vital functions of the plants themselves. Water is taken in by the rootlets and escapes from the leaves. The amount of water returned to the atmosphere in this manner from areas clothed with luxuriant vegetation is surprisingly great. It has been stated that to grow a ton of hay the grass plants must drink in two to three hundred tons of water.[1]

[1] J. W. Powell, *National Geographic Monographs*, vol. i., p. 69, published by the American Book Co., New York, 1895.

The *run-off*, as the escape of rain-water by surface streams is termed, in plant-covered regions is retarded and the volume of the draining streams rendered more uniform than it would be should the vegetation be removed. The work of streams is thus checked in two conspicuous ways by vegetation: first, by the decrease in surface waters due to evaporation, and second, by diminishing floods.

When a mat of vegetation mantles the ground, as especially when broad areas are deeply moss-covered, as in much of Alaska and about the shores of Puget Sound, the surface waters are filtered of practically all material in suspension and gather into rills which are clear, although frequently amber-coloured on account of organic matter in solution, and hence have but slight powers to abrade the rocks over which they flow.

The influence of the roots of trees, and particularly of willows, alders, cottonwoods, etc., which flourish along the margins of streams, on erosion of the banks is well known. Such vegetation assists particularly in retaining the sediment of streams when they expand and flood the adjacent land, thus assisting materially in the formation of natural levees.

The evil effects of removing the forests from a mountainous region are seen especially in the quicker and greater run-off of the waters falling on it. This is accompanied by more rapid erosion in the upper courses of the stream and aggrading in the valleys lower down. Flood-plains are thus raised where the gradients of the streams decrease, and previously fruitful areas along the borders of the rivers may be converted into barren tracts of gravel and sand, which remain for a long time unavailable for agriculture.

PLATE XII.

FIG. A.   Beaver Dam, Wyoming.

(Photograph by W. H. Jackson.)

FIG. B.   Dam of Drift-Wood, Teanaway River, Washington.

The influence of vegetation on stream development, as shown even by this hasty and incomplete review, is highly complex. In fact the influences of vegetation counteract each other, as when dense plant growth and a layer of decaying leaves and branches retard mechanical corrasion, but by supplying organic acids to percolating waters, promote chemical corrasion.

In forest-covered regions, especially where the ground is encumbered with undergrowths, or where mosses and lichens form a thick mantle, the run-off is retarded and stream development delayed. When the land is grass-covered, as in prairie regions, where in general the rain-fall is moderate, erosion is checked. In many instances, no mechanical erosion occurs in prairie regions, because all the water that falls is absorbed by the deep porous soil and evaporated largely through the agency of plants, or percolates slowly away.

In regions imperfectly clothed with desert shrubs, and where the bunch-grass common to such localities does not form a sod, as in the thousands of sage-brush valleys of the arid regions of North America, the scanty rain-fall is apt to come in the form of violent storms and copious downpours. The water being unchecked by vegetation gathers quickly into streams wherever the surface slope is favourable, and rushes along bearing with it heavy loads of debris. Between the infrequent storms the stream channels become clogged with debris swept in by the wind or slowly creeping down their sides under the influence of changes of temperature and other agencies. When the next " cloud-burst " comes, perhaps after the lapse of scores of years, the accumulated debris is again swept onward.

The conditions most favourable for general mechanical degradation and stream corrasion and deposition, so far as vegetation is concerned, are when land is bare or but scantily clothed with plants of any kind. If, in addition, the annual rain-fall is spasmodic, instead of the same amount of water falling on a given area being evenly distributed throughout the year, exceedingly favourable conditions for the development of streams result, providing the requisite slopes are present.

These conditions are more nearly fulfilled in the arid, south-west portion of the United States than in any other part of North America, and it is there that the labours of Newberry, Powell, Gilbert, Dutton, and others have been fruitful in such great results in the way of interpreting the origin of topographic forms.

Drift-Wood.—In considering the mechanical work of streams from either an engineering or a purely geographical point of view, account needs to be taken of the influence of the drift-wood carried by them. In many instances, the amount of floating timber and of trees lodged against the bottom and sides of a stream is so great as seriously to impede navigation, and not infrequently to render it impossible. Drift-wood, also, in one way or another, both assists and retards erosion, and by diverting streams from their channels leads to important geographical changes.

As is well known, streams flowing through forested regions receive great numbers of trees which fall into them principally on account of the undercutting and consequent caving of their banks. Fallen trees are swept into streams during floods, and when ice-gorges occur great destruction of timber sometimes results. In ascending such rivers as the Mississippi or the Yukon, one frequently sees whole trees, with branches and roots attached, floating with the current. In many such instances, the branches or roots drag on the bottom and disturb the mud or sand, and thus aid in the transportation of rock debris. At times the drifting trees become water-logged, and sink to the bottom in such a manner as to become anchored at one end, and being swayed by the current again assist corrasion by causing eddies in the water, as well as by the direct agitation of the material in which their roots or branches are embedded.

Drift-wood carried by swift streams, and especially during floods, tends to leave the belt of most rapid flow and accumulate along the banks, thus greatly increasing the chances of its becoming lodged. Trees that have fallen from the bank of a stream, but are yet held by their roots, cause obstructions and retard the progress of floating timber. In these and still other ways the trees which fall into streams have a conservative influence and tend to retard lateral corrasion.

The conservative tendencies of drift-wood are also seen on lake and ocean shores where it is thrown on the beach, and, becoming partially or wholly buried in sand and mud, serves to bind the shore accumulations together and counteract the force of the waves. The protection afforded by stranded drift-wood is especially well illustrated on the borders of the Laurentian lakes, and on the beaches of Puget Sound. At each of these localities one may frequently walk for several miles by stepping from one stranded log to another. In each of the instances referred to, however, the natural

16

accumulation of drift-wood is augmented by the waste from saw-mills.

The process by which the beaches of lakes, sounds, etc., are protected by stranded timber is in action also along river banks, but the ability of the currents in removing such obstructions is then usually more pronounced.

The conservative influence of drift-wood on river banks is well shown at numerous localities along the Yukon, more especially where the river divides so as to enclose islands. Where small branches of the river, or bayous, leave the main stream, as has already been mentioned, there are frequently large accumulations of stranded drift-wood. These " wood-yards " are in numerous instances several acres in area, and from fifteen to twenty or more feet deep. In many localities, as has been observed by the writer, the entrances to bayous have been completely closed by these accumulations, the interstices between the logs and broken branches being clogged with mud and sand, so that practically no water enters the side channels except when the river is in flood. When the up-stream ends of the bayous are dammed in this manner, their down-stream extremities become silted up and they are transformed into lakelets. The accumulation of drift-wood thus tends to confine the river to its main channel and retard lateral corrasion.

In mountainous regions where forests thrive, the streams are sometimes completely dammed by accumulations of drift-wood and forced to excavate new channels. These dams are usually started by the falling of a large tree across a stream, which holds drift-wood brought from above. In this way a skeleton dam, as it were, is formed, but the openings are apt to become clogged with smaller branches and leaves, and then more or less completely filled with sand and mud. Several instances of this nature have come under the writer's notice in the Cascade Mountains. The middle fork of Teanaway River, Washington, for example, in several localities has been completely turned from a former course by dams of the nature just described, and caused to excavate a new channel. A view of one of these natural log-dams is presented on Plate XII. In this instance, a former channel has been filled with drift-wood to a depth of about twenty feet for a distance of some three hundred yards and the stream completely diverted. At the upper end of the obstruction, sand and gravel have been deposited against the drift-wood to the depth of several feet, and now form the bank of the stream where it leaves its former course.

The most remarkable example of the influence of accumulations of drift-wood on the behaviour of streams yet reported in North America is probably furnished by the timber rafts, as they are termed, in Red River, Louisiana. These rafts are several square miles in area, and have been in existence so long that soil has formed on them in which trees have taken root and flourished so as to produce a floating forest. It is stated by Humphreys and Abbot [1] that these rafts contain an immense accumulation of tree-trunks, some floating, and others so water-logged as to sink and thus still more effectually to block the channel. From the rotting of the logs at the lower ends of the rafts and fresh accumulations at their upper ends, they are gradually migrating up stream. These obstructions tend to pond the

[1] *Report on the Mississippi River*, 1861, p. 37.

river and cause it to form lake-like expansions, which some-times discharge through new outlets. The influence of the rafts on Red River is much the same as in the smaller instance noted above in the case of Teanaway River, and illustrates the disturbances which the streams of forested regions frequently experience.

SUPERIMPOSED STREAMS

The reader is already aware that a consequent stream follows a predetermined course inherited from pre-existing surface conditions, and is at first not influenced by the structure of the rocks beneath the surface. It also happens that a stream may have its course determined by rocks that existed above the surface now exposed, but which have been removed, and may simulate a consequent stream.

If we imagine an ice-sheet to have covered a region of mild relief, and that streams flowing over the surface of the ice were slowly lowered upon the land beneath as the ice melted, they might entrench themselves in the rocks so as to hold their former courses after the ice entirely disappeared. The streams might have their direction of flow determined to some extent by the surface features of the land uncovered by the melting of the ice, but they would be uninfluenced by the structure of the rocks underlying the exposed surface.

Not only glaciers, however, but geological formations are removed from the superficial portions of large areas.

To present another hypothetical case: imagine a region of folded and faulted rocks to have been worn down to a peneplain and then submerged beneath the ocean and covered with a horizontal sheet of sediment. Should such an area be again upraised, consequent streams would be developed on its surface and begin an orderly sequence of changes as they advanced with the task of again reducing the land to baselevel. If the buried peneplain was above the new baselevel, the master streams would cut through the covering, presumably of soft rocks, resting on the old peneplain and sink their channels into it. Should the covering of soft rock be now removed, the streams would flow across the uncovered region in courses determined by the surface slope of the cover on which they originated, and without reference to the surface features of the exposed plain or to the structure of the rocks beneath it. A drainage system inherited in this manner by one geological terrane from another is said to be *superimposed*.

Such a history as has just been outlined furnishes an explanation of the geography of certain regions which cannot be satisfactorily accounted for in any other way.

In east-central New Jersey we have a coastal plain some twenty-five to thirty miles broad. Rising from this plain there are long, narrow ridges of hard igneous rock, such as the double ridge known as the Watchung Mountains, the Palisades of the Hudson, and several other smaller hills and ridges of the same general character. These ridges have remarkably even crest-lines, but are notched in places by water-gaps and wind-gaps. As has been admirably worked out by Davis and Wood,[1] the tops of these ridges are por-

---

[1] W. M. Davis and J. Walter Wood, " The Geographical Development of Northern New Jersey," in *Boston Society of Natural History, Proceedings,* vol. xxiv., pp. 365–423, 1889.

tions of an ancient peneplain which has been upraised somewhat irregularly, and eroded so as to leave the edges of the
sheets of hard rock which traverse it in bold relief. Previous
to the upraising of the peneplain it was depressed beneath
the sea and soft sedimentary beds spread over it, which
reached nearly if not completely across the central part
of the State. The peneplain with its cover of soft rock
was then raised and a system of consequent streams came
into existence. The streams cut through in the soft surface beds, were lowered to the concealed peneplain beneath, and continued to deepen their channels. The
streams flowed across the edges of the hard beds and carved
notches in them. When the soft surface-sheet was finally
removed and the formerly buried peneplain exposed, some
of the streams maintained their courses and still flowed
through water-gaps in the ridges, while others, by the system
of adjustment to rock structure discussed on a previous
page, were diverted to easier courses, leaving notches, or
wind-gaps.

The process by which streams are inherited by one series
of rocks from a higher series, is simulated in some of its
features by a reverse process. When the roof of a cavern
crumbles and falls in, a subterranean avenue of drainage
becomes an open channel, and the stream flowing through
it becomes a surface stream. Such a stream is an inheritance from a lower series of rocks by a higher series. If a
name were desired for this minor feature of the drainage of
certain regions, it might be termed *subimposed*. I believe,
however, that the nomenclature of geography should grow
slowly and spontaneously and not be forced.

MIGRATION OF DIVIDES

When the feeding rivulets of two rivers flow in opposite directions from the crest of a mountain range, the line separating them is termed a water-parting, or, more briefly, a *divide*. In general, then, a divide is the common boundary between two adjacent drainage systems. In the Rocky Mountain region we have the " continental divide," which parts the waters flowing to the Atlantic and Pacific respectively.

A divide, however, is not necessarily a mountain range, but may be a plateau or a plain. Neither is it a sharply defined line, but may be a broad surface and the actual water-parting indefinite. For example, a portion of the divide between the waters flowing to Red River and thence to Lake Winnipeg and Hudson Bay, and those finding their way to the Mississippi, is in a region of mild relief and is not only broad but varies with seasonal changes. During certain seasons when the streams are swollen, there is no true divide, the valley being flooded in such a manner that steamboats may pass from the Mississippi to the Red River, or in the reverse direction. Thus, at times, direct river navigation is possible from the Gulf of Mexico to Hudson Bay.

The divides between adjacent drainage slopes and the ridges between neighbouring streams belonging to the same river system, although geographically of great importance and among the most persistent features in the topography of the land—since corrasion along them is reduced to a minimum,—are yet, like all other elements in a landscape, subject to change.

The laws governing the migration of divides have already been briefly considered in discussing river piracy, but their importance is sufficient excuse for some repetition. The slopes on the opposite sides of a divide, it is safe to say, are never the same. The streams descending the steeper side will have the greater velocity and will tend to deepen their channels and to extend their branches by backward cutting more rapidly than their rivals flowing down more gentle slopes, and hence cause what is termed a migration of the divide. If other conditions are the same, but the streams flowing in one direction from a divide have a shorter course to the sea than their opposite neighbours, the task before them, in order to cut down their channels to baselevel, will be less, and consequently sooner accomplished. Hence, as the work of the opposite-flowing stream progresses, the divide between them will be shifted toward the one that works more slowly. The area drained by the shorter stream will be enlarged at the expense of its less active neighbour. Again, if the rocks on one side of a divide are softer, or more easily dissolved than those on the opposite side, other conditions being the same, the streams flowing over the softer rock will evidently progress with their task more rapidly than those having to cut down their channels in more resistant material, and hence will be enabled to extend their head branches more rapidly than their opponents and capture new territory. In other words, the divide will be shifted toward the side where the hard rocks occur.

Should the rain-fall on one side of a divide be heavier than on the opposite side, the streams on the rainy side will be larger than on the other side, and, in general, will lower their channels more rapidly than their weaker opponents. Should inequality in precipitation be the controlling condition, manifestly the divide would migrate toward the side having the smaller rain-fall. Yet another condition which might cause the migration of a divide, if not controlled by other circumstances, is the structure of the rocks forming the water-parting. If the rocks are in layers and gently inclined toward one drainage slope, as is frequently the case in ridges due to faulting, the streams descending the longer slope will have to remove more rock in order to reach base-level than the swifter streams flowing over the broken edges of the strata exposed in the steeper side of the ridge. In nature, also, the conditions just postulated are usually coupled with others which favour the more rapid cutting of the edges of the inclined beds. The declivity of a ridge formed of inclined beds is usually steeper on the side in which the edges of the strata are exposed; the streams on that side are thus given a steeper grade and flow more swiftly than their opponents, thus favouring more rapid corrasion. If alternating hard and soft beds occur, this again favours the work of the streams flowing over their broken edges, by allowing them to remove the exposed portions of the soft layers, thus undermining the more resistant beds and favouring their removal by sapping.

The Sierra Nevada is, in the main, a great monoclinal ridge of the character just described. The strata dip westward and form a long and comparatively gentle slope on that side, but present a bold escarpment formed of the broken edges of the strata upraised along a belt of faulting to the eastward. The streams flowing westward are larger than those descending the steep eastern slope for the reason that they drain greater areas, and also because the rain-fall on the western is more abundant than on the eastern slope. But in spite of these advantages the eastward-flowing streams, having steeper gradients, and far less rock to remove in order to cut to the same depth, have been enabled to extend their head-waters by backward corrasion so as to cut through what was formerly the divide at the crest of the range and acquire territory on the western slope. The water-parting is now west of the topographic crest-line of the mountain and is still migrating westward. The existence of large glaciers on the higher portions of the range, at a comparatively recent date, interfered with stream development, but did not change the conditions so far as the westward migration of the divide between the Pacific and Great Basin drainage is concerned.

It does not seem necessary to present other arguments in order to establish the law that when a ridge dividing two drainage systems is composed of inclined beds which slope in one direction from its longer axis, other conditions being the same, the divide will migrate, as erosion progresses, with the slope of the beds.

The outline presented in the last few pages of the laws governing the migration of divides, although brief, is sufficient to show that the conditions entering into the problem are complex. This complexity is still further enhanced when the influence of movements in the earth's crust are also brought into play. Although, as previously stated,

PLATE XIII.

Contour Map of a Portion of the Catskill Mountains, N. Y., Illustrating River Piracy.
(After N. H. Darton. Topography by U. S. Geological Survey.)

Approximate scale: 1 inch = 7000 feet. Contour Interval, 20 feet.

divides are among the most stable of the geographical features of the land, they are continually changing. This shifting of the position of the lines of parting between opposing drainage slopes is usually exceedingly slow, but under certain conditions may be a comparatively rapid process, as will be seen by reverting to the discussion of the origin of subsequent streams, and the manner in which they extend their channel by headward cutting so as to capture rival streams and divert their waters. This process leads to great and even rapid changes in the positions of divides.

Another illustration of the migration of a divide may be of interest to the reader. In the Catskill Mountains we have a table-land sloping gently westward, but presenting a bold escarpment about one thousand five hundred feet high, facing the Hudson. A portion of this plateau and its eastward-facing escarpment is shown on the map forming Plate XIII. The rocks forming the plateau are sedimentary beds of hard sandstone and soft shale, which dip gently westward and present their broken edges in the escarpment. As has been shown by Darton,[1] the regularity of the precipitous eastern border of the plateau was broken by alcoves and recesses, inherited from a preceding geographical cycle, and in these embayments eastward-flowing streams originated. Of these the Kaaters Kill and Plaaters Kill are the best examples. Streams also came into existence on the gentle western slope of the plateau and flowed westward ; the head

---

[1] N. H. Darton, "Examples of Stream-Robbing in the Catskill Mountains," in *Bulletin of the Geological Society of America*, vol. vii., pp. 505–507, Plate xxiii., 1896.

branches of one of these, Schoharie Creek, are shown on the accompanying map. The conditions are thus especially favourable for the processes of stream capture and the migration of a divide, already described.

It is evident from an inspection of the map, that the branches of Schoharie Creek were formerly longer than now, and carried away the surplus water from the plateau even to the edge of its eastern escarpment, but the Kaaters Kill and Plaaters Kill have been enabled to extend their head branches so as to capture a considerable portion of the previous western drainage. The divide has migrated westward, and some of the former branches of Schoharie Creek have been diverted. This history is brought out so graphically on the accompanying map that further explanation seems unnecessary.

One result of the process just considered is shown by the direction of flow of the higher branches of the capturing streams. Normally the branches of a stream join the main trunk at an acute angle, the flow in the branch and in the trunk near their place of union being in the same general direction. But in the case of the capturing streams instanced above, their head branches come in at more than a right angle; the captured branches maintain the direction they had when flowing to Schoharie Creek, and in general flow westward, while the trunk streams to which they are now tributary flow eastward. Such an abnormal arrangement of the branches of a drainage tree in any region should at once suggest that a recent capture has been made, but yet rock texture and other conditions might produce a similar result.

The process of stream capture, so admirably illustrated in the Catskills, furnishes an example of one method by which fishes, mollusks, etc., might be enabled to migrate from one side of a mountain range to the other. The opening of gaps in the crest of a high ridge or mountain range would also facilitate the distribution of plants and animals not dependent directly on streams for their means of travel. Important influences even on the migration of peoples may be traced to the same cause.[1]

[1] Books of reference:

HUMPHREYS and ABBOT. *Physics and Hydraulics of the Mississippi.* War Department, Washington, D. C., 1861.

THOMAS RUSSELL. *Meteorology.* Macmillan & Co., 1895. (Chapters IX., " Rivers and Floods," and X., " River-Stage Predictions.")

PARK MORRILL. *Floods of the Mississippi River.* Weather Bureau, Washington, D. C., 1897.

CHAPTER VIII

SOME OF THE CHARACTERISTICS OF AMERICAN RIVERS

THE many details that have occupied the reader's attention in the preceding chapter have perhaps diverted attention from certain general conclusions pertaining to the lives of streams. A brief review of the leading characteristics of a few of the rivers of America will possibly correct this tendency and at the same time afford an opportunity to apply some of the principles stated, perhaps too empirically, in what has gone before.

The initial slopes of large rivers must evidently be determined by the slope of the land due to upheaval. In many, and probably most, instances, however, the surface slopes that gave direction to the youthful streams have been deformed by movements in the rocks of the nature of a tilting of the land over broad areas; again, the rocks have been folded, or broken and one side of the fracture upraised above the opposite side, so as to affect the surface drainage. While these changes were in progress in many instances, the streams have maintained their positions or right of way by deepening their channels as fast as the rocks were raised, or by filling in the depressions due to subsidence; but in other instances the streams have been reversed or given other directions, owing to the modifications in conditions referred to. The present courses of even the larger rivers do not, therefore, in themselves, necessarily record the original slope of the land.

Throughout the lives of streams they have the power of extending their branches in a manner analogous to the growth of a tree by the lengthening of its terminal twigs. This process, as we have seen, leads to rivalry between neighbouring streams, and the shifting or migration of the boundary line between adjacent drainage areas. Climatic changes may also favour the extension of certain drainage areas and the diminution of others. For these and still other reasons, the boundaries of the original slopes which gave the large rivers their general directions have been greatly modified and in some instances rendered indeterminate; yet when the general changes that land areas pass through and the laws of stream development are known, much of the history of a river system can be deciphered.

Some of the modifications that have taken place in the various drainage areas of North America, due to changes in the elevation of the land, variation of climate, normal stream development, etc., can be recognised even in a general view of the present distribution of the streams. Individual rivers furnish too small a unit with which to measure the greater slopes produced in the surface of North America by upheaval, and a better idea of the character the surface of the continent would present, had there been no erosion, can be had by considering the main drainage areas. It must be remembered, however, that the upheavals which established the main divides occurred at widely separated intervals, and that in many instances, as in the Appalachians, the main rivers have been persistent through more than one geographical cycle.

DRAINAGE SLOPES

An examination of any fairly good map of North America will show that the continent is divided into nine principal drainage slopes. These may be conveniently named, as has been done on the map forming Plate XIV., after the water-bodies into which their rivers discharge. This classification is, in fact, arbitrary, and certain minor or but little-known regions, as the north-east coast of Labrador, much of the Arctic archipelago, Greenland, etc., are not included. The divisions chosen, largely for the purpose of dissecting a vast region into its component parts for convenience of study, are described below. These descriptions are brief, and intended simply to supplement the accompanying map.

Atlantic Drainage Slope.—This includes the land from Florida to Nova Scotia which drains to the Atlantic. The principal rivers are the Alabama, Savannah, Roanoke, James, Potomac, Susquehanna, Delaware, Hudson, Connecticut, Merrimac, and St. John.

St. Lawrence Drainage Slope.—The region draining to the Great Lakes and Lake Champlain, or directly to the St. Lawrence and its tributaries, is here included.

Hudson Bay Drainage Slope.—This division comprises the vast forested area of low relief lying principally in Canada, and draining through many valleys to Hudson Bay.

Arctic Drainage Slope.—Comprising the region north of

PLATE XIV.

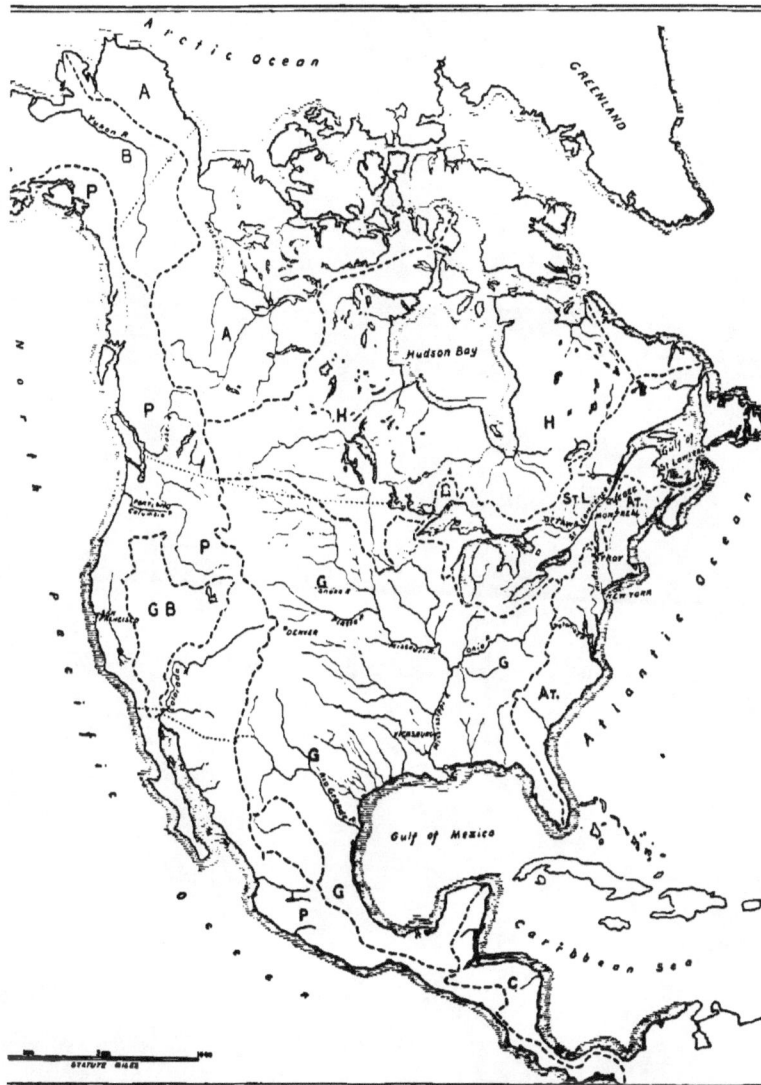

Outline Map of North America showing Drainage Slopes

A—Arctic Drainage Slope.
AT.—Atlantic Drainage Slope.
B—Bering Sea Drainage Slope.
C—Caribbean Sea Drainage Slope.

G—Gulf of Mexico Drainage Slope.
G B—Great Basin Drainage Slope.
H—Hudson Bay Drainage Slope.
P—Pacific Drainage Slope.

ST. L—St. Lawrence Drainage Slope.

the Hudson Bay drainage, several of the little-known Arctic islands, the basin of the Mackenzie, and northern Alaska.

Bering Drainage Slope.—Embracing the basins of the Yukon, Kuskoquim, and several subordinate rivers, which discharge into Bering Sea.

Pacific Drainage Slope.—The long and comparatively narrow belt of country, which discharges its drainage to the Pacific, might be subdivided under the general plan here followed, but this does not seem necessary here at present. All of the land from the Aleutian Islands to Panama, which sends its contributions of surplus waters to the Pacific, is here included. The principal rivers are the Copper, Stikine, Fraser, Columbia, Sacramento, and Colorado.

Great Basin Drainage.—The arid region embracing the eastern border of California, nearly all of Nevada, Southern Oregon, and a large part of Utah, which does not send any streams to the ocean, is here included. Similar but subordinate interior basins in Mexico are at present neglected.

Gulf Drainage Slope.—All of the land, including the vast hydrographic basin of the Mississippi, which is drained by streams flowing to the Gulf of Mexico, is here considered as a single drainage slope.

Caribbean Drainage Slope.—The region from Northern Yucatan to the junction of the Isthmus of Panama with the South American continent, from which streams flow to the Caribbean Sea, forms the most southern of the several drainage slopes here considered.

The above classification, as has been said, is in part arbitrary, but in its main features is believed to indicate condi-

17

tions which a geographer finds it convenient to have in mind.

The present extent and relationships of the drainage slopes noted above are in part due to the movements in the earth's crust, and to what may be termed the accidental inequalities of the original surface of the land, but not at a single period.   Each separate province has its own special history.   In part, also, the boundaries of the drainage slopes are dependent on present climatic conditions, as is seen in the Great Basin region.   Then, too, the character of the rocks, whether soft or hard, and the way in which the layers composing them are inclined, have had a directing influence on the migrations of the dividing lines between adjacent drainage areas.   To a marked extent, also, the boundary lines under consideration have been shifted by what is termed stream development, during which one stream extends its head-water branches so as to capture territory belonging to a neighbouring stream.   In several great regions in North America, the land has been worn down to a peneplain, and then upraised, thus making conspicuous changes in the balance of power among the streams of various drainage areas.   Again, the divides between the drainage slopes in the northern half of the continent have been modified by glacial action.   Still other complexities in the histories of the drainage slopes as we now find them will appear later.

A hasty glance at the great natural divisions of North America, as marked out by the directions of drainage, reveals the fact that the study we have undertaken is a portion of a long and still more highly complex history.   In treating such a broad subject as the nature, origin, and history of the streams of a continent, it is advisable to begin with individual streams, and to start, perhaps, with even their tiniest branches, and gradually expand our field of observation. Each of the drainage slopes enumerated has its main rivers fed by many branches. Each trunk stream and each individual branch, however small, is an active agency which is engaged in producing changes, and each trunk and branch of the many drainage systems is modified in its action by climatic, geological, and other conditions.

LEADING FEATURES OF THE SEVERAL DRAINAGE SLOPES

New England Rivers.—The Connecticut with its charming scenery, the historic Merrimac, the forest-bordered Kennebec, and many other streams in the northern portion of the Atlantic drainage slope flow through valleys sunken in a tilted peneplain. The general level to which the hills rise throughout the lower courses of these streams is itself a record of the work of rivers; for the land, during a geographic cycle long since closed, was cut away to near sea-level and then bodily upraised and tilted southward. The planation by the old streams was not complete, and the remnants of the uplands that were left rise as mountains above the general level of the plateau in which the modern rivers have entrenched themselves. The portions of the plateau surface which were once nearly smooth have been roughened by the excavation of valleys, leaving the spaces between the streams in relief.

The rivers meander through rich bottom-lands of their

own making. The borders of the valleys are frequently in steps or terraces rising one above another; each nearly flat-topped shelf furnishes sites for prosperous farms, thriving villages, or populous cities. The terraces on the sides of the present valleys are formed of gravel and sand, and show how deeply the still older valleys were filled and the progress that has been made in their re-excavation.

Not only have the valleys long and varied histories, but each roaring cascade and musical rapid, each shadowy pool and placid reach of the streams where the water loiters, and each graceful bend have a cause for their existence, and an instructive and even romantic story to tell.

A Drowned River.—The noble Hudson, in large part an arm of the sea, where the tides rise and fall, divides a mountain range. The early history of the river has not been fully traced, but apparently it had its course defined before the mountains were elevated athwart its course, and cut down its channel as fast as the land rose. Possibly it underwent a long process of adjustment to geological conditions, and experienced many vicissitudes due to changes of level, and has a far more complex history than the present features of its valley clearly indicate. At a late period it flowed far beyond the site of the great metropolis situated near its present junction with the sea, but a subsidence led to the submerging of its valley eighty miles eastward of Long Island, and transformed its upper course into an estuary as far as the city of Troy. The Hudson, in addition to its connection with American history and the wonderfully attractive scenes along its course, has a long and varied experience to relate.

Appalachian Rivers.—The Delaware, Susquehanna, Potomac, and James rise to the westward of the Appalachians and flow through the many separate ridges composing that wonderfully beautiful mountain system. They traverse the ridges in deep, narrow gorges, known as water-gaps, and enter wide-mouthed estuaries. Evidently the mountains did not exist at the time the courses of the rivers were established. The long ridges separating the picturesque and fruitful valleys in the Appalachian Mountains are level-topped, and rise in a large number of instances to the same general height. Fill the valleys to the level of the intervening uplands, and a plateau with an even surface would result. The restored plateau would slope south-eastward, and streams flowing down it would cross the tilted rock-layers composing it at right angles. The courses of the main streams, if once established on such a plane, would be maintained unless marked disturbances occurred, and would slowly deepen their channels and develop new branches. For tens of thousands of years the tireless streams would work at their task. The soft rocks would be removed with comparative ease, leaving the hard layer in bold relief. The result would be a deeply dissected plateau like that of eastern Pennsylvania or West Virginia. The filling in of this outline sketch of the origin of the bolder features so much admired by travellers over the Appalachian divisions of the Pennsylvania or the Baltimore and Ohio railroads, will give a picture of the geographical development of a large tract of rugged country embraced in the west-central portion of the Atlantic drainage slope.

The rivers flowing eastward from the Appalachians cross

a plateau composed of resistant rocks, and on its eastern border form cascades and rapids where they descend to the still lower coastal plain formed of incoherent strata. This line of cascades and rapids extends from near the Hudson to beyond the Savannah, and is frequently designated as the " fall line.'' To the west of this line the swift-flowing rivers are shallow, while to the eastward, owing in part to a subsidence of the land and the consequent drowning of their lower courses, their currents become sluggish and the water deep. These geographical conditions resulting from a long series of changes, have had a marked influence on both the savage and civilised inhabitants of the Atlantic slope. The fall line, before the arrival of Europeans, was the site of numerous Indian villages. White men coming to America in ships could ascend some of the rivers to the fall line, and there found the head of navigation. In order to penetrate farther inland a new start had to be made. At these same localities water power was discovered, and manufactories established. For these and other reasons the fall line became a line of cities. If we draw a line on a moderately small-scaled map of the Atlantic States, through the sites of Trenton, Philadelphia, Baltimore, Washington, Richmond, Weldon, Raleigh, and Augusta, it will mark out a belt of the earth's crust which has experienced repeated movements, and define with considerable accuracy the junction of the piedmont plateau with the coastal plain, and show the position of the fall line.

Rivers of Glaciated Lands.—Tens of thousands of streams in the northern part of the Atlantic drainage slope and in the region to the north and west are broken by cascades

PLATE XV.

FIG. A.   The Columbia Looking West from White Salmon, Washington.
(Photograph by J. H. Valentine.)

FIG. B.   The Hudson, from West Point, New York.
(Photograph by W. H. Rau.)
ILLUSTRATIONS OF DROWNED RIVER-VALLEYS.

and rapids and drain many thousands of lakes. These features, which add a crowning charm to northern landscapes, are almost entirely absent from the southern Appalachians and the Gulf drainage slope. Why this striking contrast ? Why should the streams from central Pennsylvania to Labrador plunge over precipices, or form foaming rapids, and the land they drain be studded with tarns, lakes, and great fresh-water seas; while the streams in an equally elevated and fully as picturesque region, but with different details, at the south, flow in evenly sloping channels except on their extreme head-waters, through a land that is completely drained and in which lakes similar to those at the north are absent ? The answer, thanks to Louis Agassiz and other students of glaciers, is that ice-sheets of vast extent gave a new surface to the land over the northern half of the continent, and to a great extent obliterated the valleys and stream channels made during a preceding period of mild climate and luxuriant vegetation.

Southern Rivers.—What charming pictures of placid rivers flowing between wooded and flower-bedecked banks, softened and partially obscured perhaps by morning mists, enrich the memories of those who have travelled in the Carolinas, Georgia, and Alabama! Whence the fascination of these sleepy streams, flowing through flat-bottomed valleys bordered by mildly roughened, plateau-like uplands ? What has subdued the broader features of the landscape in a region where every river bank reveals folded and contorted rocks, similar to those in the neighbouring mountains? The geographer sees evidence at every turn that mountains once existed, but that they have been removed. A cycle of geographical history has run its course, and a new cycle has been initiated at a comparatively recent date. The land, once rugged and mountainous, has been carved away, with the exception of certain island-like remnants or monadnocks, to a uniform level,—the horizon of the sea,—then moderately upraised and the surface of the gently tilted peneplain channelled by streams.

Alluvial Rivers.—In the low-lying regions bordering the Gulf of Mexico, the traveller finds sluggish rivers flowing through broad valleys which are flooded each springtime, or in early summer, when the snow melts on the mountains to the north and west. Every stream is margined by natural embankments or levees, which, when not modified by human agency, are built higher during each succeeding flood. With the raising of the levees the valley bottoms are inundated and a layer of fine rich soil deposited over them. Evidently the streams, instead of deepening their channels after the manner of the swift-flowing rivers of New England, are filling in previously formed depressions or making new lands along the Gulf coast. It is plain to be seen that the laying down and not the removal of material is in progress over vast areas, and that rich lands are being formed, on which rice and sugar-cane can be cultivated. No mountains or hills are in sight. The land is flat, without valleys, and except where fields have been cleared, is clothed with tangled vegetation. Cypress trees and white-trunked cottonwoods lean far over the yellow waters, their branches festooned with trailing vines and pendant lichens. Much that is interesting concerning the manner in which streams fill in their valleys during certain stages in their histories, and the way in which new areas are reclaimed from the sea, may here be studied. The process of stream excavation, most active where the land is high, the gradients steep, and the waters swift, here finds its complement where the land is low, the gradients gentle, and the waters sluggish. The rivers, although large, are unable to bear along the sediment delivered to them in their swifter upper courses, and it is laid aside in flood-plains and deltas to rest until the facilities for transportation are more favourable. The southern portion of the Gulf drainage slope furnishes abundant illustrations of the fact that an important part of the work of streams consists in depositing material and the aggrading or filling in of their channels and valleys. The streams of New England and of the Gulf region, although presenting marked contrasts, are not essentially different, but have reached different stages in their life histories, and have felt the influence of diverse modifying conditions.

The Mississippi.—Some of the characteristic features of the lower portion of this the greatest of all the rivers of North America have been included in the glance we have just given, which is all that space will allow, to the alluvial rivers of the Gulf coast. The great importance of the Mississippi as a highway of commerce and of civilisation, the vast agricultural interests of its basin, and the numerous illustrations of the behaviour of streams under widely contrasted conditions and in various stages of development furnished by it, tempt the student of American geography to visit its banks again and again, and to long to explore its entire extent with the searchlight of modern geographical methods.

The source of the central trunk of the Mississippi is in
Lake Itasca, but, as is well known, a great branch of the
drainage tree, the Missouri, far overtops the summit of its
central stem. To the geographer the true source of the
Mississippi is at the as-yet-unknown fountainhead of the
Missouri. The waters forming the Missouri are supplied in
part by the hot springs and wonderful geysers of the Yellow-
stone Park, and in part by snow banks and small glaciers in
the more elevated valleys and amphitheatres of the Rocky
Mountains, in Idaho and Montana. To a small extent the
waters of the great river come from Canadian territory.
The countless lakes of Minnesota and Wisconsin expand
like leaves on the terminal twigs of the central trunk. The
head-waters of the Ohio, the largest branch of the Mississippi which joins it from the east, rise on the western slope
of the Appalachian uplift in West Virginia and Pennsylvania. A small portion of south-western New York is also
included in the Ohio drainage basin. The distance in a
straight line from the head-waters of the Ohio north-westward to the source of the Missouri is over eighteen hundred
miles. From the mouth of the Mississippi along its general
course to the continental divide, which limits its drainage
basin on the north-west, is about twenty-five hundred miles,
but including all of the windings of the river, the actual
distance that the waters falling on the mountains of Montana have to travel in order to reach the sea, is more than
four thousand miles. The entire area drained by the
" Father of Waters " is about 1,240,000 square miles, or
nearly one-third of the United States, exclusive of Alaska.

Additional statistics concerning the Mississippi, taken

from the report of Humphreys and Abbot and from a recent
report on the floods of that river, published by the Weather
Bureau,[1] are here inserted:

Average annual precipitation over the entire basin. . . . . . .29.8 inches.
Annual discharge. . . . . .785,190,000,000 cubic yards
Ratio of rain-fall to discharge. . . . . .0.25.
Mean discharge per second. . . . . .75,000 cubic yards.

That the Mississippi was in existence previous to the
Glacial epoch is abundantly proven by the change that occurs in its valley when traced across the southern limit of
the ice invasion, which intersects its course between the
mouth of the Missouri and the Ohio. Southward of the
glacial boundary it flows through a broad valley bounded by
bluffs. The vast flood-plain, varying in width from five to
eighty miles, lies from three to five hundred feet below the
general level of the bordering uplands. The contour of
the hard-rock bottom of the valley is but imperfectly known,
but the records of wells and borings show that an ancient
valley has been filled with alluvium to a depth of at least
one or two hundred feet in its northern part and to an increasing depth southward. For about a thousand miles
northward from the mouth of the river no hard rock appears
in its bed, and cataracts are absent. The conspicuous bluffs
of light-coloured clay-like material termed loess, bordering
the flood-plain in many places, mark the borders of an inner
valley, excavated in the material which formerly occupied
the older and broader valley from side to side. The great
outer valley, eroded in large part through nearly horizontal
beds of limestone, is a record of the preglacial work of the

[1] Park Morrill, *Floods of the Mississippi.* Washington, 1897.

river; the inner valley, formed by the removal of soft incoherent loess and sand, is of postglacial origin.

North of the glacial boundary, the river, throughout much
of its course, flows through a comparatively narrow, steep-
sided valley, bordered by precipitous bluffs of hard rock,
and in places the waters rush in foaming rapids or plunge
over ledges of limestone. ·These narrow reaches have all
the characteristics of young streams. At other times the
valley broadens and its crumbling sides are crowned by
towers and pinnacles of rock which bear every indication
of long exposure to the air. These evidences of old age
occur in what is known as the driftless area of Wisconsin
and Minnesota, where an island-like area, measuring some
ten thousand square miles, existed in the former ice-sheets.

In some instances north of the glacial boundary, where
the river flows through a narrow, rock-cut valley, deeper and
broader channels adjacent to it but now filled with glacial
debris, show that the river was turned from its preglacial
course, when reborn after the ice invasion. In such instances, the greater size and depth of the old channels, in
comparison with their modern representatives, bear evidence
that the river, previous to the advent of the glaciers, had a
greater length of time in which to carry on its appointed
task, or else worked with greater energy than since the
glaciers vanished. Many considerations tend to establish
the former of these suggestions. The Mississippi was an
aged stream before the great climatic change which permitted of the extension of glaciers from the north into its
drainage basin.

The main channel of the Ohio belongs to the extensive

PLATE XVI.

FIG. A. An Aggraded Valley near Fort Wingate, New Mexico.
Illustrative of the filling of valleys in arid regions ; the cliffs are of Triassic sandstone.

FIG. B. Water-Gaps Cut by the Potomac through Two Ridges of Hard Rock,
near Harper's Ferry, W. Va.

The point of view is on the Shenandoah peneplain ; the Potomac flows through a steep-sided
trench about 225 feet deep, sunken in this peneplain. Loudoun Heights on the left and
Maryland Heights on the right in the background.

system of branching valleys formed by the sinking into the rocks of the preglacial Mississippi drainage, but its upper portion was deeply buried by ice during the height of the Glacial epoch. When the glaciers finally melted, the reborn streams found their channels blocked, and in many instances were turned from their former courses in the same manner as in the case of the streams of Wisconsin and Minnesota.

When the Laurentian glacier retreated to the northward of the height-of-land now dividing the streams which feed the Mississippi from those flowing to Hudson Bay and the Great Lakes, several lakes came into existence, which were retained on their northern margins by the face of the retreating glacier, and supplied southward-flowing streams. One of these glacier-dammed lakes, named in honour of Louis Agassiz, occupied what is now the valley of Red River and the Winnipeg basin, and supplied River Warren which flowed to the Mississippi. Another similar lake was found in the western part of the present drainage basin of Lake Superior, and had its outlet a few miles west of the site of the city of Duluth. Other lakes in this same category occupied the southern part of the basin of Lake Michigan, and the western part of the Erie basin; the former discharged into the Mississippi through the channel now being converted into a canal, just west of Chicago, and the latter flowed through the valley now occupied by the Wabash to the west of Fort Wayne, Indiana.

During the time the Winnipeg and Laurentian basins were sending their surplus waters southward to the Mississippi, not only was the run-off from the land probably greater than now on account of heavier rain-fall, but the vast snow- and ice-sheet which covered Canada was melting, and all the stream channels leading away from it were flooded. The volume of water contributed in these several ways and flowing through the Mississippi valley to the Gulf of Mexico must at all seasons have been far in excess of the greatest of the modern floods. It has been estimated by James E. Todd [1] that the Mississippi, during the geological springtime following the great winter known as the Glacial epoch, carried annually from eleven to twenty times the volume of water now reaching the Gulf of Mexico through the same channel in a single year. Whether the current of the river during this great flood stage was vastly increased or not, depends on the former elevation of the land. These are reasons for believing that the region occupied by ice was depressed several hundred feet below its present position, and that the gradient of the Mississippi was much less than at present. The expanded rivers then resembled a great sea in which the loess and other similar deposits now occupying the greater Mississippi valley were spread out.

The long preglacial history of the Mississippi, the many changes impressed by the glaciers directly on its tributaries from the Appalachians to the crest of the Rocky Mountains, and indirectly, owing to the vastly increased water-supply, on the character of the river all the way to the Gulf, make it a most instructive subject for study. An additional chapter in the life of the river is supplied by a modern submergence which allowed the sea to reach to the mouth of the Ohio, and of still later re-elevation. The ac-

[1] *Geological Survey of Missouri*, 1896, vol. x., p. 203.

cidents, as they have been termed, in the normal development of streams, due to climatic changes and to movements
in the earth's crust, thus find numerous and graphic
illustration in the Mississippi Valley. Until the entire
basin, however, has been examined as a unit, disregarding
political boundaries, even a satisfactory outline of its entire
geographical history cannot be written.

Another phase of the wonderful story of the Mississippi
deals with its influence on the early explorations of the in-
trepid emissaries of Spain and France, and the final con-
quests of its basin by the English, the vast agricultural
importance of its rich lands, and its value as an avenue of
commerce; but the influence of geographical history on
human events pertains more properly to the domain of the
historian, and cannot be treated even briefly at this time.

Canyon Rivers.—The Colorado River, rising in the mountains of Colorado, Wyoming, and Utah, and flowing through
a high and for the most part arid table-land, has carved in
the solid rocks the most magnificent canyon that has yet
been studied. The river, with its load of sand and mud,
has been able to deepen its channel more rapidly than its
bounding walls have been lowered by rain, rills, and other
destructive agencies. The result is a steep-walled trench of
such stupendous proportions that when its sides are seen
from below they appear to be towering mountain ranges.
The tributaries of the Colorado have also deepened their
channels at approximately the same rate as the main stream
has excavated its canyon. A great river with many
branches has thus been sunken into the rocks, to the depth,
over a vast area, of about one mile. Between the larger

streams there are flat-topped table-lands, remnants of the great plateau across which the Colorado flowed in its infancy. The plateau has been slowly elevated, while the sand-charged streams, acting like saws, have dissected it. Throughout a region tens of thousands of square miles in area, every stream is in the bottom of a profound gorge of its own making. The remnants of the plateau between the canyons are waterless and desert.

The Colorado throughout a large part of its course flows through a canyon that is from four to six thousand feet deep. The canyon walls are, for the most part, of horizontally bedded rocks of many tones and tints, and various degrees of hardness. Weathering has increased the variety of colours, and rendered them more brilliant than they are in the unchanged rocks. The rain and wind have sculptured the cliffs so as to give them the greatest imaginable variety of forms. The most vivid dream-pictures of gorgeous Oriental architecture fail to rival the temple- and cathedral-like forms, incrusted with harmoniously tinted decorations, which overshadow the Colorado for hundreds of miles.

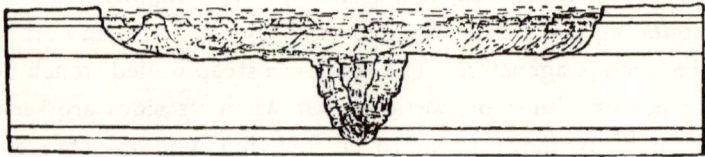

FIG. 23. Cross-Profile of the Canyon of the Colorado. (After W. H. Holmes.) Vertical and horizontal scale the same : one inch = 6375 feet.

There is nothing of the same class in the whole world, so far as is known, to compare either in extent and height, in richness of colour, or in variety and intricacy of detail with the canyon walls in the southern portion of the Pacific drainage slope. The canyon of the Colorado is not an even-sided canal, but a great valley some fifteen or more miles across. In the bottom of this greater canyon, as may be seen from the accompanying illustration, Plate XVII., reproduced from a drawing by W. H. Holmes, one of the few artists who are true to nature, is sunken a much narrower and deeper inner canyon. The reader will be able to read in this picture some of the leading events in the geographical history of the region of the Great Plateau. This outer canyon is clearly the record of a time when the land was some four thousand feet lower than now, and remained at that horizon for tens of thousands of years, while the river cut down its channel to baselevel and by lateral corrasion broadened its valley. The climate, at least near the close of this long period of uninterrupted work, was arid, as is shown by the precipitous character of the cliffs bordering the valley that was excavated. The river meandered in broad curves over the nearly level bottom of its valley, and when the land was again raised maintained its winding course, and owing to renewed energy, due to greater velocity on account of an increase in gradient, again began the task of corrading to baselevel. This new task imposed upon the river is not yet completed. The waters still flow swiftly, and vertical corrasion is still in excess of lateral wear and of weathering. The precipitous character of the cliffs bordering the inner gorge, and the details in their sculpture, indicate that the climate has had its present characteristics throughout the greater part, and probably the whole, of the time since the energy of the river was renewed.

18

The walls of the canyon of the Colorado are not even-surfaced precipices, but on either side of the river are buttressed by outstanding ridges and retaining walls, with many lateral branches.   Everywhere there are towers and pinnacles, as well as innumerable alcoves and recesses.   The main buttresses extend out for miles from the brink of the gorge and partially fill the profound chasm into which they descend.   From within the purple depth of the canyon rise wondrous temple-like forms as gorgeous in colour and as rich in fretwork and arabesque as a Moorish palace.   These shrines for Nature-worship, although minor features in the sublime panorama, tower as far above the shining stream flowing past their bases as the summit of Mount Washington rises above the sea.

As an illustration of the endless variety, both in form and colour, of architectural forms that Nature can sculpture from an upraised block of the earth's crust under certain conditions of climate and rock texture, the Colorado region is unrivalled.   The student of earth-forms there finds many illustrations of the various phases that an upraised region passes through, in what may be termed its youth.   In a review of the life histories of rivers, the Colorado furnishes an example of a stream yet young, so far as its advance in its appointed task is concerned, but one which, owing to unusual opportunities, has surpassed many older but less favoured streams in the magnificence of the results accomplished.   The Colorado is not only a young stream, but has been termed a precocious youth.   Its success, however, in producing wonderful scenery of a novel type, lies not so much in the amount of work performed, as in the fact that

PLATE XVII.

The Grand Canyon of the Colorado, at the Foot of the Toroweap, Looking East. (By W. H. Holmes, U. S. Geological Survey.)

destructive agencies have spared the canyon walls as the stream entrenched itself. The climate is arid, and the wasting of the cliffs consequently retarded.

Stupendous as are the results achieved by the Colorado, and wonderfully impressive as is the scenery along its course, the amount of work it has done—that is, the number of cubic miles of rock removed—is small in comparison with what has been accomplished in many regions of mild relief, where rivers in their old age flow sluggishly over a plain from which they have removed nearly every vestige of a former mountain range. The region of great plateaus drained by the Colorado will, under the action of the agencies now in operation, be reduced to such a plain, unless future upheaval again renews the youth of the river.

Sierra Nevada Rivers.—The numerous bright, leaping rivers of the Sierra Nevadas, flowing through valleys three to four thousand feet deep and overshadowed by pine-clothed mountains, suggest many questions in reference especially to the influence of rock texture, changes in elevation and glaciation on stream erosion, and on the origin and development of topographic forms. The valleys are narrow, with usually little if any bottom-land. The rivers are swift and strong and carry along with ease all of the debris delivered to them by the bordering slopes and tributaries. Not only do they bear away all of the fine material that reaches them, but in times of high water roll along large boulders, and yet their capacity to transport is not satisfied, and they are clear, limpid, joyous streams during a large part of the year. The conditions are there the reverse of what is so manifest in the rivers of the Gulf States, where previously

eroded valleys are being filled and broad areas of new
land have been formed.   In the Sierra Nevadas the streams
are all at work at the task of deepening their channels;
the stage in their lives when they will broaden their valleys more rapidly than they deepen them has not been
reached.   The Tuolumne, King, Truckee, and many other
rivers are not only young, but are still broken by cataracts
and rapids, and in many instances are supplied in part by
the overflow of lakes.   These are plain evidences of youth.
A little study shows one, however, that the tireless activity
of the streams is largely due to a recent uplifting of the
mountains, which has given them steeper slopes, and that
the presence of waterfalls and lakes along their courses is in
many instances due to the former existence of great snow-
fields and magnificent glaciers in all of the higher valleys.
The energy with which the streams are working is thus seen
to be due to a revival of activity, or a rejuvenation, rather
than to actual youthfulness.

The westward-flowing streams from the Sierra Nevadas
experience a sudden change on leaving the mountains and
entering the flat-bottomed valleys where they unite to form
the San Joaquin and Sacramento.   With loss of grade the
waters flow less rapidly, and their burdens are dropped.
Deposition and aggrading are then the rule instead of abrasion and valley-deepening.   Borings made in the bottom of
the broad, nearly level-floored valley of California, show
that a great depression between the Sierra Nevada and
Coast mountains has been filled to a depth of many hundreds of feet.   Much of this filling is due to the deposition
of material swept out of the bordering mountains in order

to form the gorges and canyons which give them much of their diversity and beauty. Conditions similar to those already noted on the Atlantic coast, where a subsidence of the land has transformed the river valleys into estuaries, are again manifest on the western border of the continent. The story of stream development and of changes in the relief of the land on the Pacific coast, due to the upheaval of the land, is supplemented by the effects of subsidence on the geography where land and ocean meet. The bay of San Francisco and its outlet through the Golden Gate show that valleys have been drowned, owing to a downward movement of the land. Surveys of the sea bottom adjacent to the present coast-line reveal the fact that former river courses may, in some instances, be traced over the continental border now depressed beneath the Pacific, in the same manner that soundings have demonstrated a former seaward extension of the Hudson, St. Lawrence, and other streams of the Atlantic slope.

It seems scarcely necessary to mention, so obvious is it, the intimate relation between geographical history and human activities, illustrated by the origin and marvellous growth of the metropolis of the Pacific coast on the border of a partially submerged river valley. The magnificent bay of San Francisco, one of the very finest harbours in the world, is a direct result of a long series of geographical changes. The subsidence which converted a portion of the valley of the Sacramento into an arm of the sea has had a direct and far-reaching influence not only on the lives of millions of people, but on the building of a nation. The future greatness of San Francisco, assumed by her commanding geographical position, will make her an important factor in the spread of civilisation, not in America alone, but in the countries bordering the distant shores of the Pacific.

" *Where Rolls the Oregon.*"—The Columbia and its main tributary, the Snake, rise in the Rocky Mountains, and flow across a region of small rain-fall, thus simulating some of the main conditions which have influenced the history of Colorado River.   Snake River crosses a basaltic plateau and has excavated a magnificent canyon.   Although inferior in the richness of its colouring and the profusion of details in its sculptured cliffs, it is comparable in many ways with the Grand Canyon of the Colorado.   The walls of Snake River canyon are composed mainly of black basalt in horizontal layers, which assumes a great variety of cathedral-like and monumental forms on weathering.   The architecture is locally varied where granite and schist are exposed in the lower portions of the profound gulf, but throughout hundreds of miles of great escarpments the dark basalt gives a sombre and even an oppressive gloom to the strange scenery. In its deepest portion, on the east flank of the Blue Mountains, the canyon is about four thousand feet deep and fifteen miles broad.   As in the vast canyon carved by the Colorado, ridges and abutments from the main walls extend from either side far into the profound depths, and fill the depression so as to make it appear much narrower and deeper than it is in reality.

The Columbia also flows in a canyon-like valley for much of its course after leaving the Rocky Mountains.   In its wild passage through the Cascade Mountains, it is bordered by some of the most rugged river scenery to be found on the Pacific coast, but nowhere has it formed a canyon comparable with that traversed by Snake River.

The main subjects of interest to admirers of bold scenery as well as to the student of topographic forms and of stream development, presented by the vast region drained by the Columbia, centre in the relation of the drainage lines to the disturbances which have affected the rocks. In the Appalachians, as we have seen, many of the rivers flow across folded rocks and have cut water-gaps through the ridges; in the region drained by the Columbia the streams frequently cross rocky ridges formed by the upraised edges of tilted blocks of the earth's crust, and also give origin to water-gaps. In several instances sharp-crested walls of rock from a few hundred to two or three thousand feet high, have been upraised directly athwart the course of the Columbia or of its branches, but the rivers have not been turned aside. As the blocks were tilted and their edges slowly elevated, the rivers deepened their channels as fast as the land rose and thus maintained their right of way. In other instances, the waters were held in check for a time by the rising land, and caused lakes to form, but the barriers were slowly cut across by the out-flowing streams, and again, what may be termed gateways were opened through the ridges. The thickness of ancient lake sediments over broad areas in the region under discussion shows that earth-movements, similar to those which influenced the character of the present topography, have been long in progress and have produced profound geological as well as geographical changes.

The tilting of blocks of the earth's crust in the region drained by the Columbia has not only produced ridges of the nature just referred to, but in certain instances the surface has been depressed, thus lessening the grade of the streams and causing them to deposit their loads and aggrade their valleys.   Broad areas have for this reason been transformed into nearly level alluvial plains.

In the instructive Columbian region, and especially in that portion of central Washington known as the Big Bend country, where the climate is now arid and the rate of general waste from the surface due to atmospheric agencies small, lines of fracture and of moderate faulting have determined the direction of the stream courses.   The streams flow along lines of fracture and in some instances have excavated canyons with one wall higher than the other.   This is the only region in North America, so far as has been recognised, where the relation of streams to fractures in the earth's crust favours the once prevalent idea that valleys are due to breaks in the rocks, instead of resulting from the wearing action of streams.   Even these minor examples, however, of the influence of fractures on drainage fail to support the hypothesis referred to, since the breaks simply gave direction to the streams which subsequently excavated the valleys, instead of directly producing the depressions.

Another feature of especial interest in the land of the " Oregon," illustrating the influence of climate on the lives of streams, is furnished by the Grand Coulée, a deep, steep-sided canyon which cuts across the plateau partially enclosed by the Big Bend of the Columbia.   The Columbia once flowed through this great trench, having been turned from its present channel by the advance of a glacier from the mountains to the north.   This dam of ice held the river in check and caused it to rise and form a long, narrow lake, the outlet of which was through the previously eroded canyon now known as the Grand Coulée.

The Columbia flows directly through the Cascade Mountains nearly at right angles to their trend, in a wild and exceedingly picturesque water-gap, the greatest of its class on the continent. The complete history of this most impressive topographical feature has not been made out, but the facts in hand suggest that the mountains, like the narrow, sharp-crested ridges to the eastward, are due to the upraising of a block or a series of blocks of the earth's crust, along a line or belt of faulting, and that the river deepened its channel as fast as the rocks rose. Possibly the elevation of the land was not uniform, but progressed by stages, and that when most rapid, the river, unable to maintain its grade, was ponded and lakes formed. This explanation of the origin of the Dalles of the Columbia, and other gorges both above and below, must not be accepted too hastily, however, as the possibility of cross-fractures having given direction to the river and assisted it in its task has not been fully considered.

Where the Columbia nears the ocean its waters lose their energy and expand into an estuary, in which the tides rise and fall for a distance of about one hundred and forty miles from the ocean.' From what has been said concerning the

---

' Rev. Earl M. Wilbur of Portland, Oregon, has informed the writer by letter, on the authority of government engineers, "that the tide is felt in the Columbia as far as the Lower Cascades, which is, I believe, about 140 miles from the mouth of the river; the extreme range there being about six inches.

" In the Willamette, the Columbia's largest affluent, the tide is felt as far as Oregon City, where there are falls; about 115 miles from the ocean.

" The extreme range noted at Portland, about 100 miles from the ocean, is 3.2 feet."

drowning of stream-cut valleys both on the Atlantic and
Pacific coasts, it will be readily seen that a modern subsidence has recently affected a great extent of the coastal
region of the North-west, including south-eastern Alaska,
and has allowed the sea to encroach on the land and trans-
form the lower courses of many valleys into tideways.

The extremely interesting problems presented by the
region drained by the Columbia, and the magnificence and
novelty of the scenery existing there, tempt me to detain
the reader and consider more fully the origin of the massive cliffs and of the terraces and landslides on their faces.
There are yet other connections between the elements of
scenery and the work of streams, and a wonderful story of
the time when the land was again and again inundated by
floods of molten lava, but as the object of this fireside reconnoissance is simply to indicate some of the more instructive
features of the land which the study of streams assists in
interpreting, we must hasten on.   Our journey is northward.

Rivers of the Far North-West.—Fraser River, fed by tens
of thousands of twig-like branches on the western slope of
the Cordilleran Mountain system, furnishes much information in reference to the manner in which a broad, high
region becomes dissected by the streams flowing from it.
Many of the branches of this splendid river have their
sources in fine glaciers, high up among the glorious peaks
of the Selkirks and neighbouring ranges, flow through wild,
steep-sided gorges and valleys and unite to form a trunk
stream which has sunken three or four thousand feet into
the rocks.   In following the steep bank of the Fraser, while
making the transcontinental journey over the Canadian

Pacific, one sees on every hand evidences of the work of streams. The topography is yet young, although deeply and boldly cut, but the valleys are narrow, barely wide enough to give the rushing, foaming waters a passageway.

Throughout much of the trunk portion of the Fraser drainage-tree, the grade is sufficiently steep to insure a rapid current. The debris brought from glaciers, and fed by tributary rills and creeks, supplies the swiftly running waters with an abundance of tools with which to deepen their channels. Many conditions favour rapid work, and it is not surprising that the swift, debris-charged river has literally sawed a great mountain system into blocks, and is progressing rapidly with the task of removing the masses still remaining between its branches. The walls of its main canyon, although less precipitous than the bordering cliffs of the Colorado or the Snake, are wonderfully varied and picturesque. When seen from below they appear like deeply sculptured, forest-clothed mountain ranges. The river is yet young, but has accomplished a herculean task, and is still working with the energy of youth. As in the case of Snake River, the Fraser was interrupted in its work of corrasion during the Glacial epoch and its canyon deeply filled; more recent corrasion has removed much of the alluvium, however, leaving well-marked terraces, as is illustrated on Plate VIII. Its canyon, although three or four thousand feet deep, has not yet reached the limit to which down-cutting is possible. Vertical corrasion is still in excess of lateral wear and weathering, and the great trench is V-shaped in cross-section instead of being broadly U-shaped, as will be the case in its mature life. Like the streams of

the Sierra Nevadas, its energy is not all consumed in transporting the debris delivered to it, and for a large part of
the year it rushes along as a foaming, roaring torrent carrying its load easily until it enters the coastal region, where
a recent depression of the land causes a decrease in grade
and a consequent loss of velocity. The river is shorter
than formerly, for the reason that its trunk near the sea
has been transformed into an estuary. The drainage-tree
has been betrunked by subsidence and drowning.

Glacier-Born Rivers.—North of the Fraser, and similar to
it in the chief points of their histories, are the Stickine,
Taku, Alsec, and other rivers which have their sources to
the east and north of the mountains near the coast and flow
through rugged and as yet but little-known lands to the sea.
Probably all of the region drained by these rivers was ice-
covered at a comparatively recent date, and thousands of
glaciers still remain. Many are the lessons illustrated by the
·ugged landscapes of British Columbia and Alaska of the
manner in which streams and glaciers modify topography,
and the way that a subsidence of a deeply dissected land
leads to the production of a ragged coast-line fringed with
islands. This region includes the highest mountain and the
largest glaciers in North America. The chief lesson that
invites the geographer amid the ice-covered mountains near
the coast is the influence of climate and of topography on
the birth, growth, and decline of glaciers. This theme has
been considered in a preceding volume.[1]

The streams, many of them veritable rivers, flowing beneath the glaciers, make highly interesting deposits of

[1] I. C. Russell, *Glaciers of North America.* Ginn & Co., Boston, 1897.

gravel in the tunnels they occupy, and form alluvial cones and broad sand-plains after escaping from the ice. The study of these peculiar accumulations, still in process of formation, furnishes an explanation of many riddles in formerly glaciated lands.

To the north of the narrow coastal portion of southern Alaska, where the surface waters are discharged directly to the Pacific, lies the great region drained principally by the Yukon, which forms the Bering drainage slope. The hydrographic basin of the Yukon embraces about 440,000 square miles, and the volume of the river, although as yet unmeasured, is comparable with that of the Mississippi.

The Yukon presents many of the characteristics of the rivers of more southern latitudes, and also possesses certain features peculiar to the streams of northern countries. Flowing, as it does in its upper course, from south to north, the wave of sunshine and warmth that sweeps from the equatorial to polar regions each recurring springtime reaches the lands drained by its head-waters and loosens the icy grasp of winter, while its lower portion is still ice-bound. The melting of the snow and ice and the spring rains at the south cause the streams to rise in floods, which advance laden with floating ice upon the still frozen country to the northward. Ice-dams are formed, and the streams expand and inundate the forest-covered valley bottoms. The rising waters finally break the ice-dams and rush on down the valleys carrying destruction in their paths. Trees are uprooted, or cut off by the floating ice as with a scythe. Vast quantities of earth and stones, enclosed in the ice that formed in shallow water, are borne along and deposited in part over the flood-plains of the streams when the ice melts. The energy with which the Yukon modifies its banks, on account especially of the ice-laden floods, is unrivalled by any more southern river.

Another important variation in what may be considered as the normal action of streams arises, in the Alaskan region, from the constantly frozen condition of the soil. Throughout nearly the whole of the area drained by the Yukon the soil in the low lands is continually frozen. The winters are long and severe, the summers short and hot. The soil at a depth of a few inches beneath the usual covering of moss, shrubs, and trees is perennially frozen. The thickness of the frozen subsoil is not known, but excavations twenty-five feet in depth have failed to penetrate it. Ice-cliffs along the Kowak River, in North-western Alaska, reveal a thickness of fully two hundred feet of dirt-stained ice beneath a thin layer of black mucky soil on which grasses and other vegetation thrive. From these and other observations, and especially the records of certain borings made in a similar region in Siberia, it is safe to assume that the average thickness of the frozen layer in Alaska is probably in excess of one hundred feet and possibly two or three hundred feet or more in depth. These conditions have an important bearing on the work of streams. Frost renders otherwise loose and inadherent material as firm as solid rock. The action of flowing waters on the land is thus checked, and stream development as well as rock disintegration and decay and general surface erosion greatly retarded.

The climatic conditions in the region under discussion are such that the ground almost everywhere is covered with a dense growth of mosses and lichens, which make a living mat through which the surface waters percolate as through a layer of sponges, and are filtered of all matter in suspension. Thus, again, the work of the streams is delayed, for the reason that sand and silt, which ordinarily constitute the principal tools with which flowing waters abrade the rocks, are removed. This process of filtering the water is illustrated by the contrasts in the character of the tributaries of the Yukon which come to it from the north and from the south. Every stream, so far as is known, which joins the great river along its right bank is clear, although usually amber-coloured on account of the organic material contained in solution; while the tributaries entering from the left, or, in general, the southern bank, are mostly turbid and heavily loaded with sediment, for the reason that they have their sources in glaciers. White River, one of the principal tributaries of the Yukon from the south, is charged with material in suspension not only because it is fed by melting glaciers, but for the reason that it flows through a region that is covered with fine volcanic dust, some of which is washed into the stream by every rain. The accidents to streams, as they have been termed, due to glacial and to volcanic agencies here find abundant illustration.

The valley of the Yukon and of several of its important tributaries, particularly to the east of the Alaskan boundary, are marked by conspicuous terraces. A part of these are lake terraces, formed at a time when the waters were held in check by a lava dam, but other and equally conspicuous terraces were formed by the streams, and record changes in the altitude of the land, or the overloading of the waters with detritus during a time when glaciers near their sources were much more abundant and of far larger size than now. The head-branches of the Yukon drainage-tree rise in a country which was formerly covered with a continuous ice-sheet, but in its middle and lower courses evidence of former ice occupation is wanting. Marked differences in the scenery beheld in journeying from one of these regions to the other have been noted by several travellers.

Bering Sea, into which the Yukon empties, is shallow, at least in the portions bordering Alaska, and is without strong currents or high tides. The great river on entering the sea drops its heavy burden of silt, and has built up a delta comparable in extent with that of the Mississippi. The river divides into many branches, or sends off several distributaries in the delta portion of its course. The first of these diverging channels leaves the main river about a hundred miles from its mouth. The low, swampy area built by the stream is treeless, but clothed in summer with a dense growth of mosses, lichens, grasses, rushes, and a great variety of less conspicuous flowering plants. This luxuriant garden of brilliant flowers and luscious green fronds and leaves is but a veneer of verdure concealing a frozen morass. This is a portion of the vast treeless tract of perennially frozen ground known as the *tundra*, which fringes the shores of Bering Sea and the Arctic Ocean. The several distributaries of the river flow through this new-made land in meandering courses, and enter the sea at various localities, over a breadth of seventy miles of coast.

With the exception of the delta portion of the Yukon, its **banks** are fringed with spruce trees, cottonwoods, and willows. The annual floods and ice-gorges cause large numbers of trees to be swept into the river, and the swift current at numerous localities cuts away the banks in such a way as to undermine the trees growing on them and cause them to fall into the waters with roots and branches attached. Great quantities of drift-wood are thus contributed to the river, as has already been described. The conservative influence both of growing trees and of stranded drift-wood on the banks of the river are well marked and important, as are also the destructive tendencies of the same agencies. The trees on being uprooted tear away the banks, and on being stranded frequently deflect the current so as to cause it to cut away neighbouring shores and increase the number and extent of the windings of the river.

Arctic Rivers.—Of the streams flowing down the Arctic drainage slope but little can be said, for the reason that no traveller especially interested in the study of modern geography has visited that region. The Mackenzie probably illustrates the characteristics of a northward-flowing Arctic river even better than the Yukon. Much of the region it traverses is forested, and vast floods occur each spring when the thick ice of winter breaks up and is swept northward. The sudden changes that occur at the turn of the annual tide of temperature must be even grander than along the Yukon, but in this connection but little information is available. On entering the Arctic Ocean when the tides are low and currents produced by the winds mostly lacking, owing to the fact that the sea is covered with ice-floes throughout the year, the river deposits its sediment and is engaged in building a large delta. The three great delta-making rivers of North America are the Mississippi, Yukon, and Mackenzie.

Rivers of the " Great Lone Land."—On the Hudson Bay drainage slope there are tens of thousands of lakes, which, for the most part, .occupy basins due in one way or another to the former occupation of the land by glacial ice. There are also many rivers, but the way in which they illustrate the principles of stream development has received but slight attention. The reports of explorers, especially those connected with the Geological and Natural History Survey of Canada, show that the drainage is immature. The streams have not cut down their channels so as to furnish direct and ready avenues of discharge for the surface waters. This is demonstrated especially by the countless lakes. The streams are not only young, having come into existence or having been rejuvenated since the last retreat of the glaciers, but have developed slowly on account of adverse circumstances. Among the conditions that have retarded stream development may be noted the general low altitude of the land, and, consequently, gentle gradients of the stream channels and lack of energy in the flowing waters. The winter climate is severe, and the streams either ice-covered or frozen to their bottoms for several months each year. Snow protects the ground in winter. The subsoil, as in the Yukon basin, remains solidly frozen in many places even during the warm season. Erosion and the transportation of debris by the streams is thus limited to one half, or even less, of the year. Forests with undergrowths of mosses, lichens, and other plants shield the soil in summer from the beating of rain, and filter the percolating surface waters.

thus robbing them of the means of abrading the rocks over which they flow. There are no glaciers to supply the streams with sediment. The vegetation retards the gathering of the waters into rills, and equalises the flow of the streams in such a manner that the floods caused by melting snow have their energy diminished. The river banks are clothed with trees and shrubs, especially willows and alders, and their roots bind the soil and increase its ability to resist the attacks of the flowing waters. Drift timber lodged against the sides of the streams, especially fallen trees which still retain a hold on the land, also protect the banks. For these and still other reasons, the work of the streams has progressed slowly. They illustrate retarded stream development, or a long-continued youthful stage. In this respect they afford a marked contrast to the Colorado, where the opportunities for development have been unusually great. There is still another reason for the slow development of the streams flowing to Hudson Bay, although its full significance has not been determined. That is, the region toward which they flow is believed to be a rising area. The upward movement of the land is slow, although the rate is not known. An elevation of a very few inches a century would have a decided effect on the flow of the streams in a region of such mild relief.

A glance at a map of North America suggests that a large number of islands into which the land is broken on the north-eastern border of the continent is due to a recent subsidence. There is geological evidence that over a vast area at the north, the land was depressed during the Glacial epoch and has since been slowly rising, but has not regained the position it held previous to the birth of the ice-sheets which once covered it. This re-elevation is thought to be still in progress, and should this conclusion be maintained it will furnish an additional reason for the present immature condition of the northward-flowing streams just referred to.

Rivers Flowing to Fresh-Water Seas.—The St. Lawrence drainage slope, with its great lakes and magnificent rivers, affords numerous features of interest to the geographer besides its beautiful scenery. Soundings made in the Gulf of St. Lawrence, and even well to the eastward of the most easterly cape of Nova Scotia, have revealed the fact that the submerged channel of the St. Lawrence River may be traced on the floor of the ocean as far as the submarine escarpment marking the true continental border. From the eastern extremity of this submerged channel through the Gulf of St. Lawrence and up the narrowing estuary to near Montreal, where the river at present meets tide-water, is more than a thousand miles. The Saguenay River, bordered by towering walls, occupies a canyon excavated by a branch of the Greater St. Lawrence. The same conditions are recorded in a less marked way by the Ottawa and other branches of the present river. We have here the most remarkable example of a drowned river-system that is known. The marginal portion of the continent with broad valley near the sea, leading inland to deep canyons, has been depressed in recent times so as to allow the sea to encroach on the land. The valleys have become gulfs, bays, and estuaries, and the canyons narrow tideways; highlands, that separated the former river valleys, when not completely submerged have been transformed into capes and headlands, and in part surrounded by the sea so as to form islands.

The influence of the geographical history of the St. Lawrence on the course of human events is even more strongly marked than in the case of similar changes along the Atlantic border to the southward. The estuary of the St. Lawrence furnished an easy passageway, reaching far inland, for early explorers, and its connection, by means of the unsubmerged portion of the ancient river, with the Great Lakes tempted the Jesuit missionaries to make bold canoe journeys into the very heart of the continent. This same route led to the establishment of missions and the planting of white settlements and trading stations on the shore of the Great Lakes and in the Mississippi valley before the passes in the Appalachians to the southward became known. In later years, a series of canals to facilitate navigation between the St. Lawrence estuary and the Great Lakes stimulated industry by bringing tens of thousands of square miles of forest and of rich agricultural land into communication with the markets of Europe. Far-reaching plans for establishing deep waterways along this general course of early canoe navigation are now being matured, and the influence of geographical conditions favourable to commerce will be felt still more potently in the future than they have been in the past.[1]

To the south of the St. Lawrence estuary lies the charming valley of Lake Champlain, which was excavated by a stream tributary to the Greater St. Lawrence when the land

[1] I. C. Russell, "Geography of the Laurentian Basin," in *Bulletin of the American Geographical Society*, vol. xxx., pp. 226–254, 1898.

stood higher than now. After acquiring about its present form, the Champlain valley was depressed and became an arm of the sea, which was inhabited by marine mollusks and frequented by whales. A tideway reaching southward connected with the submerged Hudson River valley, making New England an island. A partial re-elevation of the land caused the former gulf to be separated from the ocean, so as to form a saline lake. The rains and feeding streams furnished a supply of fresh water in excess of the amount lost by evaporation, and the salt waters were flooded out and the present stage in the history of the valley initiated. This marvellous transformation of a broad and well-developed river valley to an arm of the sea, to a saline lake, and then to a fresh lake, in which the blue Adirondack Hills and the equally picturesque mountains of Vermont are reflected, is one of the most instructive pages in the later geographical history of America.

The story of the St. Lawrence valley and its tributary branches is supplemented by the no less instructive history of the basins of the Great Lakes, some account of which has been given in a companion to the present volume.[1]

The student of river development and of the changes made by streams in the topography of the land, as he sails the Great Lakes and visits the thriving cities on their shores, sees records of a time when rivers flowed through the now water-filled basins, and for ages worked slowly at their appointed task of deepening and widening their valleys. This great task, when far advanced, was more than once interrupted by the invasion of the entire St. Lawrence region by

[1] I. C. Russell, *Lakes of North America.* Ginn & Co., Boston, 1895.

glaciers from the north. Conditions now characteristic of central Greenland then prevailed where millions of homes are now situated, and where fruitful farms have replaced the desolation of ice-fields. When the great geological winter had passed, the former stream channels were clogged with debris, so as to retard the waters and cause them to choose new courses. Elevation and depression of the land over tens of thousands of square miles still further complicated the difficulties that the re-born streams had to contend with. The surface waters were held in check, and formed vast lakes in the partially obstructed and warped and deformed preglacial river valleys.

When one marshals in fancy the changes that the St. Lawrence drainage slope has passed through from the time when it was more elevated than now and supplied a well-developed river-system,—that is, a river with many branches, which had cut down its channel nearly to sea-level, so as to have a low gradient for two thousand miles or more, and had broadened its valley so as to form a wide, open plain which extended far into the many tributary valleys,—through the marvellous changes incident to the glacial invasions, and the partial submergence beneath the sea, and the partial re-elevation of the drowned portion, the damming of the stream by glacial debris, and the changes due to warping of the earth's crust, the brief time that civilised man has been acquainted with the region becomes insignificant. In this hasty outline of a million or more years of geographical history, although seemingly crowded with important events, all of the changes experienced by the St. Lawrence drainage slope have not been included. There is evidence that the

St. Lawrence basin has been in communication with the
Mississippi River drainage. In the development of these
two great river-systems, there has been a struggle for the
possession of the land where they approach each other
(analogous in some ways to the wars of the French and
English for the possession of the same territory), which will
be of interest to the reader who has followed the discussion of
the backward cutting of drainage lines in a preceding
chapter. More than this, there are suggestions that the
excavation of the basins of the Great Lakes was due in part
to streams flowing southward instead of eastward, and that
a change in direction was caused by movements in the
earth's crust which are still in progress. The student of
geography thus finds two chief lines of interest in the region
under consideration, one dealing with the origin and history
of the land forms, and the other with their bearing and influence on the current of human events.

Niagara.—The lakes that first came into existence in the
Laurentian basin during the final retreat of the glaciers
were small and numerous. Many of them were short-lived,
and were drained as the ice-dam retaining them withdrew
north-eastward; but some of them expanded with the retreat
of the ice, and became vast inland seas, larger than any of
their present representatives. At a late stage in the melting of the glaciers, the basins now occupied by Lakes Erie
and Ontario were occupied by a single great water-body.
When the ice withdrew still more and the Mohawk valley was
uncovered, a lower outlet became available and the waters
escaped so as to lower the lake and cause it to be divided.
The lake in the Erie basin overflowed across the dividing

land to the Ontario basin, and Niagara River was born. An example of the manner in which a river may originate, not previously considered in this book, is thus furnished. The many happy tourists who have listened to the thunder of mighty Niagara and wandered along the brink of the gorge occupied by the waters in their mad course below the cataract, have many illustrations thrust upon their attention of the manner in which streams modify the land. The cataract was once at the margins of the bold escarpment near Lewiston, and has slowly receded, leaving a great gorge as a record of its work. Unlike the magnificent canyon of the Colorado, or the almost equally remarkable example through which Snake River flows, the steep-walled gorge of the Niagara has not been worn out by the flow of silt- and sand-laden waters, but as already described in discussing the migration of waterfalls, illustrates another process by which the land may be deeply trenched. The waters of Niagara come directly from a great lake in which they have left all of the sediment they may once have held in suspension, and are clear. The deep tourmaline-green of the plunging cataract is never clouded. Clear streams, as we are aware, have but little power to deepen their channels, as all the debris available for transportation is soon removed, and the chemical action of the waters in dissolving the rock over which they flow is so slow that only in exceptional instances are they able to deepen their channels more rapidly than the adjacent surface is lowered by weathering. How, then, has the canyon below the Falls of Niagara been excavated ?

The energy of Niagara River available for canyon cutting is concentrated at the base of the cataract. The river came

into existence with a cataract, which was even grander when
it first leaped from the crest of the escarpment at Lewiston
than it has been since the first white man kneeled in its
awful presence.   Owing to the southward dip of the rocks,
the height of the fall has been continually decreasing and
will continue to decrease until it has receded to the lake
from which the river flows, or the westward tilting of the
land, known to be in progress, diverts its waters.   The surface rock along Niagara River is a hard limestone about
eighty feet thick; beneath this there are soft shales, much
broken by joints and easy of removal.   The dash of the
spray, the grinding of ice-blocks, and, to some extent, the
freezing of absorbed water, leads to the removal of the shale
so as to leave the limestone above projecting.   From time
to time masses of the limestone break off and fall into the
pool below.   When the plunging waters have sufficient
power to move these blocks, they are dashed against the
cliff and act as millstones in deepening and widening the
basin below.   When the descending waters do not have
sufficient power to sweep about the blocks of stone, as in
the case of the American Fall, they accumulate and form a
talus slope which protects the cliffs, and retard their seces-
sion.   This explanation, first offered by Gilbert, furnishes
a reason for the marked differences between the American
and Canadian portions of the cataract.   Many other interesting and instructive features of Niagara are described and
explained in the monograph just referred to.

Retrospect.—We have made this rapid review of the principal drainage slopes of North America for the purpose of
refreshing our memories concerning the more pronounced

geographical features of the continent due to erosion. Another aim has been to suggest questions which the student of geography will find pleasure in answering. I fear, however, our hasty journey has in some respects left an erroneous impression on the reader's mind, for the reason that in considering each drainage slope only its more pronounced features have claimed attention. If each river appears to be principally and essentially different from all other streams, and the several drainage systems present an infinite variety of disconnected facts, modifications and corrections of such ideas are necessary. A more detailed study of the behaviour of streams will show that law and order prevail. From the purling rill to the majestic river, where at first, perhaps, endless variety appears, the flow of water and the changes it produces in the relief of the land are governed by inflexible laws. The streams one and all are engaged in a definite and well-circumscribed task, which leads to an orderly succession of topographic forms. When all of the modifying conditions are taken into account, the successive changes experienced by a given land area, from the time of its upraising above the sea, to the time when it is worn down nearly to sea-level once more, are seen to be as much in obedience to law as the seasonal changes in a landscape or the development of an individual man from childhood to old age.

Although the origin of topographic forms and the many metamorphoses they undergo, claim the special attention of students of geography, the fact should be borne in mind that the knowledge thus gained is but the basis of a more profound study,—the relation of man to nature. The influence of the earth's history on human history, although in many instances not fully realised, is an underlying and ever-present source of interest and enjoyment to the geologist and geographer.

The brief review of some of the characteristics of rivers given in this chapter, it is hoped, will stimulate a desire, especially in American students, to know more of the many and varied charms of their native land.

CHAPTER IX

THE LIFE HISTORY OF A RIVER

A N application of the laws governing the behaviour of streams in interpreting the origin and history of topographic forms can be made in almost any land area on the earth. In order to group in a single panorama, however, all of the various phases which a river passes through from its birth and youth to its old age and death, the conditions presented by many streams in various stages of growth and decline have to be combined, for the reason that the life of a man is too brief to enable him to observe more than a few minor changes in the history of a single river. But knowing the laws which govern stream development, one can easily picture in his mind the leading events in the life of a majestic river whose murmurs we may be pardoned for fancying make audible the memoir of a million years.

In order to sketch in outline the life history of an ideal river, let the reader imagine that the floor of the sea in temperate latitudes over an area of a hundred square miles has been upraised so as to form an island; and trace the changes which will follow as the rain-water falls on its surface, and gathers into rills which unite one with another until a series of rivers conducts the contributions from the clouds down their shining courses to the sea.

The surface of our imaginary island is mildly irregular. In the central portion it has an elevation of a thousand feet, and slopes gradually but somewhat irregularly in all directions to the sea. In places the waters gather in hollows and form lakes. These consequent lakes are soon filled, or their overflowing waters cut notches in the rims of their basins, and they are drained. The first streams that are born of the showers, like the children of men, have their courses marked out for them in early life, or, in more prosaic language, are consequent streams. Later in life they carve out their own fortunes and influence their surroundings.

In these fireside fancies we assume the point of view granted the novelist, to whom time and distance offer no limitation. A Scott or a Hawthorne tells us with confidence the most secret thoughts of a prisoner in his cell a century before they themselves were born. We accept the illusion so long as the laws governing human nature are not violated. Why should a similar privilege be denied the geographer ? Let us, then, trace the changes that our island will undergo in obedience to the laws of the inanimate world, accepting the remark of Lamarck applied to the development of species, that " time is nothing." The only supernatural condition which I will ask the reader to accept, is that the promontory on which we keep our vigil remains unchanged.

Looking across the shimmering sea of fancy, we see the new-born consequent streams appearing like shining threads of silver when the skies are clear, but when the rain descends in torrents and the soil is loosened and disturbed they become yellow with sediment. Already changes are in progress. The streams charged with silt and sand are corrading their channels. The lines thus produced are delicate at first, but soon become more and more deeply engraved. These infant streams have their sources not at the summits of the island, but in general midway down its sides. The deepening of the channels leading from the higher portions of the island to the sea makes the waters flowing down them master streams. As they sink deeper and deeper into the rocks, lateral streams are developed on the original interstream areas. These branches become swifter as the main streams deepen their channels, and in turn develop branches to which they themselves are masters. The secondary and tertiary branches cannot excavate below the level of the stream to which they contribute their waters, but the down-cutting at their mouths may keep pace with the lowering of the receiving channel. This process of throwing out new branches and the growth of each branch by terminal budding, as it were, soon lead to the complete drainage of the land. Water falling on any portion of the island finds a system of channels, delicately adjusted in size in accord with the part they have to play, which lead it back to the sea.

Our island, we will assume for simplicity, is composed of nearly horizontally bedded rock of various degrees of hardness. The influence of the dip of the beds beneath the original surface, discussed in a previous page in connection with the adjustment of subsequent streams and the development of drainage systems under the conditions there described, need not be repeated.

The headward growth of the feeding rills and brooks of

the main consequent streams brings them into rivalry with each other. The boundaries between opposite-flowing streams in the central portion of the island become more and more sharply defined, and the positions of the divides can be easily traced. From these divides the descent into the valleys on either side is steep. Hard layers in the nearly horizontal beds cause many cascades. The young, joyous streams fill the air with laughter. The cascades came into existence low down the course of the streams and gradually retreated toward the centre of the uplift, leaving shadowy gorges as records of their migrations. It is only when the streams in their lower courses have deepened their channels nearly to sea-level that they cease to be whitened by cataracts and rapids.

As we watch the growth of the streams we note that they deepen their channels most rapidly not at their mouths, nor at their sources, but at some locality between, which differs in its relative position, in various instances, with the size of the stream. The rate at which the streams we are observing entrench themselves depends, as we know, on their volume, the declivity of their channels, and on the amount and character of the loads they carry. It is the resultant of these main conditions, rock texture being essentially the same throughout their courses, which determines at what locality conspicuous changes will first appear. Near their sources the grade is steep, but the waters are divided, flowing in numerous channels, and the work they are enabled to accomplish is not so great as farther down the slopes where many tributaries have united their energies. We need not again consider the various elements of a stream energy, but from the fact that the channels through which they flow become conspicuously deeper midway up the slopes of the island, it is evident the most rapid corrasion is there taking place.

Below the locality of most rapid corrasion the slope is less precipitous, and although the volume of water is greater, the rate at which the streams corrade decreases all the way to the sea. The amount of rock that has to be removed in order to admit of the sinking of the channels to base-level, however, is less and less the nearer they approach the coast-line. The streams near their mouths are thus enabled to reach the downward limit of their task sooner than at any locality higher up their courses, in spite of the fact that they there work more slowly than elsewhere, except perhaps at their extreme head-waters. Whatever the conditions, it is evident that any portion of a stream at a distance from its mouth cannot be lowered to baselevel more quickly than the portion nearer the sea, unless possibly by solution, as the material removed would in such a case have to be carried up instead of down a gradient.

As we watch the changes in progress, we note that after the first adjustment to inherited conditions is made, all of the material removed where the stream beds are steep, is not carried directly to the sea. At first, perhaps, the slopes were such that the debris contributed to the master streams could be carried all the way to their mouths, but such an adjustment of gradient to load at the start would be of the nature of chance. The probabilities of a stream's inheriting a gradient perfectly adapted to its needs are almost infinitely small. Throughout the life of a stream, even

20

though external conditions remain unchanged, there is a constant process of adjustment of gradient to suit the changing conditions due to corrasion and sedimentation in various portions of its channel, and also to variations in volume and load.

This process of adjusting the gradient of a stream channel in its several parts to particular conditions of volume and load, is so delicate that no two of the streams we are watching will carry on their work in precisely the same way. In most instances, the debris removed midway down the course of a stream, where corrasion is most active, will in part be deposited lower down and aggrading begin. Other streams will deepen their channels at their mouths to baselevel, and then begin to broaden their valleys and spread out flood-plains. As the streams grow older, the portions of their courses where corrasion is in progress will slowly recede up stream and be followed, at least for a time, by an extension in the same direction of the increasing flood-plains.

Clouds gather about our island from time to time, and it experiences all the vicissitudes of climate entailed by the position it occupies on the earth's surface. Vegetation springs into existence, and the land is clothed with grasses and flowers, or deeply shadowed by forests. The length of our vigil is so great that possibly the character of the flora undergoes many variations owing to climatic changes. Although these modifications in conditions vary the lives of the streams, they do not stop their work.

When the streams have deepened their channel where they approach the sea nearly or quite to baselevel, vertical corrasion ceases and is followed by aggrading, while lateral corrasion continues.

If we select one of the several larger consequent streams for special study, we find during the earlier stages of its life, that debris is continually being supplied by its swift upper branches in excess of the amount the sluggish current in its main trunk can carry away. In consequence, the flood-plain downstream, from the localities where corrasion is in progress, is built higher and higher. During high-water stages accompanying heavy rains, the stream meanders at will over the flat bottom it has given to its valley, and divides into many branches. The position of the stream is unstable, for the reason that abundant deposition of debris raises its bottom and borders, thus elevating it above the adjacent areas. When floods occur, the stream breaks through its levees and chooses a new channel, which is built upon as before, and the process repeated.

At this stage in its history the stream to which we have directed special attention will have many high-grade branches, in which corrasion is in active progress, and a low-grade trunk portion where debris is being deposited. When the stream is corrading, the valleys or gorges are steep-sided and present V-shaped cross-profiles, but below the region of waste where a flood-plain is being formed, the valley is wide, essentially flat-bottomed, and has flaring sides. It is to be noted also that in the alluvial-filled valley there are no terraces. During this still youthful stage the trunk stream has many curves, and divides into several branches during floods, so as to enclose low, sandy islands.' These changes in the position of the main channel are irregular, and frequently rapid.

The grading up of the main valley in the manner just

noted, was necessitated by the high grade of its tributaries.   The aim, we may say, was to make an approximation to the easiest attainable pathway for the debris on its
journey to the sea.   Theoretically, such a pathway would
be what is known as the " curve of quickest descent."   But
the down-cutting of the stream channels in their upper
courses continually changes the conditions, and a continual
process of adjustment in the lower and flatter portions of
the curve is thus necessitated.   As the grade of the tributary streams is thus reduced, the region of previous aggrading must also be modified.   Hence there comes a time
when the stream in its trunk portion begins to excavate a
channel through its previously formed flood-plain.

In this stage of adjustment, centuries being numbered as
hours, we see the river writhing in its course through its
more level tract; now cutting away the rocks on one side
of its valley and then swinging bodily across its flood-plain
and attacking the opposite bluff.   Each of these migrations
is accompanied by a multitude of minor contortions.   Its
course is always serpentine.   On each of the minor bends
we note that the immediate river bank is steepest on the
concave side of the curve made by the stream, while on the
opposite or convex side the bank slopes gently upward to
the level of the flood-plain.   The stream is plainly at work
in removing material from the concave, and making additions
to the convex, side of each curve.   It soon becomes apparent that the stream is working over the material forming at
least the surface portion of its flood-plain.   With each disturbance of the detritus previously deposited, it is carried
farther on its way to the sea, but each journey is short for

all but the very finest material, which is taken in suspension and may be borne to the sea with but short rests on the bed of the stream. This process, as we know, leads to an assorting of the debris of which the flood-plain is formed : the coarsest portions are dropped first, and on them finer and finer sediment is laid down, the last addition to the plain being the finest of all. With each period of rest in the flood-plain, the debris undergoes chemical changes, and is more or less affected by frost and variations of temperature, which softens and weakens it so as to favour more rapid wear when next it is removed.

The increase in the curvature of the minor bends of the meandering stream leads from time to time to the cutting through of the neck of land between two adjacent curves, and the straightening of the contorted channel. A shorter course is thus made for the waters, which is followed by readjustment of grade both up and down stream, and the former abrupt curve is left as a bayou, the entrance and exit to which soon become closed and an " ox-bow lake " is formed.

A single migration of the river across its flood-plain requires thousands of years. But during this time its channel sinks deeper and deeper into the previously deposited debris, and an entire migration from one side of the valley to the other and back again is not always completed before a second swing is begun. The portion of the flood-plain not worked over during one of these incomplete migrations remains as a terrace. With each migration a flood-plain is spread out, and wherever a flood-plain formed during the preceding migration is not completely worked over, a terrace is left as a record of the unfinished task.

The branches of the river have now cut down their chan
nels so as to have a comparatively low grade, except at their
extreme head-waters, and the trunk of the drainage-tree is
contorted and bordered by alluvial terraces.

While the changes outlined above have been in progress,
the fine debris carried by the river to its mouth has been
deposited so as to form a low-grade delta, which makes an
addition to the land, thereby increasing the distance to
which the river has to carry its load before it can finally lay
it aside. Even the depositing of debris in a delta, however,
can scarcely terminate the influence of the river upon it, as
the surface of the delta is but a continuation of the flood-
plain, and future adjustments to ever-changing conditions
may necessitate its removal and re-deposition in a later
seaward extension of the land.

The growth of the delta, by increasing the length of the
river, necessitates that its gradient throughout the portion
where flood-plains occur should be raised in order to facilitate the transportation of fresh debris over it. A continual
check is thus placed on the process of down-cutting in the
alluvial filling of the valley, necessitated by the constantly
decreasing grade of the corrading tributaries. This continual re-adjustment of the gradients throughout a drainage
system, be it a meadow brook or the Mississippi, with ever-
changing conditions of corrasion and sedimentation, is one
of thousands of illustrations of the harmony of Nature. It
was the result of this process of continual adjustment which
forcibly impressed Hutton and Playfair, nearly a century
ago, as is shown by the passage quoted on a prefatory page
of this book.

During the centuries that have passed while we have been considering the work of the streams flowing from the island before us, wonderful changes have taken place in the topography of its surface. The sinking of the stream channels, but partially counteracted by aggrading, has left ridges between the drainage lines. The land has been roughened by the cutting of valleys and canyons. The degree of this roughening depends mainly on the altitude of the land, the stage of development reached by the streams in various portions of their courses, and the amount the land has been lowered by general erosion. The streams are yet young, but, as already noted, have advanced farthest with their task of removing the rocks down to sea-level in their seaward portions. In the regions of low relief, near the sea, the streams have already passed the youthful stage, and are subduing the landscape not only by lateral corrasion but by deposition. In this portion of the island, also, vertical corrasion having ceased, the tendency of weathering to reduce the interstream areas to the level of the adjacent valleys is no longer counteracted. In the higher portions of the island the divides between the main streams and between neighbouring branches of the same trunk drainage-line, are sharp-crested ridges. There is a wonderful and beautiful system displayed by these ridges. They are not level-topped, but marked by peaks and downward-curving saddles. On each ridge, whether a main divide or the crest of a branching spur, where two streams head against each other, there is a sag or saddle in its crest-line, and, where lateral spurs or secondary or tertiary ridges join the main divides or a secondary ridge, there are peaks or rounded knobs. The upland with its multitude of crest-lines and many peaks resembles a vast tent supported by many poles. The place of each support is marked by a peak, rounded and given a convex curvature by weathering, and between the peaks the tent-cloth descends in gracefully curving folds.

The branches of the stream are most numerous where the original slopes were steep; the interstream areas are there narrow and sharp crested; farther toward the sea, where the slopes are more gentle, the interstream areas are broader and flatter. There are two principal reasons for these differences. On the steeper slopes the run-off is greater in proportion to the total rain-fall than on lower slopes, because the less the slope the longer the waters are retained on the surface and the greater the loss from evaporation and percolation. A more important result, perhaps, is that on steep slopes corrasion is rapid in proportion to weathering and general degradation, while with progressively decreasing declivity weathering more and more nearly keeps pace with corrasion.

The ridges between adjacent streams not only lose their even crests as determined by the original slope of the land, with the progress of stream sculpturing, but if we look down on them from a point vertically above, it is apparent that they are sinuous lines. The eating back into the uplands of opposite-flowing streams has not been uniform, but the divides have been pushed one way or another according to the rate at which the rival streams have been enabled to progress with their work. The divides migrate toward the weaker streams. The ridges forming both the main and secondary divides are sharp and steep-sided where opposing streams have eaten back the farthest, and are broader and have more gentle slopes where diverging ridges meet. The hills as well as the valleys are ever changing and record the workings of laws which produce infinite variety with the constant preservation of harmony and beauty.

At a more advanced stage in the history of our island, the peaks standing at the junction of lateral ridges become more and more prominent as the saddles between them are deepened. Those well down the general slope in time become so far isolated that they stand as individual eminences, and their connection with the central system is at the first glance not apparent.

The island has now reached its greatest topographic diversity, and, unless the orderly progression is disturbed, as by renewed elevation, for example, future changes will be in the direction of subduing its relief and smoothing out its contours.

The process of broadening the valleys in their lower courses is extended farther and farther toward their sources. Broad flood-plains in time reach well into the central group of hills.

In the uplands, valley-deepening continues, but the ratio of corrasion to general erosion becomes less and less with decrease in the gradients of the streams. With decrease in elevation, general erosion or degradation also diminishes, and both corrasion and degradation cease when baselevel is reached.

As the gradient of the streams in their upper courses diminishes, the loads they carry to lower tracts also become less, and the streams are enabled to cut still deeper into their previously formed flood-plains. With the advance of old age the gradients of the streams become less and less throughout their lengths, but are always steeper near their sources than at any locality farther downstream.

Our island now consists of two portions in reference to topographic development: a central region of prominent peaks and ridges, and a surrounding baselevel plain, covered with a sheet of stream-deposited debris.

If at this stage a comparatively sudden elevation of the whole island occurs, which carries it up, we will assume, one hundred feet, conspicuous changes will follow. The gradients of the streams at their mouths will be increased. Some of them may plunge into the sea over escarpments, thus forming cascades, which will recede up stream, leaving sharply cut ravines. The gradients of the streams will be re-adjusted to meet the requirements of the changed conditions. Their revived energy will enable them to corrade throughout their length and to quickly deepen their channels, especially in the previously alluvial-filled valleys. This rapid deepening will lead to the abandoning of portions of previously occupied flood-plains, and terraces will appear. The streams flowing through their new steep-sided channels will at first retain the positions they chanced to have at the time of the uplift, and will be sinuous, but their increased energy will tend to straighten their courses. The terraces left by the sinking of the streams will be broad in the coastal plain and become narrower and narrower farther inland. At the same time the vertical elevation of each terrace above the adjacent portion of the new stream channel will decrease from the sea margin inland to where the stream it borders ceases to be a depositing stream and the tract where corrasion is in progress is reached.

At this stage in the history of the island, its marginal t'ıct is an upraised peneplain, surrounding a group of hills, or monadnocks.

The streams again broaden their valleys in their lower courses, the broadening terraces are removed, and this change sweeps inland until perhaps all records of the once conspicuous peneplain disappear.

While we are pondering on the changes produced by slowly acting forces when the time limit is ample, our island, ¡n obedience to unseen causes deep within the earth, is depressed two hundred feet. The sea encroaches on the land, and, extending far up the valleys, converts them into estuaries. The highlands between the valleys become capes, and possibly some of the outer members of the central group of hills are entirely surrounded by water and are transformed into islands. The coast-line, which previous to the subsidence, was conspicuously regular and formed long, sweeping curves, is now markedly irregular. The sea-water, extending far up the deeper and more thoroughly developed valley, forms long, narrow estuaries or downward valleys, of the type of the Hudson estuary. In some instances the drowning of the valleys has extended above where the lower branches of the former stream joined the main trunk, and the lower courses of the tributary valleys are now bays on the side of the main estuary. These are estuaries of the Chesapeake type. In such instances the trunks of the former river systems have disappeared, and only their dismembered branches remain. The drainage-trees have been betrunked by subsidence. At this stage of greatest geographical diversity, so far as the relations of sea

and land are involved, the shores of the island are indented
by numerous bays, many of them having flat alluvial lands
at their heads.

In fancy we have clothed our island with a varied flora.
The picture presents a pleasing grouping of swelling hills
with rounded summits and gradually sweeping sides, wide
valleys with gently sloping borders, separated in part by
broad but yet well-drained plains. These various forms are
modulated and their details concealed beneath a living mantle of vegetation. Seasonal changes, recurring like the figures in a dance of merry children, come and go with the
ebb and flow of the annual tide of temperature. Each
springtime the willow-fringed brooksides blush with the
pulsations of renewed youth. Flowery banks and shadowy
vistas in the forests reveal cool retreats in summer, when in
the stillness of the evening we hear the distant mellow song
of the wood-thrush. The deep, strong, harlequin colours of
autumn make the island a garden of gorgeous flowers edged
about by the silvery surf. In winter the babble of the brooks
is hushed beneath icy coverings, and the bare trees are etch-
ings on the white pages of the snow. These minor har-
monies are interwoven all through the melody of the ages.
Like the white fretwork on the waves of the sea, they ac-
company the greater changes wrought by unseen agencies.
We are overpowered by the multitude of questions suggested
by this great drama of Nature. We long to know what the
end may be. Why all this beauty and variety in form and
colour ? Why the scented breeze, the hum of insects, the
songs of birds, the music of the brooks, the coming and
going of hills and valleys, and the thousands of other evi-

dences of harmoniously working laws ? Was the elevation
of the land in a far distant time, the crumbling and decay of
the rocks, the long journeys of the finer fragments down the
streams, and their deposition in alluvial lands, but to form
a soil in which violets and lilies might take root and furnish
nectar for the bees ? We trace the origin and development
of material things to intangible laws. These at first seem
but the children of our own brains. We soon learn, however, that they are not only external to ourselves, but sway
and guide us. Man, too, gathers honey from the flowers.
Such a mighty vision rises before the mind as we watch our
island passing through its orderly transformations or glance
upward at the changing constellations above it, that we
pause, fearing to go farther, lest our fancy lead us astray.
Our studies have brought us to the threshold of a vast
temple: to explore it we must grope our way at first and
laboriously gather facts to guide us in the same manner as
in attempting to trace the life history of a river.

We are recalled from dreamland by a new element in the
scene before us. A canoe, buoyant and graceful, rounds a
distant headland, traverses the belt of dark water just out-
side the beating surf, enters one of the sheltered bays, and
touches the shore. Dark men clad in skins step upon the
beach. The light canoe is drawn part way out of the water.
Soon a column of blue smoke rises above the tree-tops,
spreads inland, and vanishes in the steady blow of the
breeze from the sea. As time passes, other savages come
to the island. Villages are built. Fires sweep through the
forests leaving black ruin in their wakes. The soil is
stripped of its natural covering, and for a time erosion is

accelerated. Large quantities of soil and other rock debris
are washed down from the hills and encumber the more
level lands below, destroying for a time their fertility.
Generations of savages come and go, until a change of as
great moment to them as was their coming to the animals
and plants of the island takes place.

For the first time a sail breaks the even sky-line of the
sea. A *Half-Moon* borne proudly on by gentle breezes
nears the island and enters one of its forest-fringed harbours.
The changes which follow the coming of civilised man need
not be dwelt upon. Chief among the events due to the
greater wants of civilised than of savage men, is the removal
of the forests. The land is cleared of its trees and shrubs.
Other plants which grew beneath their shelter are extermin-
ated. Ploughing greatly facilitates the work of the rills and
rivulets. The precious layer of soil, thin at best, is more
rapidly removed than formerly, and the sources of its renewal to a great extent destroyed. In time, fields become
too impoverished to repay cultivation while virgin lands can
still be had on neighbouring shores for the taking, and are
abandoned. Destruction follows apace. Gullies and deep
canyon-like trenches are cut in the sides of the hills, and
even greater desolation results in the plains below than followed the wild-fire started by the Indians. The island
loses its archaic loveliness. Its flora is largely laid waste,
or supplanted by the growth of seeds brought intentionally
or by accident from other lands. The native birds and
animals disappear, or, like the plants, are displaced by others
and in part alien, species. The changes are so profound that
they are felt not only throughout the fauna and flora, but

impress themselves on the topography of the land. No
longer a source of immediate gain, the island is neglected
and abandoned.

The rivers with their increased freight due to the debris
washed from abandoned fields, progress more rapidly with
their appointed tasks than before the forests were removed.
Deltas are formed at the mouth of the streams, the estuaries
are filled, and in time the waters of the sea are displaced,
and broad grassy plains due to construction make their appearance. The coast-line again becomes a series of sweeping curves. Tens of thousands of years elapse before the
last of the conspicuous results due to elevation and subsidence become obliterated, and during this interval marked
changes have taken place in the group of monadnocks
forming the central highland of the island. Some of the
original consequent streams were larger or had shorter
courses to the sea than their competitors, and were enabled
to develop more rapidly. The divides at the heads of
the more energetic streams receded and new territory is
added to their hydrographic basins. This process of capture and diversion leads to still greater diversity in the
topography. The struggle between streams for the possession of territory in progress along every divide is not unlike
the struggle for existence and the survival of the fittest in
the animal world. The streams develop in accordance with
their environment. Those most favoured capture the
waters of their less favoured neighbours and wax stronger
at the expense of the weak.

In its old age our island loses the roughness of surface
produced by stream corrasion. The ridges and peaks be-

come subdued and their outlines more flowing, and the valleys broader. In time low mounds alone remain to mark the site of once picturesque peaks, and in the broad valleys sluggish streams meandering in sweeping curves carry off the decreased water supply. Even the hills, after a prolonged old age, disappear, and an undulating plain but slightly elevated above the encircling sea remains. A geographical cycle has run its course. The resulting peneplain has even less diversity than the surface of the new-born island. The streams, now flowing sluggishly on account of the lowering of their gradients, are too feeble to carry burdens, and run clear, but their chemical activity is undiminished, and they still bear invisible loads in solution. Chemical degradation, previously of minor importance in reference to the work of mechanical agencies, now becomes the more potent, and the final reduction of the land to sea-level is secured by the removal of its material in solution.

The waves and currents of the sea have been active throughout this long history in producing changes which, however, are beyond the limits of the present discussion.

After the streams ceased to bring debris to the shore, which, we may presume, either in part or wholly counteracted the attacks of the sea on the land, the low coastal plains are washed away, and finally the waves roll over the site of the vanished island.

INDEX

Æolian corrasion, mention of, 29

Ages of terraces, relative, 170, 171

Aggrading, explanation of the term, 98

Alaska, characteristics of the rivers of, 284-289

Alluvial cones, description of, 101-109

— fans, reference to, 101

— rivers, characteristics of, 264, 265

Alsec River, Alaska, mention of, 284

Analyses of river-water, average, 80

— table of, 78

Analysis of rain-water, 75

Anchor ice, influence of, on stream transportation, 25-28

Anticlinals, influence of, on topography, 198

Appalachian Mountains, stream adjustment in, 195-203

— rivers, brief account of, 260, 261

Arctic drainage slope briefly defined, 256, 257

Atlantic drainage slope briefly defined, 256

Babb, C. C., observations by, 74

Baselevel, definition of, 47

Baselevelling, discussion of, 46-50

Bear River, Wyoming, analysis of the water of, 78

Beheaded streams, explanation of the term, 191

Bering drainage slope briefly defined, 257

Big Bend of Columbia River, Washington, mention of, 280

Big Wills Creek, Alabama, adjustment of, 208-213

Bischof, G., cited on water analyses, 79

Blatchley, W. S., reference to writings of, 96

Bonneville, Lake, reference to deltas of, 125

Bottom loads of streams, 68-70

— terraces, origin and nature of, 166, 167

Branner, J. C., reference to work of, x., 11

Breccia, due to faulting, mention of, 4

Calcium carbonate, solubility of, 92

Call, R. E., reference to writings of, 94

Campbell, M. R., reference to work of, x.

Canada, characteristics of the rivers of, 290-292

Canadian Geological Survey, reference to, xi.

Canyon of Snake River, Washington, reference to, 160

— rivers, characteristics of, 271-275

Caribbean drainage slope briefly defined, 257

Carrollton, Mississippi, sediment in the Mississippi at, 71, 72

Cascade Mountains, reference to waterfalls of, 57, 61

— streams of, 280

Catskill Mountains, migration of divides on, 251-253

Cephalonia, Greece, reference to "sea-mills" of, 95

Chamberlin, T. C., reference to the work of, x.

Chandler, C. F., water analyses by, 78

Characteristics of American rivers, 254–299

Chattanooga, Tenn., geography near, 208–214

Chelan, Lake, Washington, terraces near, 182

Chemical degradation, 82–84

— denudation, discussion of, 80, 81

— disintegration, discussion of, 6–11

Chesapeake Bay, map of, 219

Chipaway River, reference to, 138

Clarke, F. W., water analyses by, 78

Climate, influence of, on streams, 140–142

Climatic changes, influence of, on streams, 223–233

— on terrace-making, 158–160

Colorado River, characteristics of, 271–275

— reference to, 133

— still corrading, 45

Columbia River, characteristics of, 278–282

— terraces of, 180–182

Corrasion, discussion of, 28–36

— lateral, discussion of, 34–36

— stream, general process of, 142–145

Corthell, E. L., reference to writings of, 132

Crevasses, origin and nature of, 120

Crosby, F. W., reference to writings of, 95

— W. O., reference to writings of, 95

Croton River, New York, analysis of the water of, 78

— material carried in suspension by, 79

Cumberland River, Tennessee, analysis of the water of, 78

Current terraces, origin and nature of, 167–169

Curves made by streams, 36–39

Danube River, data concerning, 74, 75

— material carried in suspension by, 79

Darton, N. H., cited on drainage of Catskill Mountains, 251

— reference to the work of, x.

Davis, W. M., cited on lakes, 122

— cited on peneplains, 48

— cited on stream development, 187

— references to the writings of, x., 41, 42, 214

— and J. W. Wood, cited on superimposed drainage, 243

Decay of rocks, 1–11

Deflection of streams owing to the earth's rotation, 39–43

Degradation of the land, general rate of, 81–84

Delaware River, analysis of the water of, 78

Delta of the Yukon River, brief account of, 288

— terraces, origin and nature of, 167–169

Deltas, origin and structure of, 123–142

Deposition, stream, general process of, 142–145

Deposits made by streams, variations in the, 136–142

Development of streams, 63–66

Diller, J. S., reference to the work of, x.

Discharge of the Mississippi, 267

Disintegration of rocks, 1–11

Distributaries, explanation of the term, 103

Diverted streams, explanation of the term, 192

Divides, migration of, 247–253

Dodge, R. E., cited on terraces, 157, 158

Drainage slopes of North America briefly defined, 256, 257

Drew, F., reference to the writings of, 101

Drift-wood, influence of, on stream development, 240–244

Drowned rivers, examples of, 260

Dunes, influence of, on streams, 139

Dutton, C. E., reference to explorations by, x.

Earth's rotation, influence of, on streams, 39–43

Elevation, effects of, on stream development, 215–217
England, rate of land degradation in, 83
Erosion, baselevel of, discussed, 46–50
— general discussion of, 46–51

" Fall line " of the Atlantic coast, brief account of, 261
Fault breccia, mention of, 4
Fergusson, J., reference to the writings of, 37
Ferrel, W., cited on the rotation of the earth, 41
Flood-plains, origin and nature of, 110–116
Floods in rivers, brief account of, 229–233
Fluctuations of streams, discussion of, 229–233
Forshey, Professor, observations by, 70
Fraser River, British Columbia, characteristics of, 282–284

Ganges River, data concerning, 75
Geikie, A., references to the writings of, 18, 74
Genesee River, New York, analysis of the water of, 78
Geographical cycles, definition of, 49
Gilbert, G. K., cited on Niagara Falls, 59, 60
— explorations by, x.
— reference to writings of, 31, 42, 125
Glacial corrasion, mention of, 29
— meal, contribution of, to streams, 14
— terraces, origin and nature of, 169, 170
Glaciated lands, rivers of, 262, 263
Glaciers, influence of, on stream development, 234–236
Grand Coulée, Washington, mention of, 280
Great Basin, climatic condition of, 178, 179
— drainage, brief account of, 257
Great Falls, Canada, mention of, 58
Great Lakes, rivers flowing to, 292–300

Great Plateaus, references to, 44, 45
Green River, Kentucky, references to, 88–90, 94
Ground ice, influence of, on stream transportation, 25–28
Gulf drainage slope briefly defined, 257

Hayes, C. W., cited on geography of Southern Appalachians, 208–214
— references to the work of, x., 207, 208
Hicks, L. E., cited on flood-plains, 118
— cited on profiles of streams, 146, 150
High Plateaus, reference to, 45
Hitchcock, E., cited on delta terraces, 167
Hoang Ho River, data concerning, 75
Holmes, W. H., cited on Colorado River, 273
Hosford, E. N., water analysis by, 78
Hovey, H. C., references to the writings of, 94, 96
Hudson Bay drainage slope briefly defined, 256
Hudson River, New York, analysis of the water of, 78
— brief account of, 260
— cited as an example of a drowned river, 218
— material carried in suspension by, 79
Humboldt River, Nevada, analysis of the water of, 78
Humphreys and Abbot, cited in reference to the Mississippi, 70, 73, 253, 267 ; cited on drift-wood, 243
— cited on Mississippi delta, 132
Hunt, T. S., water analysis by, 78
Hydration, influence of, on rock disintegration, 6

Ice, influence of, on stream transportation, 22–28
— weight of, 23
Indian Creek, California, reference to, 111
Invisible load of streams, 75–81

Irrawaddy River, data concerning, 74

James River, Virginia, analysis of the water of, 78
Jones, W. J., water analysis by, 78
Jordan River, Utah, analysis of the water of, 78
Jukes-Browne, A. J., reference to the writings of, 18
Julian, A. A., references to the writings of, 11, 76

Keyes, C. R., cited on the meanderings of streams, 113
Kittatinny peneplain, brief account of, 200, 206
Kowak River, Alaska, mention of, 286

Lake Pepin, Wisconsin – Minnesota, reference to, 138
— St. Clair, delta in, 133
— Tahoe, California–Nevada, analysis of the water of, 78
Lakes, climatic changes indicated by, 220
Laurentian Basin, rivers of, 292–300
Le Conte, J., references to the writings of, 18, 19
Levees, natural, origin and nature of, 116–123
Life history of a river, 301–320
Limestone, solubility of, 92
Loads of streams, how obtained, 13–16
Loew, O., water analysis by, 78
London, England, analysis of rain-water at, 75
Lookout Mountain, Tennessee-Alabama, drainage of, 208–214
Los Angeles River, California, analysis of the water of, 78
Lost rivers, reference to, 226
Lupton, N. T., water analysis by, 78
Luray Cavern, Virginia, references to, 93, 94
Lyell, C., reference to the writings of, 22

Mackenzie River, delta of, 133
Maine, coast topography of, 218
Mammoth Cave, Kentucky, brief account of, 88, 89, 91, 94

Marsh, G. P., reference to the writings of, 11
Mason, W. P., references to the writings of, 75, 76
Matapediac River, New Brunswick, anchor ice in, 25–27
Material in suspension, measures of, 70–75
Maumee River, Ohio, analysis of the water of, 78
Maxwell, W., reference to the writings of, 11
McGee, W. J., reference to the work of, x.
Meandering streams, discussion of, 36–38
Mechanical disintegration of rocks, 2–6
Merrill, G. P., cited on hydration, 6
— references to the writings of, 9, 11
Migration of divides, discussion of, 247–253
— of waterfalls, discussion of, 60–63
Mississippi River, analysis of the water of, 78
— characteristics of, 265–271
— Commission, reference to map by, 122
— data concerning, 74, 75
— delta of, 131
— influence of earth's rotation on, 42
— inundation of, 119–121
— material carried in suspension by, 79
— rate of degradation in basin of, 83, 84
— sediment in waters of, 70–74
Missouri River, an aggrading stream, 43, 44
Mohawk River, New York, analysis of the water of, 78
Monadnock, definition of, 49
— Mount, New Hampshire, reference to, 49
Montmorenci Falls, Canada, reference to, 58
Morrill, P., cited on the Mississippi, 267
— reference to the writings of, 121, 253
Moses Lake, Washington, reference to, 139
Moulins, mention of, 34

Murray, J , cited on water analyses, 80

Natural Bridge, Virginia, reference to, 94
— levees, origin and nature of, 116–123
Newberry, J. S., explorations by, x.
New England rivers, characteristics of, 259, 260
New Orleans, Louisiana, depth of delta deposits at, 132
Niagara Falls, profile and section at, 60
— reference to, 62
Niagara River, characteristics of, 296–298
Nile River, data concerning, 74, 79
Nita crevasse, Louisiana, an account of the, 121, 122

Ottawa River, Canada, analysis of the water of, 78
— mention of, 292

Pacific drainage slope, brief account of, 257
Passaic River, New Jersey, analysis of the water of, 78
Peneplain, definition of, 48
Peneplains, ancient, in the Appalachians, 205–207
Platte River, Nebraska, an aggrading stream, 43, 44
Po River, Italy, data concerning, 74, 75
Porcupine River, Alaska, ice-work on banks of, 24
Pot-holes, origin and nature of, 33, 34
Potomac River, Virginia, data concerning, 74
— rate of degradation by, 82
Powell, J. W., cited on baselevel, 47
— cited on moisture necessary for vegetation, 237
— cited on rapids in Colorado River, 138
— reference to explorations by, x.
Precipitation, influence of variations in, on streams, 224–228
Profiles of streams, 145–151

Rain-water, impurities in, 75, 76

Reade, T. M., cited on chemical degradation, 82
Red River, Louisiana, lakes on the sides of, 122
Regolith, meaning of the term, 9
Reversed streams, explanation of, 192
Rhine River, material carried in suspension by, 79
Rhone River, data concerning, 74, 75, 79
Rio Grande, data concerning, 74
Rio Grande del Norte, analysis of the water of, 78
River piracy, discussion of, 203–205
Rocky Mountains, reference to waterfalls of, 57
Rotation of the earth, influence of, on streams, 39–43
Roth, Professor, cited in water analysis, 79
Russell, I. C., cited on glaciers, 236
— cited on Laurentian basin, 293
— cited on Laurentian lakes, 294
— cited on terraces of the Columbia, 180–182
— references to the writings of, 11, 24, 123, 124, 134, 137, 174
— T., reference to the writings of, 253

Sacramento River, California, analysis of the water of, 78
St. Anthony Falls, Minnesota, reference to, 62
St. Clair Lake, delta in, 133
St. Lawrence drainage slope briefly described, 256
St. Lawrence River, analysis of the water of, 78
— character of, 43
— submerged portion of, 218
Salisbury, R. D., reference to the writings of, x., 170
Schooley peneplain, reference to, 205
Screes, explanation of the term, 109
Shaler, N. S., cited on caverns, 90
Shenandoah peneplain, brief account of, 200
Shoshone Falls, Idaho, reference to, 62
Sierra Nevada, reference to waterfalls of, 57

Sierra Nevada rivers, characteristics of, 275–278
Sink-holes, reference to, 93
Snake River, Idaho–Washington, characteristics of, 279, 280
Snickers Gap, Virginia, character and origin of, 200, 201
Southern rivers, characteristics of, 263, 264
Stevenson, D., reference to the writings of, 18
Stickine River, Alaska–Canada, mention of, 284
Stream conquest, discussion of, 203–205
— deposition, discussion of, 97–151
— development, discussion of, 184–195
Subimposed drainage, term suggested, 246
Subsequent streams, origin and nature of, 184, 185
Subsidence, effects of, on stream development, 217–221
Superimposed drainage, explanation of, 244–246
Synclinal mountains and anticlinal valleys, 207–214
Synclinals, influence of, on topography, 198

Tahoe Lake, California–Nevada, analysis of the water of, 78
Taku River, Alaska, mention of, 284
Talus slopes, origin and nature of, 109, 110
Tarr, R. S., cited on drowned rivers, 219
— cited on young valleys, 55
— reference to the work of, xi.
Teanaway River, Washington, dam of drift-wood on, 243
Temperature, influence of variation in, on streams, 228, 229
Terraces, origin and nature of, 152–183
Thames River, England, material carried in suspension by, 79
Thompson, W. G., cited on anchor ice, 25–27
Tides in Columbia River, 280
Todd, J. E., cited on the Mississippi, 270

Transportation by streams, discussion of, 14–28
Trenton Falls, New York, reference to, 58
Troy, New York, impurities in rain-water at, 76
Truckee River, Nevada, analysis of the water of, 78
Tundra of Arctic shores, brief account of, 133, 288

Underground streams, 84–96
United States Geological Survey, reference to work of, xi.
Uruguay River, data concerning, 74

Vegetation, influence of, on stream development, 236–244
Visible loads of streams, 67–75
Volcanic agencies, influence of, on stream development, 231–233
Volcanic dust, contributed to streams, 14
Von Hosen, J., table of analyses compiled by, 78

Wales, rate of land degradation in, 83
Walker River, Nevada, analysis of the water of, 78
Walla Walla River, Washington, reference to, 137
Waller, E., water analysis by, 78
Water, weight of, 23
— analyses, table of, 78
Waterfalls, nature and history of, 54–62
Water-gaps, origin of, 199–205
Watkins Glen, New York, reference to, 58
Wheeler, W. H., reference to the writings of, 73
White River, Washingson, mention of, 287
Wilbur, E. M., cited on tides in Columbia River, 280
Willis, B., cited on stream adjustment, 198
— reference to the work of, xi.
— reference to the writings of, 200
Wills Creek, Alabama, adjustment of, 208–213

Wind-gaps, explanation of the term, 199–205

Wurtz, H., water analysis by, 78

Wyandotte Cavern, Indiana reference to, 93

Yazoo River, Louisiana, reference to, 123

Young valleys, illustrations of, 55

Yukon River, ice-work on the banks of, 24

— drift-wood on, 242

Putnam's
Science Series

~The Study of Man. By Professor A. C. HADDON, M.A., D.Sc
M.R.I.A. Fully illustrated. 8°, net $2.00.

"A timely and useful volume. . . . The author wields a pleasing pen and knows
how to make the subject attractive. . . . The work is calculated to spread among its
readers an attraction to the science of anthropology. The author's observations are
exceedingly genuine and his descriptions are vivid."—*London Athenæum.*

2.—The Groundwork of Science. A Study of Epistemology. By
ST. GEORGE MIVART, F.R.S. 8°, net $1.75.

"The book is cleverly written and is one of the best works of its kind ever put before
the public. It will be interesting to all readers, and especially to those interested in the
study of science."—*New Haven Leader.*

3.—Rivers of North America. A Reading Lesson for Students of Geography and Geology. By ISRAEL C. RUSSELL, Professor of Geology,
University of Michigan, author of "Lakes of North America," "Glaciers of North America," "Volcanoes of North America," etc. Fully
illustrated. 8°, net $2.00.

"There has not been in the last few years until the present book any authoritative,
broad résumé on the subject, modified and deepened as it has been by modern research
and reflection, which is couched in language suitable for the multitude. . . . The text
is as entertaining as it is instructive."—*Boston Transcript.*

4.—Earth Sculpture; or, The Origin of Land-Forms. By JAMES
GEIKIE, LL.D., D.C.L., F.R.S., etc., Murchison Professor of Geology
and Mineralogy in the University of Edinburgh; author of "The
Great Ice Age," etc. Fully illustrated. 8°, net $2.00.

"This volume is the best popular and yet scientific treatment we know of of the origin and development of land-forms, and we immediately adopted it as the best available
text-book for a college course in physiography. . . . The book is full of life and vigor.
and shows the sympathetic touch of a man deeply in love with nature."—*Science.*

5.—Volcanoes: Their Structure and Significance. By T. G. BONNEY,
F.R.S., University College, London. Fully illustrated. 8°. Revised
and Enlarged Edition. Illustrated. Net $2.00.

"It is not only a fine piece of work from a scientific point of view, but it is uncom-
monly attractive to the general reader, and is likely to have a larger sale than most books
of its class."—*Springfield Republican.*

6. Bacteria : Especially as they are related to the economy of nature, to
industrial processes, and to the public health. By GEORGE NEWMAN,
M.D., F.R.S. (Edin.), D.P.H. (Camb.), etc., Demonstrator of Bac
teriology in King's College, London. With 24 micro-photographs of
actual organisms and over 70 other illustrations. 8°, net $2.00.

"Dr. Newman's discussions of bacteria and disease, of immunity, of antitoxins, and
of methods of disinfection, are illuminating, and are to be commended to all seeking in
formation on these points. Any discussion of bacteria will seem technical to the uniniti
ated, but all such will find in this book popular treatment and scientific accuracy happily
combined."—*The Dial*

7.—A Book of Whales. By F. E. BEDDARD, M.A., F.R.S. Illustrated. 8°. Net, $2.00.

"Mr. Beddard has done well to devote a whole volume to whales. They are worthy of the biographer who has now well grouped and described these creatures. The general reader will not find the volume too technical, nor has the author failed in his attempt to produce a book that shall be acceptable to the zoölogist and the naturalist."—*N. Y. Times*

8. Comparative Physiology of the Brain and Comparative Psychology. With special reference to the Invertebrates. By JACQUES LOEB, M.D., Professor of Physiology in the University of Chicago. Illustrated. 8°. Net, $1.75.

"No student of this most interesting phase of the problems of life can afford to remain in ignorance of the wide range of facts and the suggestive series of interpretations which Professor Loeb has brought together in this volume."—JOSEPH JASTROW, in the *Chicago Dial.*

9.—The Stars. By Professor SIMON NEWCOMB, U.S.N., Nautical Almanac Office, and Johns Hopkins University. 8°. Illustrated. Net. $2.00.

"The work is a thoroughly scientific treatise on stars. The name of the author is sufficient guarantee of scholarly and accurate work."—*Scientific American.*

10.—The Basis of Social Relations. A Study in Ethnic Psychology. By DANIEL G. BRINTON, A.M., M.D., LL.D., Sc.D., Late Professor of American Archæology and Linguistics in the University of Pennsylvania ; Author of " History of Primitive Religions," " Races and Peoples," " The American Race," etc. Edited by LIVINGSTON FARRAND, Columbia University. 8°. Net, $1.50

" Professor Brinton his shown in this volume an intimate and appreciative knowledge of all the important anthropological theories. No one seems to have been better acquainted with the very great body of facts represented by these sciences." —*Am. Journal of Sociology.*

11.—Experiments on Animals. By STEPHEN PAGET. With an Introduction by Lord Lister. Illustrated. 8°. Net, $2.00.

"To a large class of readers this presentation will be attractive, since it gives to them in a nut shell the meat of a hundred scientific dissertations in current periodical literature. The volume has the authoritative sanction of Lord Lister."—*Boston Transcript.*

12 — Infection and Immunity. With Special Reference to the Prevention of Infectious Diseases. By GEORGE M. STERNBERG, M.D., LL.D. Surgeon-General U. S. Army (Retired). Illustrated. 8°. Net, $1.75

" A distinct public service by an eminent authority. This admirable little work should be a part of the prescribed reading of the head of every institution in which children of youths are gathered. Conspicuously useful."—*N. Y. Times.*

13.—Fatigue. By A. MOSSO, Professor of Physiology in the University of Turin. Translated by MARGARET DRUMMOND, M.A., and W. B. DRUMMOND, M.B., C.M., F.R.C.P.E.; extra Physician, Royal Hospital for Sick Children, Edinburgh ; Author of " The Child, His Nature and Nurture." Illustrated. 8°. Net, $1.50.

" A book for the student and for the instructor, full of interest, also for the intelligent general reader. The subject constitutes one of the most fascinating chapters in the history of medical science and of philosophical research."—*Yorkshire Post.*

14.—Earthquakes. In the Light of the New Seismology. By CLARENCE E. DUTTON, Major, U. S. A. Illustrated. 8°. Net, $2.00

" The book summarizes the results of the men who have accomplished the great things in their pursuit of seismological knowledge. It is abundantly illustrated and it fills a place unique in the literature of modern science."--*Chicago Tribune.*

15.—The Nature of Man. Studies in Optimistic Philosophy. By ÉLIE METCHNIKOFF, Professor at the Pasteur Institute. Translation and introduction by P. CHAMBERS MITCHELL, M.A., D.Sc. Oxon. Illustrated. 8°. Net, $1.50.

" A book to be set side by side with Huxley's Essays, whose spirit it carries a step further on the long road towards its goal."—*Mail and Express.*

16.—The Hygiene of Nerves and Mind in Health and Disease. By AUGUST FOREL, M.D., formerly Professor of Psychiatry in the University of Zurich. Authorized Translation. 8°. Net, $2.00.

A comprehensive and concise summary of the results of science in its chosen field. Its authorship is a guarantee that the statements made are authoritative as far as the statement of an individual can be so regarded.

17.—The Prolongation of Life. Optimistic Essays. By ÉLIE METCHNIKOFF, Sub-Director of the Pasteur Institute. Author of " The Nature of Man," etc. 8°. Illustrated. Net, $2.50. Popular Edition. With an introduction by Prof. CHARLES S. MINOT. Net, $1.75.

In his new work Professor Metchnikoff expounds at greater length, in the light of additional knowledge gained in the last few years, his main thesis that human life is not only unnaturally short but unnaturally burdened with physical and mental disabilities. He analyzes the causes of these disharmonies and explains his reasons for hoping that they may be counteracted by a rational hygiene.

18.—The Solar System. A Study of Recent Observations. By Prof. CHARLES LANE POOR, Professor of Astronomy in Columbia University. 8°. Illustrated. Net, $2.00.

The subject is presented in untechnical language and without the use of mathematics. Professor Poor shows by what steps the precise knowledge of to-day has been reached and explains the marvellous results of modern methods and modern observations.

19.—Heredity. By J. ARTHUR THOMSON, M.A., Professor of Natural History in the University of Aberdeen ; Author of " The Science of Life," etc. 8°. Illustrated. Net, $3.50.

The aim of this work is to expound, in a simple manner, the facts of heredity and inheritance as at present known, the general conclusions which have been securely established, and the more important theories which have been formulated.

20.—Climate—Considered Especially in Relation to Man. By ROBERT DeCOURCY WARD, Assistant Professor of Climatology in Harvard University. 8°. Illustrated. Net, $2.00.

This volume is intended for persons who have not had special training in the technicalities of climatology. Climate covers a wholly different field from that included in the meteorological text-books. It handles broad questions of climate in a way which has not been attempted in a single volume The needs of the teacher and student have been kept constantly in mind.

21.—Age, Growth, and Death. By CHARLES S. MINOT, James Stillman Professor of Comparative Anatomy in Harvard University, President of the Boston Society of Natural History, and Author of " Human Embryology," " A Laboratory Text-book of Embryology," etc. 8°, Illustrated. $2.50 net.

This volume deals with some of the fundamental problems of biology, and presents a series of views (the results of nearly thirty years of study), which the author has correlated for the first time in systematic form.

22.—The Interpretation of Nature. By C. LLOYD MORGAN, LL.D., F.R.S. Crown 8vo. Net, $1.25.

Dr. Morgan seeks to prove that a belief in purpose as the causal reality of which nature is an expression is not inconsistent with a full and whole-hearted acceptance of the explanations of naturalism.

23.—Mosquito Life. The Habits and Life Cycles of the Known Mosquitoes of the United States; Methods for their Control; and Keys for Easy Identification of the Species in their Various Stages. An account based on the investigation of the late James William Dupree, Surgeon-General of Louisiana, and upon the original observations by the Writer. By EVELYN GROESBEECK MITCHELL, A.B., M.S. With 64 Illustrations. 8°. Net, $2.00.

This volume has been designed to meet the demand of the constantly increasing number of students for a work presenting in compact form the essential facts so far made known by scientific investigation in regard to the different phases of this, as is now conceded, important and highly interesting subject. While aiming to keep within reasonable bounds, that it may be used for work in the field and in the laboratory, no portion of the work has been slighted, or fundamental information omitted, in the endeavor to carry this plan into effect.

24.—Thinking, Feeling, Doing. An Introduction to Mental Science. By E. W. SCRIPTURE, Ph.D., M.D., Assistant Neurologist Columbia University, formerly Director of the Psychological Laboratory at Yale University. 189 Illustrations. 2d Edition, Revised and Enlarged. 8°. Net, $1.75.

"The chapters on Time and Action, Reaction Time, Thinking Time, Rhythmic Action, and Power and Will are most interesting. This book should be carefully read by every one who desires to be familiar with the advances made in the study of the mind, which advances, in the last twenty-five years, have been quite as striking and epoch-making as the strides made in the more material lines of knowledge."— *Jour. Amer. Med. Ass'n.*, Feb. 22, 1908.

25.—The World's Gold. By L. DE LAUNAY, Professor at the École Supérieure des Mines. Translated by Orlando Cyprian Williams. With an Introduction by Charles A. Conant, author of "History of Modern Banks of Issue," etc. 8°. Net, $1.75.

M. de Launay is a professor of considerable repute not only in France, but among scientists throughout the world. In this work he traces the various uses and phases of gold; first, its geology; secondly, its extraction; thirdly, its economic value.

26.—The Interpretation of Radium. By FREDERICK SODDY, Lecturer in Physical Chemistry in the University of Glasgow. Third Edition, rewritten, with data brought down to 1912. 8°. With 33 Diagrams and Illustrations. $2.00 net.

As the application of the present-day interpretation of Radium (that it is an element undergoing spontaneous disintegration) is not confined to the physical sciences, but has a wide and general bearing upon our whole outlook on Nature, Mr. Soddy has presented the subject in non-technical language, so that the ideas involved are within reach of the lay reader. No effort has been spared to get to the root of the matter and to secure accuracy, so that the book should prove serviceable to other fields of science and investigation, as well as to the general public.

27.—Criminal Man. According to the Classification of CESARE LOMBROSO. Briefly Summarized by his Daughter, Gina Lombroso-Ferrero. With 36 Illustrations and a Bibliography of Lombroso's Publications on the Subject. 8°. Net $2.00.

Signora Guglielmo Ferrero's résumé of her father's work on criminal anthropology is specially dedicated to all those whose office it is to correct, reform, and punish the criminal, with a view to diminishing the injury caused to society by his anti-social acts; also to superintendents, teachers, and those engaged in rescuing orphans and children of vicious habits, as a guide in checking the development of evil germs and eliminating incorrigible subjects whose example is a source of corruption to others.

28.—The Social Evil. With Special Reference to Conditions Existing in the City of New York. A Report Prepared in 1902 under the Direction of the Committee of Fifteen. Second Edition, Revised, with New Material Covering the Years 1902–1911. Edited by EDWIN R. A. SELIGMAN, LL.D., McVickar Professor of Political Economy in Columbia University. 8vo. $1.75 net.

A study that is far from being of merely local interest and application. The problem is considered in all its aspects and, for this purpose, reference has been made to conditions prevailing in other communities and to the different attempts foreign cities have made to regulate vice.

29.—Microbes and Toxins. By ETIENNE BURNET, of the Pasteur Institute, Paris. With an Introduction by Elie Metchnikoff, Sub-Director of the Pasteur Institute, Paris. With about 71 Illustrations. $2.00 net.

A well-known English authority said in recommending the volume: "Incomparably the best book there is on this tremendously important subject. In fact, I am assured that nothing exists which gives anything like so full a study of microbiology." In the volume are considered the general functions of microbes, the microbes of the human system, the form and structure of microbes, the physiology of microbes, the pathogenic protozoa, toxins, tuberculin and mallein, immunity, applications of bacteriology, vaccines and serums, chemical remedies, etc.

30.—Problems of Life and Reproduction. By MARCUS HARTOG, D. Sc., Professor of Zoölogy in University College, Cork. 8vo. $2.50 net.

The author uses all the legitimate arms of scientific controversy in assailing certain views that have been widely pressed on the general public with an assurance that must have given many the impression that they were protected by the universal consensus of biologists. Among the subjects considered are: "The Cellular Pedigree and the Problem of Heredity"; "The Relation of Brood-Formation to Ordinary Cell-Division"; "The New Force, Mitokinetism"; "Nuclear Reduction and the Function of Chroism"; "Fertilization"; "The Transmission of Acquired Characters"; "Mechanism and Life"; "The Biological Writings of Samuel Butler"; "Interpolation in Memory"; "The Teaching of Nature Study."

31.—Problems of the Sexes. By JEAN FINOT, Author of "The Science of Happiness," etc. Translated under authority by Mary J. Safford. 8vo. $2.00 net.

A masterly presentation of the attitude of the ages toward women and an eloquent plea for her further enfranchisement from imposed and unnatural limitations. The range of scholarship that has been enlisted in the writing may well excite one's wonder, but the tone of the book is popular and its appeal is not to any small section of the reading public but to all the classes and degrees of an age that, from present indications, will go down in history as the century of Woman.

32.—The Positive Evolution of Religion. Its Moral and Social Reaction. By FREDERIC HARRISON. 8vo. $2.00 net.

The author has undertaken to estimate the moral and social reaction of various forms of Religion—beginning with Nature Worship, Polytheism, Catholicism, Protestantism, and Deism. The volume may be looked upon as the final word, the summary of the celebrated author's philosophy—a systematic study of the entire religious problem.

33.—The Science of Happiness. By JEAN FINOT, Author of "Problems of the Sexes," etc. Translated from the French by Mary J. Safford. 8°. $1.75 net.

In this work, which was crowned by the Academy, the author considers a subject, the solution of which offers more enticement to the well-wisher of the race than the gold of the Incas did to the treasure-seekers of Spain, who themselves doubtless looked upon the coveted yellow metal, however mistakenly, as a key to the happiness which all are trying to find. "Amid the noisy tumult of life, amid the dissonance that divides man from man," remarks M. Finot, "the Science of Happiness tries to discover the divine link which binds humanity to happiness through the soul and through the union of souls." The author considers the nature of happiness and the means of its attainment, as well as many allied questions.

34—Genetic Theory of Reality. Being the Outcome of Genetic Logic as Issuing in the Æsthetic Theory of Reality Called Pancalism. By JAMES MARK BALDWIN, Ph.D., D.Sc., LL.D., Foreign Correspondent of the Institute of France, Author of " History of Psychology," etc.

The author here states the general results of the extended studies in genetic and social science and anthropology made by him and others, and a critical account of the history of the interpretation of nature and man, both racial and philosophical.

The book offers an *Introduction to Philosophy* from a new point of view. It contains, also, a valuable glossary of the terms employed in these and similar discussions.

35—Mosquito Control in Panama The Eradication of Malaria and Yellow Fever in Cuba and Panama. By J. A. LE PRINCE, C.E., A. M., Chief Sanitary Inspector, Isthmian Canal Commission, 1904-1914, and A. J. ORENSTEIN, M.D., Assistant Chief Sanitary Inspector, Isthmian Canal Commission. With an introduction by L. O. HOWARD, Ph.D., Entomologist and Chief, Bureau of Entomology, United States Department of Agriculture. 8°. 95 illustrations. $2.50.

Mr. Le Prince's books will be not only of great practical importance as a guide to future work of the same character, especially in the Tropics, but also of permanent historic value.